COLLECTION EDITOR
MARK D. BEAZLEY

ASSOCIATE MANAGING EDITOR
ALEX STARBUCK

EDITOR, SPECIAL PROJECTS
JENNIFER GRÜNWALD

MASTERWORKS EDITOR
CORY SEDLEMEIER

SENIOR EDITOR, SPECIAL PROJECTS
JEFF YOUNGQUIST

COLOR RECONSTRUCTION
MICHAEL KELLEHER &
JERRON QUALITY COLOR

ART RECONSTRUCTION
POND SCUM

SVP PRINT, SALES & MARKETING
DAVID GABRIEL

EDITOR IN CHIEF:
AXEL ALONSO

CHIEF CREATIVE OFFICER:
JOE QUESADA

PUBLISHER:
DAN BUCKLEY

EXECUTIVE PRODUCER:
ALAN FINE

SPECIAL THANKS TO TOM BREVOORT,
RALPH MACCHIO, WILL GABRI-EL,
TERRY AUSTIN & JAMES CHAN

S0-CEX-912

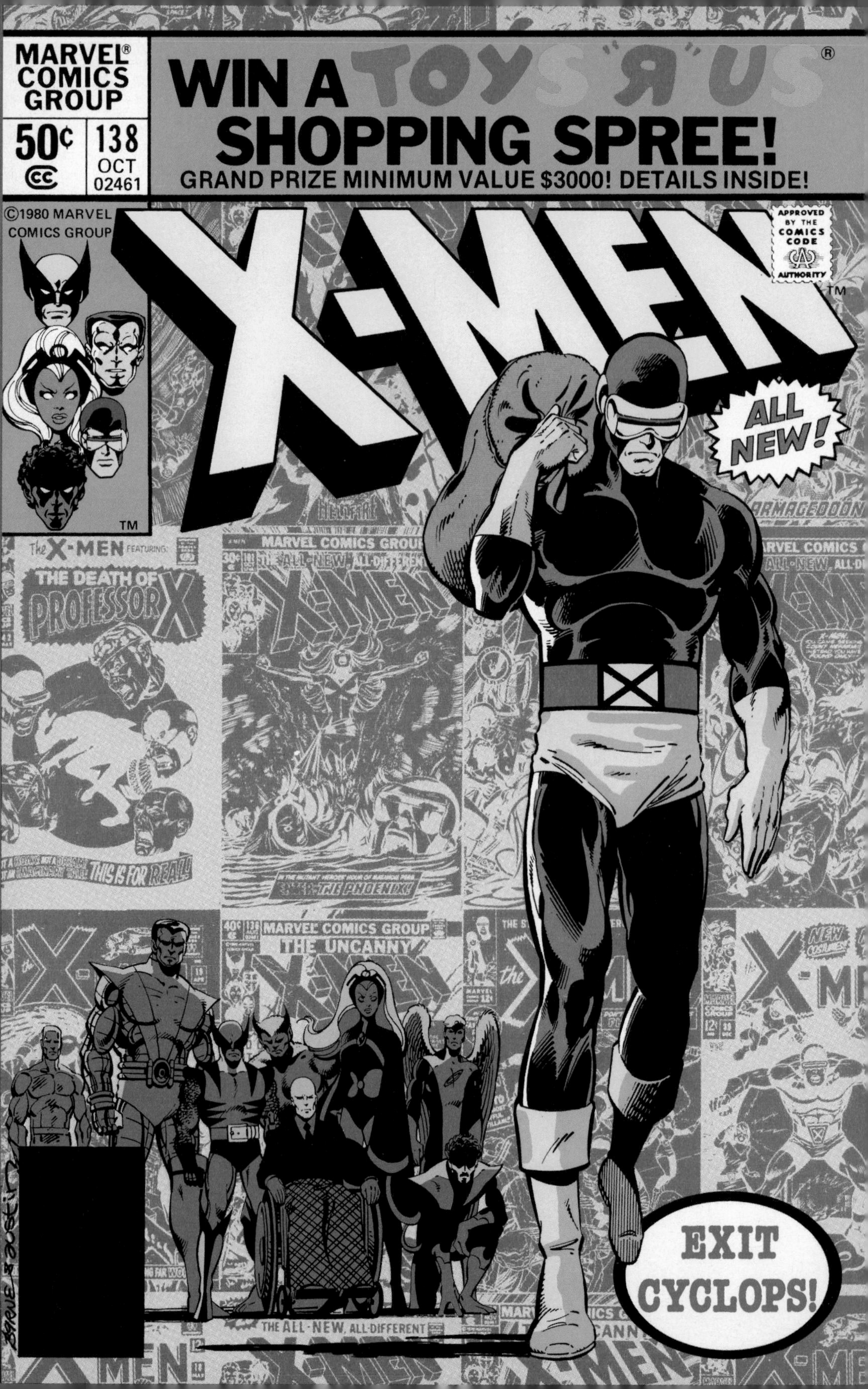

MARVEL® COMICS GROUP
50¢
138 OCT 02461
WIN A TOYS "R" US® SHOPPING SPREE!
GRAND PRIZE MINIMUM VALUE $3000! DETAILS INSIDE!
©1980 MARVEL COMICS GROUP
X-MEN™
APPROVED BY THE COMICS CODE AUTHORITY
ALL NEW!
EXIT CYCLOPS!

Cyclops. Storm. Nightcrawler. Wolverine. Colossus. Children of the atom, students of Charles Xavier, MUTANTS — feared and hated by the world they have sworn to protect. These are the STRANGEST heroes of all!

Stan Lee PRESENTS: THE UNCANNY X-MEN! ™

Elegy

"ALL MY LIFE, IT SEEMED THAT-- EVERY TIME I TURNED AROUND-- I WAS LOSING PEOPLE I LOVED: MY FOLKS, MY BROTHER ALEX, THE FEW FRIENDS I MADE AT THE ORPHANAGE. EACH TIME, THE LOSS HURT.

"LOSING YOU WAS THE LOSS I COULDN'T TAKE.

"JEAN, YOU'RE EVERYTHING TO ME -- AS NECESSARY AS THE AIR I BREATHE..."

NOW I STAND OVER HER GRAVE.

I SAID THOSE WORDS, NOT LONG AGO, TO A WOMAN I LOVED MORE THAN MY OWN LIFE.

JEAN GREY
1956·1980

HER NAME IS JEAN GREY. MINE IS SCOTT SUMMERS. THIS IS OUR STORY.

CHRIS CLAREMONT & JOHN BYRNE | TERRY AUSTIN
writer / co-plotters / penciler | inker

TOM ORZECHOWSKI | GLYNIS WEIN | LOUISE JONES | JIM SHOOTER
letterer | colorist | editor | editor-in-chief

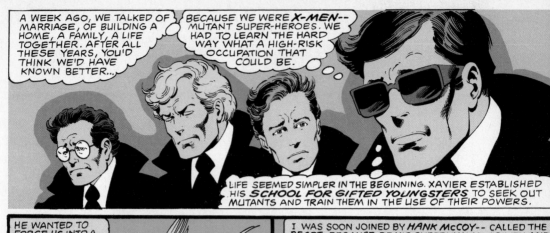

A WEEK AGO, WE TALKED OF MARRIAGE, OF BUILDING A HOME, A FAMILY, A LIFE TOGETHER. AFTER ALL THESE YEARS, YOU'D THINK WE'D HAVE KNOWN BETTER...

BECAUSE WE WERE *X-MEN*-- MUTANT SUPER-HEROES. WE HAD TO LEARN THE HARD WAY WHAT A HIGH-RISK OCCUPATION THAT COULD BE.

LIFE SEEMED SIMPLER IN THE BEGINNING. XAVIER ESTABLISHED HIS *SCHOOL FOR GIFTED YOUNGSTERS* TO SEEK OUT MUTANTS AND TRAIN THEM IN THE USE OF THEIR POWERS.

HE WANTED TO FORGE US INTO A FORCE FOR *GOOD* IN THE WORLD. *I* WAS THE FIRST X-MAN-- A RUNAWAY ORPHAN WITH *OPTIC FORCE BLASTS* THAT COULD ONLY BE CONTROLLED WITH THE AID OF A SPECIAL *RUBY QUARTZ* VISOR OR GLASSES.

I WAS SOON JOINED BY *HANK McCOY*-- CALLED THE *BEAST*, BECAUSE OF HIS SUPERHUMAN AGILITY AND DEXTERITY...

...*WARREN WORTHINGTON, III*-- CALLED *ANGEL*, THANKS TO HIS WINGS...

...AND *BOBBY DRAKE*-- *ICEMAN*, FOR OBVIOUS REASONS.

FINALLY, THERE WAS *JEAN GREY*-- *MARVEL GIRL*. SHE WAS A *TELEKINETIC*, ABLE TO MOVE SOLID OBJECTS SOLELY BY THE POWER OF HER OWN MIND.

A *REDHEAD!* LOOK AT THAT FACE... AND THE *REST* OF HER!

ALL OF A SUDDEN, I'M IN NO HURRY TO GRADUATE FROM THIS PLACE.

A GIRL... *BIG DEAL!*

WITHIN HOURS OF JEAN'S ARRIVAL, WE EMBARKED ON OUR FIRST MISSION-- AGAINST A MAN WHO WAS TO BECOME OUR DEADLIEST FOE: *MAGNETO*, MUTANT MASTER OF MAGNETISM!

FOOLS! I CAN DEFEAT *ANY* FOE... NO MATTER *HOW* SUPER-HUMAN HE MAY BE!

ALTHOUGH WE WERE UNABLE TO STOP HIM, WE FORCED MAGNETO TO ABANDON HIS ASSAULT ON THE CAPE CITADEL MISSILE BASE.

OUR BAPTISM OF FIRE HAD LASTED LESS THAN FIFTEEN MINUTES, AND WE'D EMERGED UNSCATHED, AND VICTORIOUS!

IT SEEMED SO EASY, ALMOST LIKE A GAME

6

WE THOUGHT WE WERE PRETTY HOT STUFF-- UNTIL WE FOUGHT THE *VANISHER*. FOR ALL OUR VAUNTED PROWESS, IT STILL TOOK PROFESSOR X'S PSI-POWERS TO DEFEAT HIM. GOOD AS WE WERE, WE STILL HAD A *LOT* TO LEARN.

AS TIME PASSED, I BECAME INCREASINGLY ATTRACTED TO JEAN -- YET I SAID NOTHING, DID NOTHING. I'D BEEN HURT TOO OFTEN, TOO DEEPLY, IN THE STATE ORPHANAGE WHERE I GREW UP. I WAS DETERMINED NOT TO BE HURT AGAIN.

THEN, MAGNETO RE-APPEARED.

ALSO, I FELT I HAD NO RIGHT TO LOVE *ANYONE* SO LONG AS MY OPTIC BLASTS REMAINED UNCONTROLLABLE.

THIS TIME, HE WASN'T ALONE. TOGETHER WITH QUICKSILVER, THE SCARLET WITCH, MASTER-MIND AND THE TOAD, HE FORMED A *BROTHERHOOD OF EVIL MUTANTS*.

THEY TRIED TO OVERTHROW THE SOUTH AMERICAN REPUBLIC OF SAN MARCO. WE STOPPED THEM, BUT OURS WAS A *PYRRHIC* VICTORY.

THE BATTLE LEFT THE PROFESSOR BADLY INJURED, HIS PSI-ABILITIES APPARENTLY *GONE*. WHEN MAGNETO AMBUSHED US IN NEW YORK, WE WERE ON OUR OWN FOR THE FIRST TIME.

THAT FIGHT RAGED FROM THE LEXINGTON AVENUE SUBWAY, THROUGH GRAND CENTRAL STATION, WHERE ANGEL WAS CAPTURED--

--TO *ASTEROID M*, MAGNETO'S ORBITING HEADQUARTERS. AGAIN, AS THEY HAD BEFORE, QUICKSILVER AND HIS SISTER SURREPTITIOUSLY *HELPED* US. THEY WERE TORN BY CONFLICTING LOYALTIES.

THEY OWED MAGNETO THEIR LIVES, YET IN THEIR HEARTS, THEY *HATED* WHAT HE MADE THEM DO.

MONTHS LATER, THEY LEFT MAGNETO TO BECOME HONORED MEMBERS OF THE *AVENGERS*.

WE RESCUED ANGEL, DESTROYED ASTEROID M, AND RETURNED TO EARTH RELATIVELY UNSCATHED. IN RETROSPECT, I MARVEL AT OUR LUCK.

MAGNETO, OF COURSE, *ESCAPED*.

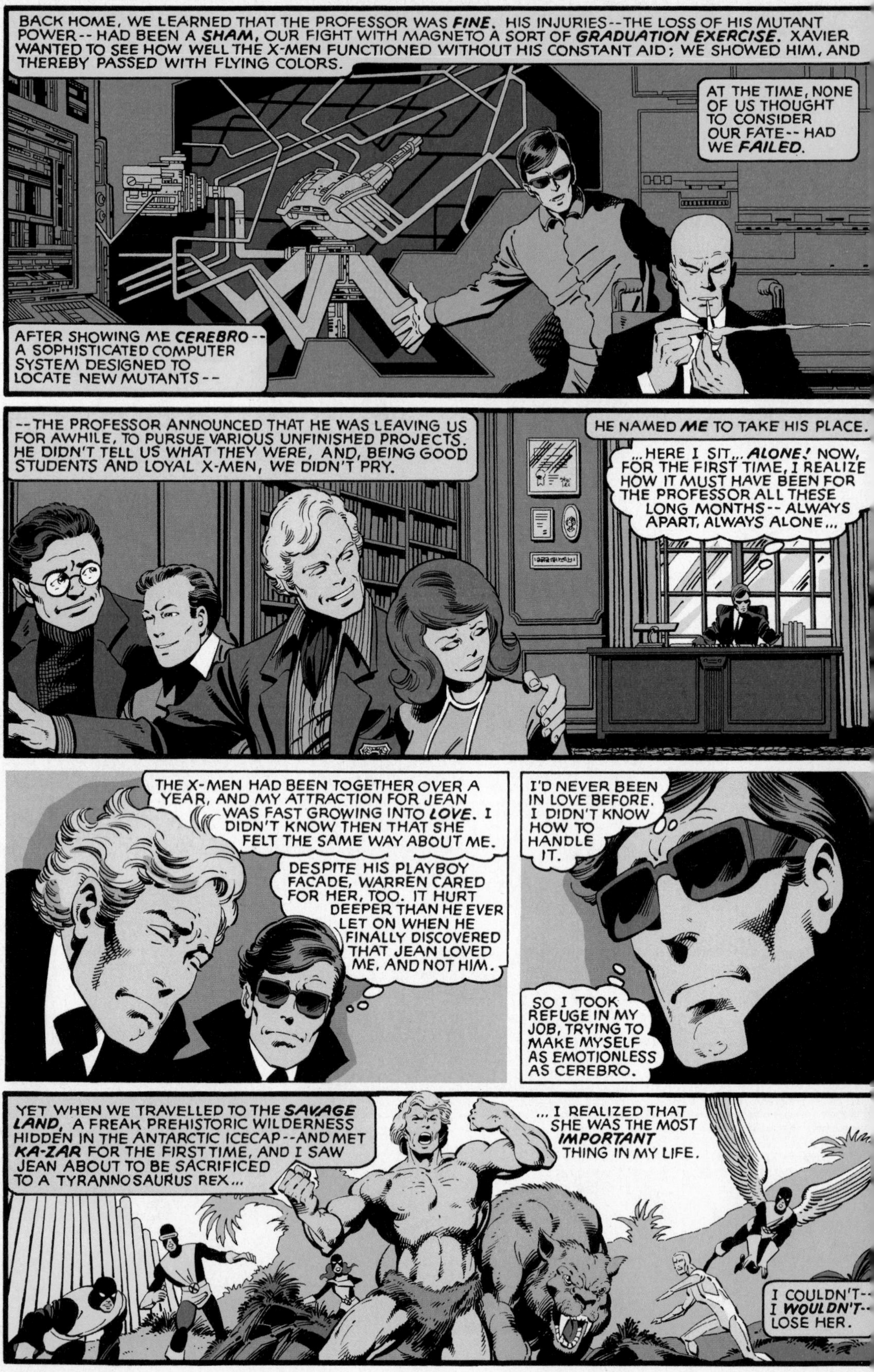
BACK HOME, WE LEARNED THAT THE PROFESSOR WAS FINE. HIS INJURIES--THE LOSS OF HIS MUTANT POWER--HAD BEEN A SHAM, OUR FIGHT WITH MAGNETO A SORT OF GRADUATION EXERCISE. XAVIER WANTED TO SEE HOW WELL THE X-MEN FUNCTIONED WITHOUT HIS CONSTANT AID; WE SHOWED HIM, AND THEREBY PASSED WITH FLYING COLORS.
AT THE TIME, NONE OF US THOUGHT TO CONSIDER OUR FATE--HAD WE FAILED.
AFTER SHOWING ME CEREBRO--A SOPHISTICATED COMPUTER SYSTEM DESIGNED TO LOCATE NEW MUTANTS--
--THE PROFESSOR ANNOUNCED THAT HE WAS LEAVING US FOR AWHILE, TO PURSUE VARIOUS UNFINISHED PROJECTS. HE DIDN'T TELL US WHAT THEY WERE, AND, BEING GOOD STUDENTS AND LOYAL X-MEN, WE DIDN'T PRY.
HE NAMED ME TO TAKE HIS PLACE.
...HERE I SIT... ALONE! NOW, FOR THE FIRST TIME, I REALIZE HOW IT MUST HAVE BEEN FOR THE PROFESSOR ALL THESE LONG MONTHS--ALWAYS APART, ALWAYS ALONE...
THE X-MEN HAD BEEN TOGETHER OVER A YEAR, AND MY ATTRACTION FOR JEAN WAS FAST GROWING INTO LOVE. I DIDN'T KNOW THEN THAT SHE FELT THE SAME WAY ABOUT ME.
DESPITE HIS PLAYBOY FACADE, WARREN CARED FOR HER, TOO. IT HURT DEEPER THAN HE EVER LET ON WHEN HE FINALLY DISCOVERED THAT JEAN LOVED ME, AND NOT HIM.
I'D NEVER BEEN IN LOVE BEFORE. I DIDN'T KNOW HOW TO HANDLE IT.
SO I TOOK REFUGE IN MY JOB, TRYING TO MAKE MYSELF AS EMOTIONLESS AS CEREBRO.
YET WHEN WE TRAVELLED TO THE SAVAGE LAND, A FREAK PREHISTORIC WILDERNESS HIDDEN IN THE ANTARCTIC ICECAP--AND MET KA-ZAR FOR THE FIRST TIME, AND I SAW JEAN ABOUT TO BE SACRIFICED TO A TYRANNOSAURUS REX...
...I REALIZED THAT SHE WAS THE MOST IMPORTANT THING IN MY LIFE.
I COULDN'T--I WOULDN'T--LOSE HER.

MAGNETO WAS NEVER ONE TO SUFFER DEFEAT LIGHTLY. EACH SETBACK MERELY STRENGTHENED HIS DETERMINATION TO DESTROY US. FINALLY, HE CONTACTED A MYSTERIOUS BEING WHO CALLED HIMSELF THE "STRANGER" AND TRIED TO ENLIST HIS AID...

... ONLY TO DISCOVER THAT HE'D BITTEN OFF FAR MORE THAN HE COULD CHEW. BOTH HE AND PROFESSOR X ASSUMED THE STRANGER TO BE A MUTANT. THEY WERE WRONG.

HE WAS AN ALIEN.

HE TOOK MAGNETO AND THE TOAD WITH HIM TO HIS HOME AMONG THE STARS. HE SAID THEY WOULD NEVER RETURN.

I CAN'T SAY I WAS SORRY TO SEE THEM GO.

BUT IF WE THOUGHT OUR LIVES WOULD GET ANY EASIER WITH MAGNETO'S ABRUPT DEPARTURE, WE WERE SOON RUDELY DISILLUSIONED. ALMOST IMMEDIATELY, CEREBRO'S MUTANT ALARM HERALDED THE ARRIVAL OF A FOE WHOSE RAW POWER AND FEROCITY WERE AS AWESOME AS HIS HATE.

HIS NAME WAS CAIN MARKO. HE WAS PROFESSOR XAVIER'S HALF-BROTHER.

WE CAME TO KNOW HIM BETTER AS--
JUGGERNAUT!

WE THREW EVERYTHING WE HAD AT HIM. NOTHING WORKED. AFTER A DESPERATE FIGHT, ANGEL, WITH THE AID OF THE HUMAN TORCH, MANAGED TO REMOVE MARKO'S HELMET, THEREBY RENDERING JUGGERNAUT VULNERABLE TO THE PROFESSOR'S TELEPATHIC ATTACK.

WE'D SURVIVED, WE'D TRIUMPHED, BY THE SKIN OF OUR TEETH. WE DIDN'T KNOW THAT THERE WAS FAR WORSE YET TO COME.

9

AN ANTHROPOLOGIST NAMED *BOLIVAR TRASK* SPOKE OUT AGAINST THE *"MUTANT MENACE"*, AND, SEEMINGLY OVERNIGHT, THE X-MEN BECAME VIRTUAL PUBLIC ENEMIES. TRASK HAD CREATED GIANT ROBOTIC *SENTINELS* TO COMBAT THIS *"MENACE"*, BUT THINGS QUICKLY GOT OUT OF HAND. INSTEAD OF PROTECTING HUMANITY, THE SENTINELS-- LED BY THEIR *MASTER MOLD*-- SET OUT TO CONQUER IT.

LOOKING BACK ON THOSE DAYS, IT SEEMS LIKE WE WERE CONSTANTLY FIGHTING SOME NEW MUTANT MENACE OR SUPER-VILLAIN.

TRASK SACRIFICED HIS LIFE TO DESTROY HIS REBELLIOUS CREATIONS--AND THAT EPIC BATTLE ALMOST KILLED *ICEMAN* AS WELL.

NO MATTER HOW HARD WE TRIED TO LIVE OUR OWN LIVES, BEING AN X-MAN ALWAYS SEEMED TO TAKE PRECEDENCE. I DIDN'T MIND, THEN. PERHAPS I SHOULD HAVE.

JEAN WAS AN UNDERGRADUATE STUDENT AT METRO UNIVERSITY. I WAS DESPERATELY AFRAID OF LOSING HER, YET TERRIFIED OF TELLING HER SO. THE NIGHT OF BOBBY'S 18th BIRTHDAY, I RESOLVED TO LET HER KNOW HOW I FELT. I THINK I'D HAVE RATHER FACED JUGGERNAUT SINGLE-HANDED.

A *SURPRISE PARTY*-- IN GREENWICH VILLAGE! HOW LUCKY CAN A GUY *BE?!*

HI, CREW! I WANT YOU TO MEET A VERY GOOD FRIEND OF MINE-- *CANDY SOUTHERN!*

HEADS UP, GROUP! WARREN'S HERE!

AND LOOK AT THE GAL HE BROUGHT WITH HIM!

I'M VERY GLAD TO MEET ALL OF YOU!

10

IT WAS A BEAUTIFUL EVENING, PERFECT FOR A LOVERS' STROLL THROUGH CENTRAL PARK. WE MUST HAVE WALKED AND TALKED FOR HOURS.

I DON'T REMEMBER MUCH OF MY CHILDHOOD, EXCEPT IN... NIGHTMARES. I USED TO HAVE A LOT OF THEM. I'D BE FALLING THROUGH FLAMES; I'D SEE FACES-- A MAN, A WOMAN, MY FOLKS I GUESS. I'LL NEVER KNOW FOR SURE.

I WAS IN THE HOSPITAL FOR OVER A YEAR, AFTER I WAS FOUND. THE DOCTORS SAID I SUFFERED SOME BRAIN DAMAGE. THAT ACCOUNTS FOR MY AMNESIA, AND, THE PROFESSOR THINKS, FOR WHY I CAN'T CONTROL MY OPTIC BLASTS.

I WAS NEVER ADOPTED. THE ORPHANAGE WAS THE ONLY HOME I KNEW... UNTIL I RAN AWAY. SAYING ALL THIS ISN'T EASY, JEAN... I...

I... LOVE YOU. I'VE LOVED YOU FROM THE MOMENT I SET EYES ON YOU.

AND I, YOU, SCOTT, WITH ALL MY HEART!

THAT SAME NIGHT, THE PROFESSOR WAS KIDNAPPED BY A GROUP OF DEADLY VILLAINS CALLING THEMSELVES *FACTOR 3.* THEY WERE THE UNWITTING PAWNS OF THEIR LEADER, "MUTANT MASTER," WHO TURNED OUT TO BE A "BUG-EYED MONSTER" FROM A PLANET IN THE SIRIUS SYSTEM.

WHILE WE SEARCHED FOR THE PROFESSOR WE FACED A NUMBER OF THREATS THAT HAD NOTHING TO DO WITH HIS KID-NAPPING.

IN THE END WE TRIUMPHED OVER THEM ALL. "MUTANT MASTER" WAS DEFEATED AND THE PROFESSOR WAS RETURNED HOME, SAFE AND SOUND.

SOMETHING OF A TREAT AWAITED US AT HOME-- COURTESY OF THE PROFESSOR AND JEAN-- NEW UNIFORMS!

"THE X-MEN ARE SCARCELY *CHILDREN* ANYMORE!" XAVIER TOLD US. "THEY'VE EACH PROVED THEMSELVES A *HUNDRED* TIMES.

"IT'S TIME THEY LOOKED LIKE *INDIVIDUALS*-- NOT PRODUCTS OF AN *ASSEMBLY LINE!*"

IN A SENSE, OUR NEW COSTUMES *DID* MARK OUR COMING OF AGE. CERTAINLY IT MARKED THE BEGINNING OF A *GRIM* CHAPTER IN OUR HISTORY.

IN THE SUBWAYS BENEATH MANHATTAN, WE FACED A SUBTERRANEAN POWER-HOUSE NAMED *GROTESK*.

HE WAS THE LAST SURVIVOR OF A RACE EXTERMINATED BY RADIATION FROM NUCLEAR TESTS. HE WISHED TO PAY HUMANITY BACK IN KIND. WE STOPPED HIM, BUT IT COST US FAR MORE THAN WE'D EXPECTED...

PROFESSOR CHARLES XAVIER.

WITH THE PROFESSOR'S DEATH, THE HEAD AND HEART AND SOUL OF THE X-MEN HAD BEEN DESTROYED. WE WOULD LEARN TO LIVE WITH OUR LOSS, BUT NOTHING WOULD EVER BE QUITE THE SAME FOR US AGAIN. AT THE GOVERNMENT'S REQUEST, THE TEAM SPLIT UP.

BOBBY DRAKE ENDED UP IN SAN FRANCISCO, WHERE HE MET A LOVELY YOUNG LADY NAMED *LORNA DANE.*

HER GREEN HAIR MARKED HER AS A MUTANT...

...BUT WHAT KIND--AND HOW POWERFUL--A MUTANT WE DIDN'T LEARN UNTIL SHE WAS SUBJECTED TO MESMERO'S MUTANT ENERGY STIMULATOR. SHE EMERGED AS *POLARIS*, MISTRESS OF MAGNETISM--

--DAUGHTER OF *MAGNETO!*

THIS LAST PROVED TO BE A VICIOUS DECEPTION. MAGNETO--WHO HAD PREVIOUSLY ESCAPED FROM THE STRANGER'S WORLD-- WAS *NOT* LORNA'S FATHER...

...HE MERELY *CLAIMED* TO BE, IN ORDER TO ENTICE HER INTO JOINING HIS CAUSE. HE FAILED.

FBI EDICT OR NO, WE BEGAN TO DRIFT BACK TOGETHER. SEPARATING THE X-MEN HADN'T REALLY WORKED OUT. IT MERELY PROVED WHAT WE ALREADY KNEW, THAT THE WHOLE OF THE TEAM WAS GREATER THAN THE SUM OF THE PARTS.

WE WERE MORE THAN A SIMPLE FIGHTING TEAM. THE X-MEN WERE A *FAMILY.* IN MY CASE, THE ONLY FAMILY I HAD--

-- SAVE FOR MY YOUNGER BROTHER, *ALEX.*

I INTRODUCED THE X-MEN TO HIM --AND HIM TO THEM --THE DAY HE GRADUATED FROM LANDON COLLEGE.

WE'D BEEN SEPARATED IN THE ORPHANAGE-- HE'D BEEN ADOPTED WHILE I'D BEEN IN THE HOSPITAL, IN A COMA. PROFESSOR X HELPED ME TRACK HIM DOWN, AND WE'D STAYED IN CLOSE TOUCH EVER SINCE. I KNEW HE WAS A MUTANT, BUT-- AS WITH LORNA-- WE DIDN'T DISCOVER THE NATURE AND EXTENT OF HIS POWERS...

...UNTIL HE WAS KIDNAPPED BY THE *LIVING PHARAOH.*

THE TWO WERE *SYMBIOTES,* EACH DRAWING POWER FROM COSMIC RAYS AND FROM EACH OTHER.

AS ALEX'S ABILITY WAXED, THE PHARAOH'S WANED-- AND VICE VERSA. A FULL CHARGE TRANS-FORMED THAT EGYPTIAN MADMAN INTO THE *LIVING MONOLITH.*

BUT WHEN HE WAS DEFEATED, ALL THAT RAW ENERGY FLOWED INTO ALEX. AND WHAT I FEARED MOST CAME TO PASS.

HE COULDN'T CONTROL IT.

IN HIS OWN WAY, HE WAS AS POTENTIAL-LY DANGEROUS AS I. UNABLE TO COPE WITH THAT DREAD REALIZATION--AND, TO BE HONEST, I CAN'T SAY I BLAME HIM-- HE FLED FROM THE X-MEN... RIGHT INTO THE ARMS OF A *SENTINEL.*

13

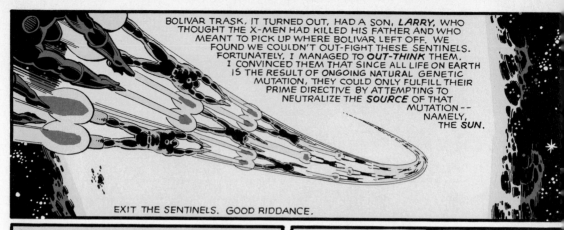

BOLIVAR TRASK, IT TURNED OUT, HAD A SON, *LARRY*, WHO THOUGHT THE X-MEN HAD KILLED HIS FATHER AND WHO MEANT TO PICK UP WHERE BOLIVAR LEFT OFF. WE FOUND WE COULDN'T OUT-FIGHT THESE SENTINELS. FORTUNATELY, I MANAGED TO *OUT-THINK* THEM. I CONVINCED THEM THAT SINCE ALL LIFE ON EARTH IS THE RESULT OF ONGOING NATURAL GENETIC MUTATION, THEY COULD ONLY FULFILL THEIR PRIME DIRECTIVE BY ATTEMPTING TO NEUTRALIZE THE *SOURCE* OF THAT MUTATION-- NAMELY, THE *SUN*.

EXIT THE SENTINELS. GOOD RIDDANCE.

BUT WE'D SUFFERED A CASUALTY... ALEX. WE RUSHED HIM TO A COLLEAGUE OF THE PROFESSOR'S, *DR. KARL LYKOS*... NOT ONE OF OUR BRIGHTER MOVES. LYKOS, UNFORTUNATELY, WAS A NON-MUTANT VARIENT WHO EXISTED BY ABSORBING THE LIFE FORCE FROM OTHER BEINGS. DOING THAT TO ALEX...

...TRANSFORMED LYKOS INTO *SAURON*-- A HUMANOID PTERODACTYL WITH HYPNOTIC/ILLUSION POWERS THAT PUT BOTH MESMERO AND MASTERMIND TO SHAME.

LYKOS WAS A DRIVEN, TORMENTED SOUL, BUT BASICALLY A GOOD MAN. HE WANTED ONLY TO BE WORTHY OF *TANYA ANDERSSEN*, THE WOMAN HE LOVED. SAURON, THOUGH, WAS A CREATURE OF *PURE EVIL*.

WE FOUGHT HIM IN NEW YORK, AND FOLLOWED HIM WHEN HE FLED TO HIS HOME IN *TIERRA DEL FUEGO*.

KARL!!

THERE, RATHER THAN SURVIVE BY KILLING TANYA, LYKOS TOOK HIS OWN LIFE.

OUR UNSUCCESSFUL QUEST TO RECOVER LYKOS' BODY LED TO KA-ZAR'S SAVAGE LAND, AND YET ANOTHER CONFRONTATION WITH MAGNETO.

HE FOUGHT HARD, AS USUAL. HE LOST.

NO SOONER HAD WE RETURNED HOME THAN WE FACED YET ANOTHER MUTANT THREAT, A JAPANESE YOUTH: *SHIRO YASHIDA-- SUNFIRE!*

HE WASN'T EVIL, MERELY MISGUIDED-- BUT IT TOOK THE VIOLENT DEATH OF HIS FATHER TO SHOW HIM THE ERROR OF HIS WAYS.

14

WE WERE DOG-TIRED, AND IN NO CONDITION... MENTALLY OR PHYSICALLY... FOR THE SURPRISE AWAITING US AT THE MANSION: PROFESSOR XAVIER... *ALIVE!*

GROTESK HAD MURDERED A MUTANT SHAPE-CHANGER-- THE *CHANGELING*-- WHO HAD TAKEN THE PROFESSOR'S PLACE, WHILE HE WORKED ON A SUPER-SECRET PROJECT. XAVIER *SAID* IT WAS A *NECESSARY* DECEPTION.

I WONDERED. ALL THE PAIN, THE GRIEF WE SUFFERED-- IT HAD ALL BEEN FOR *NOTHING.*

I THOUGHT IT *CRUEL.*

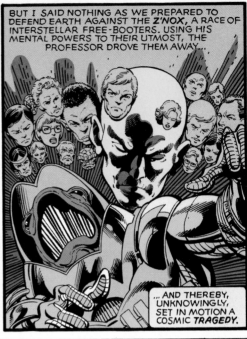

BUT I SAID NOTHING AS WE PREPARED TO DEFEND EARTH AGAINST THE *Z'NOX*, A RACE OF INTERSTELLAR FREE-BOOTERS. USING HIS MENTAL POWERS TO THEIR UTMOST, THE PROFESSOR DROVE THEM AWAY...

... AND THEREBY, UNKNOWINGLY, SET IN MOTION A COSMIC *TRAGEDY.*

CONSIDERING THE CIRCUMSTANCES, WHAT ALTERNATIVE DID HE HAVE? GOOD OR BAD, HE DID WHAT HE THOUGHT BEST.

AS HANK DID WHEN HE LEFT THE X-MEN SOON AFTER THAT TO GO TO WORK FOR THE BRAND CORPORATION.

SOMETHING HAPPENED TO HIM THERE-- HE STILL WON'T SPEAK OF IT. HE MUTATED PHYSICALLY, FROM A PERSON WITH THE *ABILITY* OF A BEAST, TO ONE WITH THE *LOOK* OF A BEAST AS WELL.

EVEN NOW, HE'S HIDING HIS TRUE FEATURES UNDER A MASK OF HIS OLD FACE.

SINCE THEN, HE QUIT BRAND AND JOINED THE AVENGERS. I HOPE HE'S *HAPPY* WITH THEM. HE DESERVES IT. WE *ALL* DO.

TIME PASSED, AND AN UNEXPECTED EMERGENCY FORCED THE PROFESSOR TO RECRUIT *NEW* X-MEN. HE FOUND:

KURT WAGNER-- NIGHTCRAWLER-- AGILE AS THE BEAST AND POSSESSING THE ABILITY TO TELEPORT. *ORORO-- STORM--* AN ELEMENTAL, ABLE TO CONTROL THE WEATHER. *PETER RASPUTIN-- COLOSSUS--* ABLE TO TRANSFORM HIS BODY INTO NEAR-INVULNERABLE ORGANIC STEEL. *JOHN PROUDSTAR-- THUNDERBIRD--* FAST, STRONG, AGILE, A SUPER-TRACKER.

WOLVERINE-- WITH THE HYPER-SENSES OF AN ANIMAL, PLUS AN UNBREAKABLE ADAMANTIUM SKELETON AND CLAWS. *SEAN CASSIDY-- BANSHEE--* MASTER OF THE SONIC SCREAM. AND *SUNFIRE--* ABLE TO GENERATE NUCLEAR FIREBOLTS.

THE *NEW* TEAM'S FIRST MISSION WAS TO RESCUE THE OLD FROM THE CLUTCHES OF A LIVING ISLAND--

--A MUTANT COLONY CREATURE THAT CALLED ITSELF *KRAKOA*.

COMBINING THE POWERS OF MYSELF, ALEX, STORM AND POLARIS, WE MANAGED TO SEVER THE GRAVIMETRIC LINES OF FORCE BENEATH THE ISLAND. FOR A MOMENT, GRAVITY THERE CEASED TO EXIST.

MOTHER NATURE DID THE REST.

CENTRIFUGAL FORCE RIPPED KRAKOA OUT OF THE SEABED AND HURLED IT INTO SPACE.

ENTER THE NEW X-MEN, *EXIT* THE OLD. THEY DECIDED THAT THE TIME HAD COME TO LEAVE, TO FINALLY BEGIN TO LIVE THEIR OWN LIVES. JEAN LEFT WITH THEM.

I STAYED. I LOVED JEAN. BUT I HAD NO LIFE-- NO PURPOSE-- OUTSIDE THE X-MEN-- HERE I FELT I WAS NEEDED. SHE UNDERSTOOD, AND FOR THAT I LOVED HER ALL THE MORE.

I HAD A MONTH TO TRAIN THESE NEOPHYTE X-MEN BEFORE OUR FIRST BATTLE-- WITH COUNT NEFARIA AND HIS ANI-MEN. THIS TEAM DIDN'T MESH AS WELL AS THE OLD. IT WAS OLDER, MORE EXPERIENCED, ITS MEMBERS MORE USED TO WORKING *SOLO* THAN AS A UNIT.

IN THE PAST, THE X-MEN HAD OFTEN MADE UP WITH LUCK WHAT WE LACKED IN EXPERIENCE, OR SKILL. THAT FATEFUL DAY, IN THE SKY ABOVE VALHALLA MOUNTAIN, OUR LUCK FINALLY *RAN OUT*.

DEFEATED, NEFARIA TRIED TO ESCAPE IN A STOLEN FIGHTER. THUNDERBIRD AND BANSHEE WENT AFTER HIM. THE PLANE BLEW UP, AND CRASHED. THUNDERBIRD DIDN'T SURVIVE.

IS THAT WHEN I BEGAN TO QUESTION-- TOO LITTLE, TOO LATE?

DID IT TAKE THUNDER-BIRD'S *DEATH* TO MAKE ME REALIZE THE TRUE COST OF A MISTAKE?

I KEEP REMEMBERING WHAT ORORO ASKED ME NOT LONG AGO -- IF *THIS* WAS THE LIFE I IMAGINED FOR MYSELF WHEN I WAS YOUNG?

WAS THIS THE LIFE *ANY* OF US IMAGINED FOR OURSELVES?

THINGS WERE RELATIVELY PEACEFUL FOR THE X-MEN AFTER THAT. THE PROFESSOR LEFT ON A VACATION. I SPENT MORE AND MORE TIME WITH JEAN. WE WERE HAPPY, CONTENT.

IT WAS TOO GOOD TO LAST. IT DIDN'T.

PREPARE TO FACE YOUR *DOOM,* MUTANTS--

--FOR THE *SENTINELS* HAVE RETURNED!

I'LL NEVER FORGET THE 72 HOURS THAT FOLLOWED. THESE NEO-SENTINELS WERE THE BRAINCHILD OF A GOVERNMENT WACKO NAMED *STEVEN LANG.* WE FOUGHT HIM IN AN ABANDONED AMERICAN SPACE STATION, AND WON. BUT DURING RE-ENTRY, WE WERE CAUGHT IN A *SOLAR FLARE.*

THE FLARE-- THE RADIATION-- IT'S STARTING TO *GET THROUGH!*

SCOTT!

EVERYONE BUT JEAN WAS IN THE SHUTTLE'S SHIELDED ANTI-RADIATION CELL. SHE WAS ON THE UNPROTECTED FLIGHT DECK, PILOTING THE SPACE-CRAFT. SHE USED HER TELEKINETIC POWER TO BLOCK THE SOLAR RADIATION AS LONG AS POSSIBLE. BUT EVEN SHE COULDN'T HOLD OUT INDEFIN

WE ALL THOUGHT SHE'D DIED. CERTAINLY NOTHING EVEN REMOTELY *HUMAN* COULD HAVE SURVIVED.

NOTHING REMOTELY HUMAN *DID.*

HEAR ME, X-MEN!

NO LONGER AM I, THE WOMAN YOU *KNEW!*

I AM *FIRE!* AND *LIFE INCARNATE!* NOW AND FOREVER --

-- I AM phœnix!

PART OF ME WISHES JEAN HAD... DIED IN THAT CRASH. AND YET... I WOULDN'T HAVE MISSED THIS LAST MONTH -- OUR LAST WEEKS TOGETHER -- FOR THE WORLD.

XAVIER SENT THE X-MEN TO IRELAND FOR A VACATION -- WHILE I STAYED WITH JEAN IN NEW YORK. SOME VACA-TION. FIRST THEY FOUGHT *JUGGERNAUT* AND HIS NEW PARTNER-- BANSHEE'S VILLAINOUS COUSIN, *BLACK TOM CASSIDY--* AND THEN MAGNETO.

AT THE SAME TIME, WE SOMEHOW GOT CAUGHT UP IN AN INTERSTELLAR CIVIL WAR. XAVIER HAD BEEN CONTACTED BY AN ALIEN PRINCESS, *LILANDRA*. ONE LOOK AND HE WAS HEAD OVER HEELS IN LOVE WITH HER, AND SHE WITH HIM.

INCREDIBLE.

HER BROTHER, EMPEROR OF THE SHI'AR, HAD LEARNED OF AN ANCIENT FORCE, KNOWN ONLY AS *"THE END OF ALL THAT IS."* HE MEANT TO MASTER IT. LILANDRA MEANT TO *STOP* HIM. THAT LED TO THE X-MEN'S INITIAL CONFRONTATION WITH THE *IMPERIAL GUARD*.

TOO LATE, WE DISCOVERED THAT THIS ANCIENT *"FORCE"* WAS A *NEUTRON GALAXY*. ONCE UNLEASHED, IT COULD NEVER BE RESTRAINED -- AND ITS MIND-BOGGLING POWER WOULD DESTROY THE ENTIRE *UNIVERSE!*

WE -- HECK, *EVERYTHING* -- WOULD HAVE PERISHED THAT DAY IF NOT FOR *JEAN*.

THE NEUTRON GALAXY WAS BOUND WITHIN A LATTICE OF LIVING ANTI-ENERGY. THANKS TO THE EMPEROR'S MEDDLING, THAT LATTICE WAS UNRAVELLING.

PHOENIX -- WITH THE SPIRITUAL SUPPORT OF THE X-MEN -- KNITTED THAT LATTICE BACK TOGETHER AGAIN.

PHOENIX SAVED THE UNIVERSE. HOW PROSAIC THAT SOUNDS. HOW... *INADEQUATE*. WORDS CAN'T DESCRIBE WHAT JEAN DID.

OR HOW I FEEL.

WHAT DO YOU SAY, WHAT DO YOU *DO*, WHEN THE WOMAN YOU LOVE BECOMES... SUPREMELY POWERFUL? WHAT DO YOU DO WHEN SHE... *DIES?*

AFTER THAT, WE ALL TRIED OUR BEST TO PUT OUR LIVES BACK IN ORDER. IT DIDN'T WORK. FIRST, THE CANADIAN GOVERNMENT -- REFUSING TO ACCEPT WOLVER-INE'S RESIGNATION FROM THEIR SECRET SERVICE --

-- SENT *VINDICATOR* TO BRING HIM HOME.

THEN, MESMERO -- WITH SURPRISING, DISCONCERTING EASE -- CAPTURED US AND TURNED US INTO CARNIVAL FREAKS. WE'D PROBABLY BE THERE STILL...

...IF THE BEAST HADN'T COME LOOKING FOR US. HE RISKED HIS LIFE AND SANITY BUSTING US FREE.

UNFORTUNATELY, THINGS QUICKLY WENT FROM BAD TO WORSE. OUR NEXT FOE WAS MAGNETO. HE BEAT US HANDS DOWN. WE REFUSED TO GIVE UP, THOUGH, AND THE RESULTANT BATTLE-ROYAL PRETTY MUCH TRASHED HIS ANTARCTIC BASE, BURIED IN THE HEART OF A LIVE VOLCANO.

FOR HANK, I GRIEVED. BUT FOR JEAN...

...I FELT *NOTHING*.

I WAS *NUMB*, HURT SO DEEPLY THAT I DARED NOT LET MYSELF FEEL IT.

BUT IN THE CONFUSION, WE BECAME SEPARATED. JEAN AND HANK MADE IT TO THE SURFACE, WHILE THE REST OF US TUNNELED OUR WAY INTO THE SAVAGE LAND. EACH GROUP THOUGHT THE OTHER DEAD.

AT THE TIME, I-- AND SOME X-MEN -- THOUGHT IT WAS BECAUSE I DIDN'T CARE.

WE WENT ON FROM THERE,... BECAUSE WE HAD TO --

-- EACH OF US DEALING WITH OUR LOSS IN HIS OWN WAY WE HELPED KA-ZAR SAVE THE SAVAGE LAND, HELPED SUN-FIRE SAVE JAPAN, AND ENDED UP IN A CRAZY DONNY-BROOK IN CALGARY WITH A CANADIAN SUPER-HERO GROUP CALLED *ALPHA FLIGHT*.

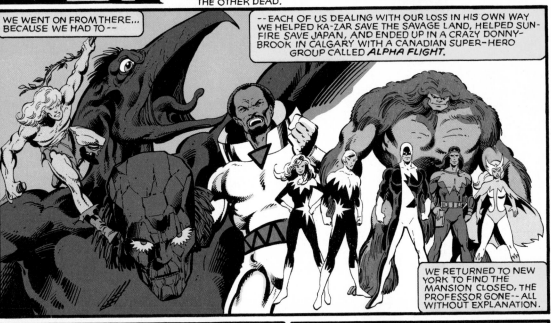

WE RETURNED TO NEW YORK TO FIND THE MANSION CLOSED, THE PROFESSOR GONE-- ALL WITHOUT EXPLANATION.

TO EASE HIS GRIEF OVER OUR SUPPOSED "DEATH," LILANDRA HAD INVITED HIM TO ACCOMPANY HER TO HER HOMEWORLD, AS HER IMPERIAL CONSORT. FEELING THAT THERE WAS NOTHING LEFT TO REALLY HOLD HIM TO THE EARTH, XAVIER *ACCEPTED*.

IN NO TIME AT ALL, WE WERE FIGHTING FOR OUR LIVES IN *MURDERWORLD* -- AN ASSASSINATION AMUSEMENT PARK RUN BY A NUT-CASE KILLER-FOR-HIRE NAMED *ARCADE*.

SIMULTANEOUSLY, IN SCOTLAND, JEAN WAS BECOMING INVOLVED WITH *JASON WYNGARDE (HIS REAL NAME, IRONICALLY ENOUGH)* -- A MAN THE X-MEN KNEW FAR BETTER AS *MASTERMIND*.

HE'D HOOKED UP WITH AN OUTFIT CALLED THE *HELLFIRE CLUB*. THEY MEANT TO RULE THE WORLD. THEY SAW THE X-MEN -- AND ESPECIALLY JEAN -- AS A MEANS TO ACHIEVING THAT END.

BUT MASTERMIND HAD MADE A *FATAL* MIS-CALCULATION. HE ASSUMED THAT PHOENIX WAS MERELY MARVEL GIRL WITH A DIFFERENT NAME AND FLASHIER COSTUME.

SHE WASN'T.

IT WAS INCREASINGLY EVIDENT TO JEAN -- AND TO *MOIRA MacTAGGERT*, XAVIER'S LONG-TIME COLLEAGUE IN MUTANT RESEARCH -- THAT THERE WAS NO COMPARI-SON BETWEEN MARVEL GIRL AND PHOENIX.

IT'S EASY TO PLAY "*WHAT IF*" GAMES, TO THINK OF WHAT *MIGHT* HAVE BEEN. MOIRA FEARED THAT JEAN'S POWER COULD GET OUT OF CONTROL. SHE MIGHT HAVE FOUND A WAY TO PREVENT THAT...

... HAD HER -- AND OUR -- ATTENTION NOT BEEN DIVERTED BY THE MENACE OF HER SON, *PROTEUS*.

TO EXIST, HE POSSESSED PEOPLE-- CONSUMING A LIFETIME'S WORTH OF BIO-ENERGY IN A MATTER OF HOURS. HE THOUGHT OF PEOPLE THE WAY WE THINK OF COWS--AS *FOOD*. IF HE HUNGERED FOR A LIFE, HE *TOOK* IT.

HE WAS THE KIND OF MUTANT THE X-MEN HAD BEEN FORMED TO COMBAT.

MY ONE REGRET WAS THAT OUR BATTLE WITH PROTEUS WAS TO THE *DEATH*. IT WAS NECESSARY, BUT I WISH THERE'D BEEN ANOTHER WAY.

THINGS HAVE A WAY OF *BALANCING* OUT, THOUGH. WE'D FOUND A TRULY EVIL MUTANT IN PROTEUS. BUT SOON AFTER THAT WE FOUND A TRULY GOOD ONE-- INDEED, A POTENTIAL X-MAN --

-- IN *KITTY PRYDE*.

SHE'S 13½, CUTE, BRIGHT, SPUNKY-- AND SHE WALKS THROUGH WALLS.

THEN,.. CAME THE HELLFIRE CLUB. MASTERMIND HAD SUCCEEDED IN SUBVERTING JEAN BY MAKING HER BELIEVE THAT SHE WAS PSYCHICALLY SLIPPING IN TIME, RELIVING AN ANCESTOR'S LIFE. THE WORLD SHE SAW WAS THAT OF *1780*, NOT 1980.

BY THE TIME SHE BROKE HIS CONTROL OVER HER, THE DAMAGE HAD BEEN DONE.

NO LONGER WAS SHE PHOENIX, CHILD OF LIGHT AND LAUGHTER. SHE WAS *DARK PHOENIX*, THE BLACK ANGEL, CHAOS-BRINGER.

RAVAGER OF WORLDS.

AT HER HANDS, AN ENTIRE STAR SYSTEM-- FIVE BILLION PEOPLE -- DIED. SHE WAS DRIVEN BY NEEDS, DESIRES, PASSIONS THAT NONE OF US CAN COMPREHEND-- AFTER ALL, WE'RE ONLY HUMAN. PHOENIX WAS A STEP BEYOND.

BUT... SHE WAS STILL THE WOMAN I LOVED. I HAD TO TRY TO SAVE HER. I TRIED TO TALK HER DOWN. I WAS REACHING HER WHEN PROFESSOR X STEPPED IN. I USED REASON...HE USED *FORCE*. WHO'S TO SAY WHICH OF US HAD THE *BETTER* WAY?

HE AND PHOENIX FACED OFF IN A *PSI-WAR*. HE WON. JEAN WAS "CURED," THE POWER OF THE PHOENIX ONCE MORE UNDER CONTROL. I ASKED HER TO MARRY ME. SHE SAID, YES. HAPPY ENDING.

NOT SO.

ENTER LILANDRA, DETERMINED TO ELIMINATE PHOENIX AS A THREAT ONCE AND FOR ALL.

WHEN HER IMPERIAL GUARD FAILED, JEAN FINISHED THE JOB HERSELF.

SCOTT!

JEAN!

THIS... IS PAIN BEYOND PAIN. I NEVER KNEW A BODY COULD HURT SO MUCH AND STILL... FUNCTION.

I'M NOT SURE I WANT TO CALL THIS *"LIVING."*

HOW ARE YOU BEARING UP, SCOTT? I KNOW HOW MUCH YOU LOVED JEAN, AND SHE YOU. I KNOW HOW HARD ALL THIS MUST BE ...

DON'T WORRY ABOUT ME, SIR. I'LL BE FINE. BUT HOW ARE *YOU?* AND *MRS. GREY?*

SURVIVING.

PROFESSOR GREY, I SPEAK FOR ALL SHI'AR WHEN I SAY HOW... SORRY WE ARE AT YOUR DAUGHTER'S DEATH. YOUR GRIEF IS OURS.

THANK YOU, YOUR ..., MAJESTY. THAT'S VERY KIND.

SO LONG AS I RULE, SO LONG AS SHI'AR ENDURES, JEAN GREY'S NAME AND MEMORY WILL BE

SHE GAVE HER LIFE, THAT THE *UNIVERSE* MIGHT LIVE.

PLEASE ACCEPT THIS GIFT. IT IS A HOLEMPATHIC MATRIX CRYSTAL. TOUCH IT, AND YOU WILL NOT ONLY SEE A 3-DIMENSIONAL IMAGE OF JEAN, BUT FEEL THE ESSENCE OF HER PERSONALITY AS WELL. THIS WAY, A PART OF HER WILL BE WITH YOU, ALWAYS.

Th- thank you.

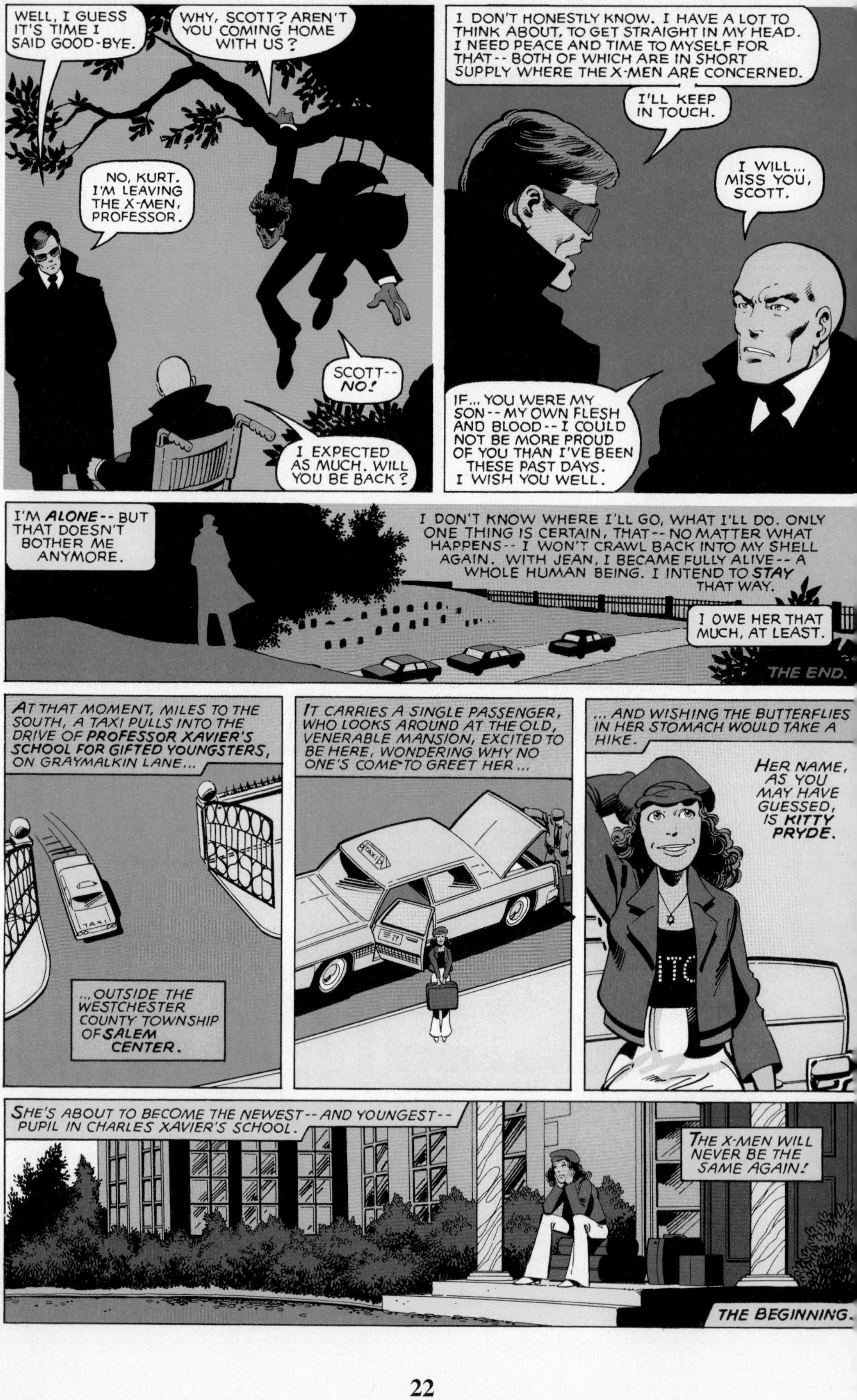

WELL, I GUESS IT'S TIME I SAID GOOD-BYE.
WHY, SCOTT? AREN'T YOU COMING HOME WITH US?
NO, KURT. I'M LEAVING THE X-MEN, PROFESSOR.
SCOTT-- NO!
I EXPECTED AS MUCH. WILL YOU BE BACK?
I DON'T HONESTLY KNOW. I HAVE A LOT TO THINK ABOUT, TO GET STRAIGHT IN MY HEAD. I NEED PEACE AND TIME TO MYSELF FOR THAT-- BOTH OF WHICH ARE IN SHORT SUPPLY WHERE THE X-MEN ARE CONCERNED.
I'LL KEEP IN TOUCH.
I WILL... MISS YOU, SCOTT.
IF... YOU WERE MY SON-- MY OWN FLESH AND BLOOD-- I COULD NOT BE MORE PROUD OF YOU THAN I'VE BEEN THESE PAST DAYS. I WISH YOU WELL.
I'M ALONE-- BUT THAT DOESN'T BOTHER ME ANYMORE.
I DON'T KNOW WHERE I'LL GO, WHAT I'LL DO. ONLY ONE THING IS CERTAIN, THAT-- NO MATTER WHAT HAPPENS-- I WON'T CRAWL BACK INTO MY SHELL AGAIN. WITH JEAN, I BECAME FULLY ALIVE-- A WHOLE HUMAN BEING. I INTEND TO STAY THAT WAY.
I OWE HER THAT MUCH, AT LEAST.
THE END.
AT THAT MOMENT, MILES TO THE SOUTH, A TAXI PULLS INTO THE DRIVE OF PROFESSOR XAVIER'S SCHOOL FOR GIFTED YOUNGSTERS, ON GRAYMALKIN LANE...
...OUTSIDE THE WESTCHESTER COUNTY TOWNSHIP OF SALEM CENTER.
IT CARRIES A SINGLE PASSENGER, WHO LOOKS AROUND AT THE OLD, VENERABLE MANSION, EXCITED TO BE HERE, WONDERING WHY NO ONE'S COME TO GREET HER...
... AND WISHING THE BUTTERFLIES IN HER STOMACH WOULD TAKE A HIKE.
HER NAME, AS YOU MAY HAVE GUESSED, IS KITTY PRYDE.
SHE'S ABOUT TO BECOME THE NEWEST-- AND YOUNGEST-- PUPIL IN CHARLES XAVIER'S SCHOOL.
THE X-MEN WILL NEVER BE THE SAME AGAIN!
THE BEGINNING.

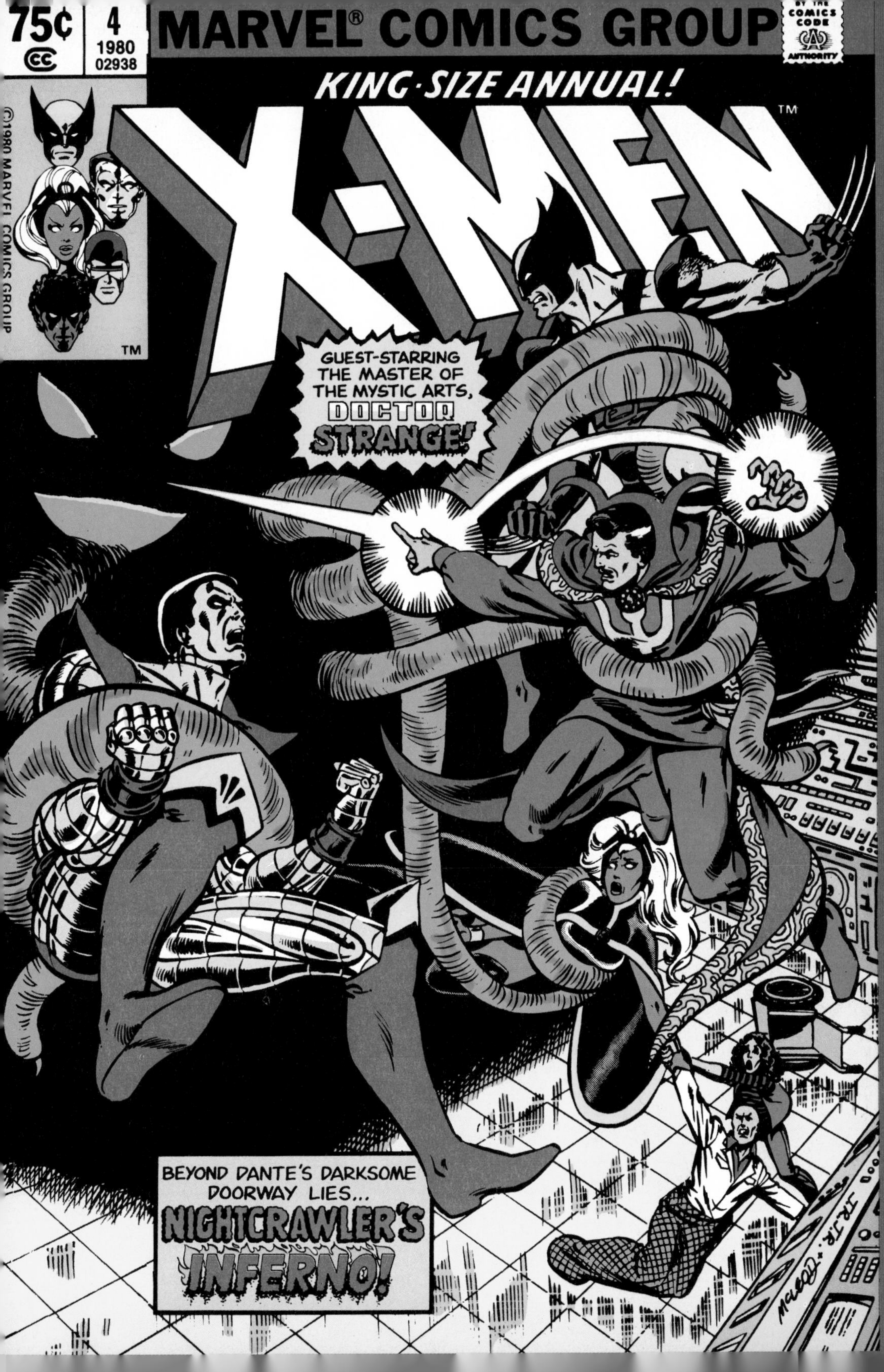

75¢
4
1980
02938
MARVEL® COMICS GROUP
APPROVED BY THE COMICS CODE AUTHORITY
KING-SIZE ANNUAL!
X-MEN™
©1980 MARVEL COMICS GROUP
GUEST-STARRING THE MASTER OF THE MYSTIC ARTS, DOCTOR STRANGE!
BEYOND DANTE'S DARKSOME DOORWAY LIES...
NIGHTCRAWLER'S INFERNO!

STAN LEE PRESENTS: **THE UNCANNY X-MEN!**™

CHRIS CLAREMONT
WRITER | JOHN ROMITA, Jr. & BOB McLEOD
ARTISTS | TOM ORZECHOWSKI, letterer
GLYNIS WEIN, colorist | LOUISE JONES
EDITOR | JIM SHOOTE
Ed.-in-CHIEF

HIS NAME IS KURT WAGNER-- ALSO KNOWN AS NIGHTCRAWLER.

Nightcrawler's INFERNO

HE GREW UP IN THE CIRCUS AND, IN THOSE DAYS, ALL HE WANTED OUT OF LIFE WAS TO BECOME THE FINEST TRAPEZE ARTIST IN THE WORLD. THAT DREAM NEVER CAME TO PASS.

WHAT THE--?!?

INSTEAD, HE BECAME A SUPER-HERO, JOINING STORM, COLOSSUS AND WOLVERINE AS ONE OF THE UNCANNY X-MEN. SINCE THAT FATEFUL DAY, HE'S SEEN MORE THAN HIS SHARE OF EXCITEMENT-- NOT TO MENTION A FEW OUTRAGEOUS SURPRISES.

24

CASE IN POINT: "Happy birthday to you, Happy birthday to you-- "Happy birthday, Kurt Wagner! Happy birthday to you!'"

OH, MY...

MY FRIENDS, MY DEAR FRIENDS...

...I DON'T KNOW WHAT TO SAY.

DON'T SAY ANYTHING, KURT.

JUST BE HAPPY.

I WILL, STORM... ORORO. I FEEL SO ASHAMED -- I WAS FEELING SORRY FOR MYSELF...

...THINKING THAT YOU HAD ALL FORGOTTEN...

FORGOTTEN-- HAH! WE HAVE BEEN PLANNING THIS FOR WEEKS, TOVARISCH.

SO THAT'S WHY YOU HAD ME RUNNING ERRANDS TODAY. I NEVER SUSPECTED A THING.

THAT WAS THE IDEA, FELLA.

THE LAUGHTER COMES EASILY, THE JOY OF CELEBRATION SHARED BY ALL...

...SAVE KITTY PRYDE. AT 13½, SHE'S THE YOUNGEST STUDENT PROFESSOR XAVIER'S SCHOOL FOR GIFTED YOUNGSTERS HAS EVER HAD.

EVERYONE HAS DONE THEIR BEST TO MAKE HER FEEL AT HOME, BUT SHE STILL DOESN'T QUITE FEEL LIKE SHE TRULY BELONGS AMONG THE X-MEN.

THAT WILL COME IN TIME, SHE HOPES.

HAVE YOU OPENED ALL THE PRESENTS, KURT?

I'M NOT SURE, PETER...

NOT QUITE, KURT. THERE SEEMS TO BE ONE LEFT, THAT BLACK BOX.

DANKE, PROFESSOR. *Hmmm* -- IT LOOKS AS SINISTER AS IT DOES STYLISH, A PACKAGE AFTER MY OWN HEART.

D'YOU THINK IT'S *FROM SCOTT?* WE HAVEN'T HEARD MUCH FROM HIM SINCE HE LEFT US. *

*SEE *X-MEN #138,* ON SALE NOW, FOR DETAILS -- LOUISE.

WOW.

A CRYSTAL FIGURINE -- OF MYSELF.

KURT -- IT'S BEAUTIFUL.

THAT IT IS, ORORO.

NO CARD, THOUGH -- NOTHING TO TELL US WHO IT'S FR--

--AARGKGH!!

POOF

THE STATUE *EXPLODED!* AND THE BLAST CAUGHT KURT FULL IN THE FACE!

KURT, ARE YOU *ALL RIGHT?!*

KURT!?!

26

WOLVERINE-- ANYTHING?!

NOT A PEEP, PROFESSOR.

WE'D BETTER GET HIM TO THE MEDILAB, FAST!

MOMENTS LATER, IN ANOTHER WING OF THE ELEGANT, VENERABLE MANSION THAT SERVES BOTH AS XAVIER'S SCHOOL, AND THE X-MEN'S SECRET HOME AND HEADQUARTERS...

PLACE NIGHTCRAWLER ON THE EXAMINATION TABLE, COLOSSUS.

STORM, WOULD YOU ASSIST ME, PLEASE? THE REST OF YOU, WAIT OUTSIDE. WE'LL BRING YOU WORD AS SOON AS WE'VE LEARNED ANYTHING.

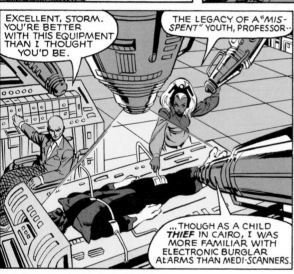

EXCELLENT, STORM. YOU'RE BETTER WITH THIS EQUIPMENT THAN I THOUGHT YOU'D BE.

THE LEGACY OF A "MIS-SPENT" YOUTH, PROFESSOR--

...THOUGH AS A CHILD THIEF IN CAIRO, I WAS MORE FAMILIAR WITH ELECTRONIC BURGLAR ALARMS THAN MEDI-SCANNERS.

STORM AND PROFESSOR XAVIER HAVE BEEN IN THE MEDICAL LABORATORY SUCH A LONG TIME!

I HATE THIS WAITING! I NEED TO DO SOMETHING, ANYTHING! KURT IS MY FRIEND-- I WANT TO HELP HIM, BUT I DO NOT KNOW HOW!

KURT IS... BEYOND OUR HELP, PETER.

WE DID ALL WE COULD, BUT--DESPITE OUR BEST EFFORTS-- HE WOULD NOT RESPOND TO TREATMENT.

NIGHT-CRAWLER'S ...DEAD?

NO.

HE IS NO LONGER ... ALIVE.

NO!!

SKRUNCH!

27

ARE YOU **SURE**, CHARLEY?! MAYBE YER MACHINES WERE ON THE FRITZ--?!

WE COVERED THAT, WOLVERINE. THE PROFESSOR TELEPATHICALLY **MIND-SCANNED** KURT, BUT RECEIVED **NO** RESPONSE. KURT'S MIND, HIS SOUL-- HIS ESSENTIAL LIFE-FORCE -- IS NO MORE.

EXCUSE ME A MOMENT, X-MEN. THERE ARE TELEPHONE CALLS-- CERTAIN... **SPECIAL** ARRANGEMENTS-- I MUST MAKE.

WHAT KILLED HIM, 'RORO? AN' WHO? AN' **WHY**?!?

I DON'T KNOW. WE FOUND NO EVIDENCE OF ANY ORGANIC OR INORGANIC TOXINS, NO SIGN OF A PSIONIC ATTACK.

THAT ACCURSED STATUE BLEW UP-- AND OUR FRIEND DIED.

WE GAVE THE PACKAGE EVERY CONCEIVABLE TEST -- TO TRY TO FIND SOME CLUE TO ITS ORIGINS. WE WERE WASTING OUR TIME.

SOME **LEADER** OF THE X-MEN I AM TURNING OUT TO BE.

Uh, GUYS, THE DOORBELL'S RINGING.

ONE OF US IS **MURDERED** BEFORE OUR EYES -- AND THERE SEEMS TO BE **NOTHING** WE CAN DO ABOUT IT!

NEVER MIND. I'LL GET IT.

I NEVER LIKED NIGHTCRAWLER MUCH. HE WAS ALWAYS NICE TO ME, BUT HE LOOKED SO... **WEIRD.**

WITHOUT MEANING TO, HE GAVE ME THE CREEPS.

BUT NOW, I WISH I'D LIKED HIM MORE.

I WISH HE WASN'T DEAD.

GOOD EVENING. MY NAME IS **STEPHEN STRANGE.** I AM A... PHYSICIAN.

I BELIEVE I AM **EXPECTED.**

OH!

Uh... um...

IT'S ALL RIGHT, KITTY. DR. STRANGE IS HERE AT **MY** REQUEST.

IT WAS GOOD OF YOU TO ANWER MY CALL SO QUICKLY, STEPHEN.

YOUR MESSAGE SOUNDED URGENT.

NO NEED TO HIDE, YOUNG LADY. I'M A FRIEND. REALLY.

PETER-- LOOK!

DID I STARTLE YOU, KITTY? MY APOLOGIES -- I SIMPLY CANCELLED THE ILLUSION-SPELL THAT MAKES MY SORCERER'S GARB APPEAR AS NORMAL CLOTHES.

"SPELL?" I THOUGHT YOU WERE A DOCTOR.

I WAS, WOLVERINE. I AM. BUT I AM ALSO--

--MASTER OF THE MYSTIC ARTS.

THOSE ARE THE SKILLS REQUIRED OF ME TONIGHT. CHARLES -- PROFESSOR XAVIER -- CAN FIND NO PHYSICAL OR PSYCHIC CAUSE FOR YOUR FRIEND'S CONDITION.

I AM HERE TO DETERMINE IF HE WAS STRUCK DOWN BY A MYSTIC ATTACK.

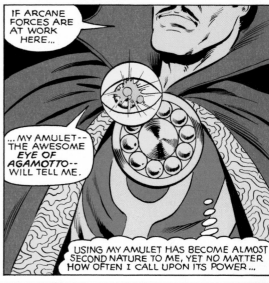

IF ARCANE FORCES ARE AT WORK HERE...

... MY AMULET -- THE AWESOME EYE OF AGAMOTTO -- WILL TELL ME.

USING MY AMULET HAS BECOME ALMOST SECOND NATURE TO ME, YET NO MATTER HOW OFTEN I CALL UPON ITS POWER ...

... I STILL FEEL THE SAME SENSE OF WONDER I FELT THE DAY MY MENTOR, THE ANCIENT ONE, PLACED IT IN MY CHARGE.

THE DAY I LOSE THAT FEELING--

-- THE DAY I BECOME SO JADED THAT I TAKE MY POWER FOR GRANTED -- IS THE DAY I WILL NO LONGER BE WORTHY OF MY DREAD RESPONSIBILITY AS EARTH'S MYSTIC DEFENDER.

FASCINATING. AT FIRST GLANCE, I ASSUMED NIGHTCRAWLER TO BE SOME HUMAN/DEMON HYBRID...

...YET THE ALL-SEEING EYE'S LIGHT OF TRUTH REVEALS HIM TO BE HUMAN IN HIS ESSENCE.

29

IT ALSO REVEALS THAT THE YOUTH IS UNDER AN *ENCHANTMENT!*

HIS *SOUL* HAS BEEN STOLEN!

SORCERY IS AT WORK HERE, MY FRIENDS -- A POWER THAT *RIVALS* MY OWN. BUT, ALTHOUGH IT IS A HOSTILE POWER -- ONE FUELED BY GREAT *HATRED* --

-- IT DOES NOT SEEM TO BE CONSECRATED TO *EVIL.*

DESPITE APPEARANCES, NIGHTCRAWLER IS NOT DEAD. HIS PHYSICAL BODY IS IN A STATE OF *SUSPENDED ANIMATION,* BUT HIS SPIRIT HAS BEEN TORN FROM HIM. SO LONG AS BODY AND SOUL ARE KEPT APART, HE CANNOT TRULY DIE... BUT NEITHER CAN HE TRULY LIVE -- *EH?*

MY MYSTIC EYE -- IT SENSES ANOTHER PRESENCE IN THE ROOM!

BY THE HOARY HOSTS OF HOGGOTH!

THE MOMENT I BEGAN TO WORK, I CAST A *SPELL OF PROTECTION* AROUND THIS LAB -- AND THE ENTIRE HOUSE -- YET NOW, SOME POWER, SOME ENTITY -- PASSES THROUGH IT WITH ALMOST CONTEMPTUOUS EASE!

I MUST BE ON MY GUARD.

BEHIND ME, X-MEN!

"IF THIS IS AN ATTACK, I WILL DEAL WITH IT.

"WHO ARE YOU, SPIRIT-FORM? WHY ARE YOU HERE? SPEAK, WOMAN -- IF WOMAN YOU TRULY BE --

"-- Dr. STRANGE *COMMANDS* IT!"

NONE COMMANDS MARGALI OF THE WINDING ROAD.

YOU ARE *KNOWN* TO ME, MAGE.

DO YOU MAKE THE X-MEN'S CAUSE YOUR OWN?

...DO. ...RELEASE NIGHTCRAWLER, SORCERESS, OR SUFFER THE CONSEQUENCES!

A PROUD CHALLENGE.

A CHALLENGE ACCEPTED!

BUT IF ANY ARE TO SUFFER IN THIS DUEL, DR. STRANGE, IT WILL NOT BE ME.

MY SPELLS ARE NOT STOPPING IT!

A NETHER-WORLD DEMON!

COLOSSUS -- ARMOR UP! THIS SUCKER'S DRAGGIN' US TOWARDS THAT WITCH-QUEEN --

--AN' I, FER ONE, AIN'T INCLINED TA GO!

BUT FOR ALL DOCTOR STRANGE'S MYSTIC MIGHT -- EVEN COMBINED WITH THE RAW STRENGTH OF A MUTANT MAN OF STEEL, AND THE RAZOR-KEEN ADAMANTIUM CLAWS THAT POP OUT OF THE BACK OF WOLVERINE'S HANDS --

--THE TENTACLED DEMON DRAWS THEM SLOWLY, INEXORABLY, INTO ITS GAPING MAW.

IT WILL BE OUR TURN NEXT. I MUST GET YOU TWO OUT OF HERE!

31

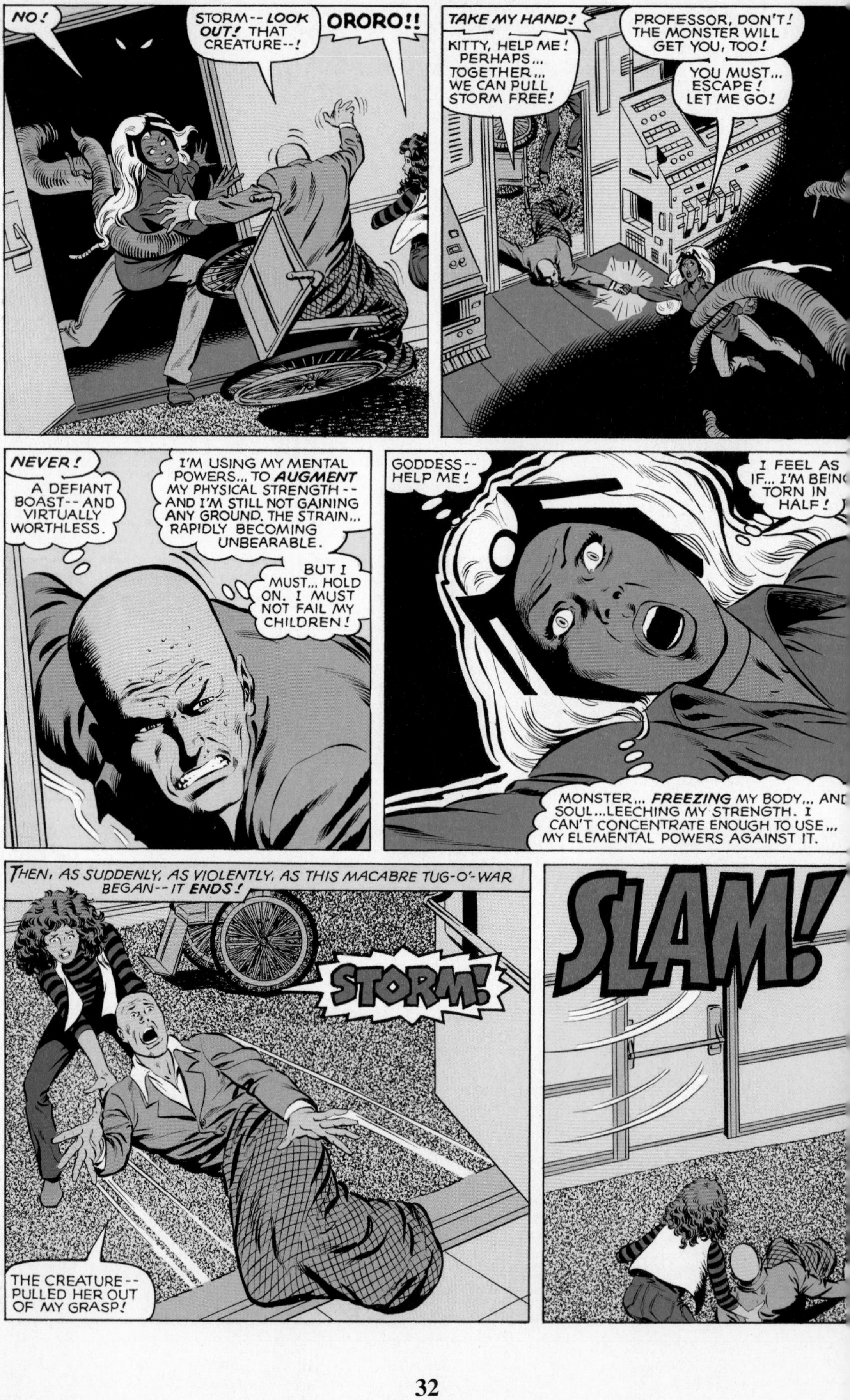
NO!
STORM--LOOK OUT! THAT CREATURE--!
ORORO!!
TAKE MY HAND!
KITTY, HELP ME! PERHAPS... TOGETHER... WE CAN PULL STORM FREE!
PROFESSOR, DON'T! THE MONSTER WILL GET YOU, TOO!
YOU MUST... ESCAPE! LET ME GO!
NEVER!
A DEFIANT BOAST--AND VIRTUALLY WORTHLESS.
I'M USING MY MENTAL POWERS... TO AUGMENT MY PHYSICAL STRENGTH--AND I'M STILL NOT GAINING ANY GROUND. THE STRAIN... RAPIDLY BECOMING UNBEARABLE.
BUT I MUST... HOLD ON. I MUST NOT FAIL MY CHILDREN!
GODDESS--HELP ME!
I FEEL AS IF... I'M BEIN TORN IN HALF!
MONSTER... FREEZING MY BODY... AN SOUL...LEECHING MY STRENGTH. I CAN'T CONCENTRATE ENOUGH TO USE... MY ELEMENTAL POWERS AGAINST IT.
THEN, AS SUDDENLY, AS VIOLENTLY, AS THIS MACABRE TUG-O'-WAR BEGAN--IT ENDS!
STORM!
THE CREATURE--PULLED HER OUT OF MY GRASP!
SLAM!

UP TO THE MOMENT THE DOOR SLAMMED SHUT, THAT WITCH-LADY WAS CACKLING HER HEAD OFF. I CAN'T HEAR HER ANYMORE.

I CAN'T HEAR *ANYTHING.*

KITTY, GET AWAY FROM THERE!

OKAY, PROFESSOR-- AFTER I'VE TAKEN A QUICK *LOOK-SEE* OF THE LAB.

BACK IN A FLASH.

NO!!

LAB 1

WITH JUST A THOUGHT, THE YOUNGEST X-MAN PHASES FIRST HER FACE, AND THEN HER ENTIRE BODY, THROUGH THE LABORATORY DOOR.

KITTY, COME BACK! YOU DON'T KNOW WHAT'S IN THERE!

MUST REACH HER *TELEPATHICALLY--* BEFORE IT'S TOO LATE!

KATHERINE PRYDE-- RETURN TO ME AT ONCE!

YOU'RE *UNTRAINED* IN YOUR POWERS. IF YOU RUN INTO SERIOUS TROUBLE, YOU MIGHT NOT BE ABLE TO *COPE!*

GET OUTTA MY HEAD, PROFESSOR!

AND QUIT YELLIN', WILLYA?! IT *HURTS!*

ALL I WANTED TO DO WAS SEE WHAT HAPPENED TO ORORO AND THE OTHERS. I WAS TRYING TO *HELP* YOU-- TO ACT LIKE A REAL *X-MAN.*

THEY'RE GONE, PROFESSOR-- *ALL* OF THEM: ORORO, WOLVERINE, PETER, KURT, THE DOCTOR. *GONE!*

LIKE THEY'D NEVER EVEN BEEN HERE.

WHAT DID THAT MARGALI AND HER PET MONSTER DO WITH THEM, PROFESSOR?! *WHERE DID SHE TAKE THE X-MEN?!?*

33

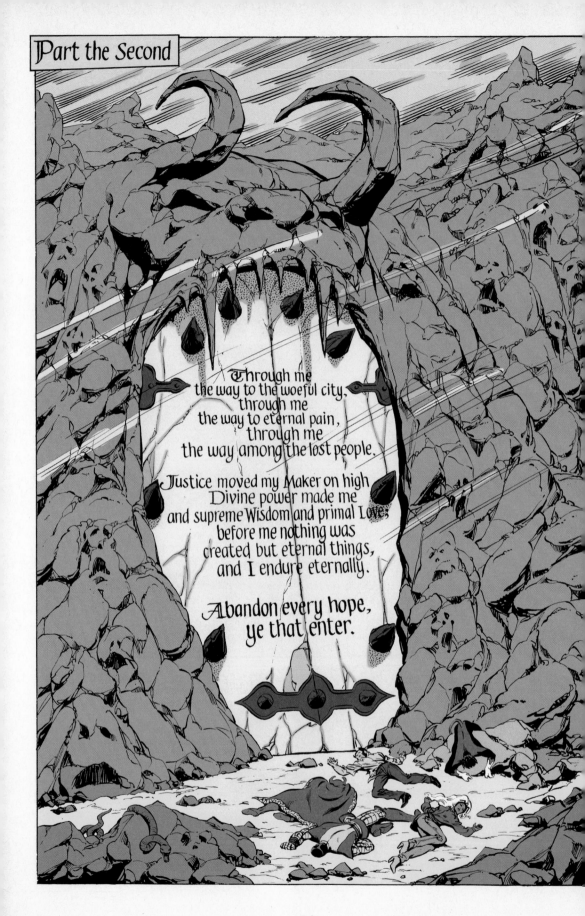

Through me
the way to the woeful city,
through me
the way to eternal pain,
through me
the way among the lost people.

Justice moved my Maker on high
Divine power made me
and supreme Wisdom and primal Love;
before me nothing was
created but eternal things,
and I endure eternally.

Abandon every hope,
ye that enter.

TIME PASSES IN THIS TIME-LESS PLACE, AND THEN...

TO COIN A PHRASE: *OUCH!* THAT WAS ONE TRIP I COULD HAVE DONE WITHOUT.

IS EVERYONE... ALL RIGHT?

NO SERIOUS INJURIES, STORM-- ONLY ACHES AND PAINS.

COMRADES-- *LOOK!* NIGHTCRAWLER IS BREATHING, MOVING! HE IS *ALIVE!*

BY THE ETERNAL VISHANTI! THAT GATE! IT-- IT *CAN'T* BE!

THE AIR-- SO FOUL-- LIKE A *CHARNAL PIT.*

WHERE *ARE* WE?!

WOULD YOU BELIEVE... *"HELL?"*

oooooohhhhhhhhhhh...

HUH?!

WHAT... HAPPENED TO ME...?

AND, AFTER A BRIEF REUNION, AND A BRIEFER EXPLANATION TO NIGHTCRAWLER OF THEIR PLIGHT...

THIS IS THE GATEWAY TO HELL, AS DESCRIBED BY THE 14th-CENTURY ITALIAN POET, *DANTE ALIGHIERI*...

...IN HIS CLASSIC POEM, THE *INFERNO."*

THAT EPIC CHRONICLED DANTE'S DESCENT INTO THE PIT, AND HIS EVENTUAL MEETING WITH *SATAN* HIMSELF.

IT SEEMS WE'RE EXPECTED TO FOLLOW IN HIS FOOTSTEPS.

THE GATE OPENS, MY FRIENDS. MARGALI MUST BE EAGER TO SEE US.

WHAT LIES ON THE OTHER SIDE, DOCTOR?

IF MEMORY SERVES ME RIGHT, STORM, THE *RIVER ACHERON.*

BRACE YOURSELVES, X-MEN. NOTHING IN YOUR EXPERIENCE CAN COMPARE WITH WHAT YOU ARE ABOUT TO FACE. TO SURVIVE-- MUCH LESS TRIUMPH-- YOU WILL NEED ALL YOUR STRENGTH, YOUR COURAGE, YOUR... HUMANITY.

IT'S *ME* MARGALI WANTS-- ME SHE *HATES.* WHY DID SHE INVOLVE THE X-MEN?!

SO WHAT ELSE IS NEW?

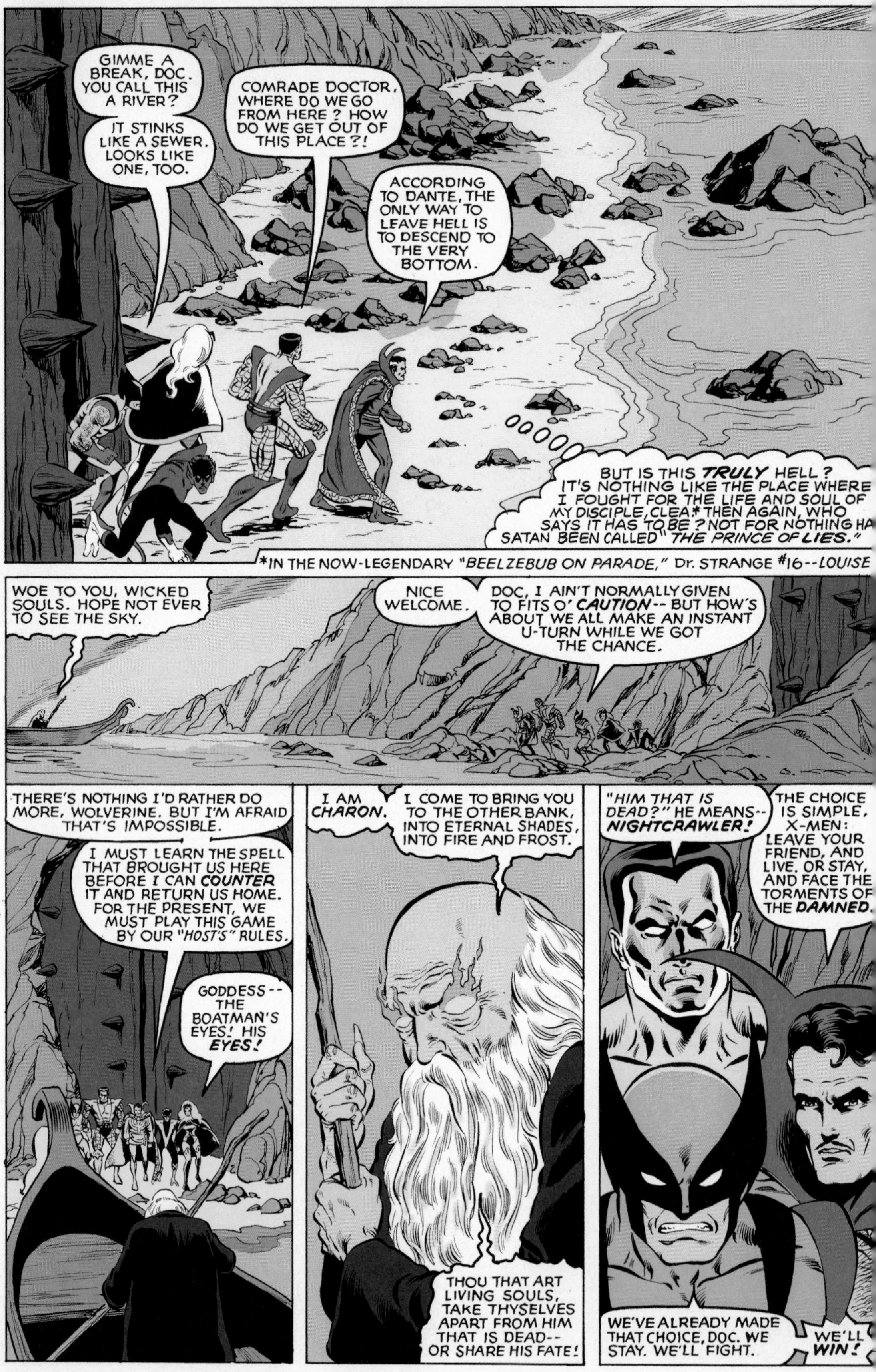
GIMME A BREAK, DOC. YOU CALL THIS A RIVER?
IT STINKS LIKE A SEWER. LOOKS LIKE ONE, TOO.
COMRADE DOCTOR, WHERE DO WE GO FROM HERE? HOW DO WE GET OUT OF THIS PLACE?!
ACCORDING TO DANTE, THE ONLY WAY TO LEAVE HELL IS TO DESCEND TO THE VERY BOTTOM.
BUT IS THIS TRULY HELL? IT'S NOTHING LIKE THE PLACE WHERE I FOUGHT FOR THE LIFE AND SOUL OF MY DISCIPLE, CLEA.* THEN AGAIN, WHO SAYS IT HAS TO BE? NOT FOR NOTHING HA SATAN BEEN CALLED "THE PRINCE OF LIES."
*IN THE NOW-LEGENDARY "BEELZEBUB ON PARADE," Dr. STRANGE #16--LOUISE
WOE TO YOU, WICKED SOULS. HOPE NOT EVER TO SEE THE SKY.
NICE WELCOME.
DOC, I AIN'T NORMALLY GIVEN TO FITS O' CAUTION-- BUT HOW'S ABOUT WE ALL MAKE AN INSTANT U-TURN WHILE WE GOT THE CHANCE.
THERE'S NOTHING I'D RATHER DO MORE, WOLVERINE. BUT I'M AFRAID THAT'S IMPOSSIBLE.
I MUST LEARN THE SPELL THAT BROUGHT US HERE BEFORE I CAN COUNTER IT AND RETURN US HOME. FOR THE PRESENT, WE MUST PLAY THIS GAME BY OUR "HOST'S" RULES.
GODDESS-- THE BOATMAN'S EYES! HIS EYES!
I AM CHARON.
I COME TO BRING YOU TO THE OTHER BANK, INTO ETERNAL SHADES, INTO FIRE AND FROST.
THOU THAT ART LIVING SOULS, TAKE THYSELVES APART FROM HIM THAT IS DEAD-- OR SHARE HIS FATE!
"HIM THAT IS DEAD?" HE MEANS-- NIGHTCRAWLER!
THE CHOICE IS SIMPLE, X-MEN: LEAVE YOUR FRIEND, AND LIVE. OR STAY, AND FACE THE TORMENTS OF THE DAMNED.
WE'VE ALREADY MADE THAT CHOICE, DOC. WE STAY. WE'LL FIGHT.
WE'LL WIN!

AT WOLVERINE'S PROUD, DEFIANT BOAST, THE AGED BOATMAN MERELY *LAUGHS*...

...AND, IN HIS CHARGE, THE X-MEN AND DR. STRANGE BEGIN THEIR DESCENT INTO THE ETERNAL PIT. SOON...

FARE... "WELL," CHILDREN OF MAN.

WE SHALL NOT MEET AGAIN.

FINE BY ME, BUB.

HERE WE PART, MORTAL FOOLS.

IN THIS PLACE WILT THOU BE JUDGED, AND PUNISHED, ACCORDING TO THY MANIFOLD SINS. AND, ONCE CONDEMNED, THERE IS NO APPEAL, NO ESCAPE.

THIS PLACE IS *HUGE*, YET IT MAKES ME FEEL AS IF I'M TRAPPED IN A TINY BOX. I'VE BEEN TERRIFIED OF CONFINING PLACES EVER SINCE I WAS BURIED ALIVE AS A CHILD. I WANT TO SCREAM, RUN AWAY, HIDE.

BUT--I WILL--OVER-COME MY FEAR!

WILKOMMEN. BIENVENUE. WELCOME.

WHAT ARE NICE PEOPLE LIKE YOU DOING IN A PLACE LIKE THIS?

WHO--?!

HIS NAME, COLOSSUS, IS *MINOS*.

AND, DESPITE HIS APPEARANCE, HE IS *GUARDIAN* OF THE *GATE OF HELL*.

YOU ARE NOT AS DANTE DESCRIBED YOU.

TIMES CHANGE, COMPADRE.

ALIGHIERI SAW ME IN TERMS OF HIS WORLD. YOU SEE ME IN TERMS OF YOURS. CONSIDERATE, hm?

I'M A WEE BIT SURPRISED, THOUGH. WE EXPECTED ONE NEW ARRIVAL: KURT WAGNER-- OR NIGHTCRAWLER-- BY NAME, SWASHBUCKLER BY TRADE, DAMSEL SAVING A SPECIALTY.

NOT THAT I MIND, Y'UNDERSTAND. IN THIS BUSINESS, AS THE SAYING GOES, THE MORE, THE MERRIER.

YOU ALL FRIENDS OF KURT'S?

THESE ARE THE X-MEN. I AM DOCTOR STRANGE, MASTER OF THE MYSTIC ARTS, SORCERER SUPREME OF EARTH. NIGHT-CRAWLER IS UNDER MY PROTECTION.

HOW NICE.

IT'S BEEN A WHILE SINCE I'VE SEEN AS FOXY A LADY AS YOU, M'DARLIN'!

YUM!

GODDESS-- HIS LOOK, HIS TOUCH, LIKE BEING CARRESSED BY MAGGOTS...

...AND YET... SOMETHING IN ME FINDS THIS OBSCENITY ...ATTRACTIVE.

YOU AIN'T SO BAD YOURSELF, KURT... DO YOU MIND IF I CALL YOU KURT?

A FINE FIGURE OF A LAD.

YOU'LL LIKE IT HERE. WE'LL LIKE HAVING YOU.

YOU ALL LOOK SHOCKED! DON'T BE.

THIS IS HELL. ANYTHING GOES.

'RORO AN' KURT LOOK LIKE THAT MINOS CREEP JUST TURNED THEIR SOULS INSIDE OUT. I'VE NEVER SEEN 'EM SO SHAKEN.

I AIN'T STANDIN' FER ANYMORE O' THIS!

38

NOW, TO BUSINESS.

YOU KNOW, OF COURSE, WHY YOU'RE HERE, KURT MY LAD. YOU'VE BEEN A NAUGHTY BOY.

BON VOYAGE!

NO!!

IN THE BLINK OF AN EYE, MINOS' TAIL--

-- IMPOSSIBLY LONG, IMPOSSIBLY POWERFUL-- GATHERS NIGHT-CRAWLER UP AND HURLS HIM OUT OF THE PALACE, HIS ACCELERATION SO GREAT THAT SHEER SPEED ALONE STUNS HIM TO NEAR-UNCONSCIOUSNESS.

A TENTACLE, FROM BENEATH THE THRONE -- GRABBING ME!

YOU'VE BROKEN THE MORAL LAWS LAID DOWN BY UPSTAIRS. SHAME ON YOU.

BUT, FOLLOWING A HEART-BEAT BEHIND...

...STORM STREAKS TO HIS RESCUE.

... AND, THEREBY, BECOMES THE FIRST OF THE X-MEN TO SEE HELL IN ALL ITS FABLED, DARKSOME MAJESTY.

GOT YOU!

LORDS OF THE EARTH AND AIR!

IT'S MY JOB-- NO, I LIE. IT'S MY PLEASURE TO, SHALL WE SAY, MAKE THE PUNISHMENT FIT THE CRIME. IN YOUR CASE, BOTH ARE CONSIDERABLE.

THE PIT--SO VAST-- IT SEEMS TO GO ON FOREVER! HOW MANY POOR SOULS ARE HERE, SPENDING ETERNITY IN TORMENT...?

AT THAT THOUGHT, A GREAT SADNESS WELLS WITHIN HER, BRINGING HER CLOSE TO TEARS...

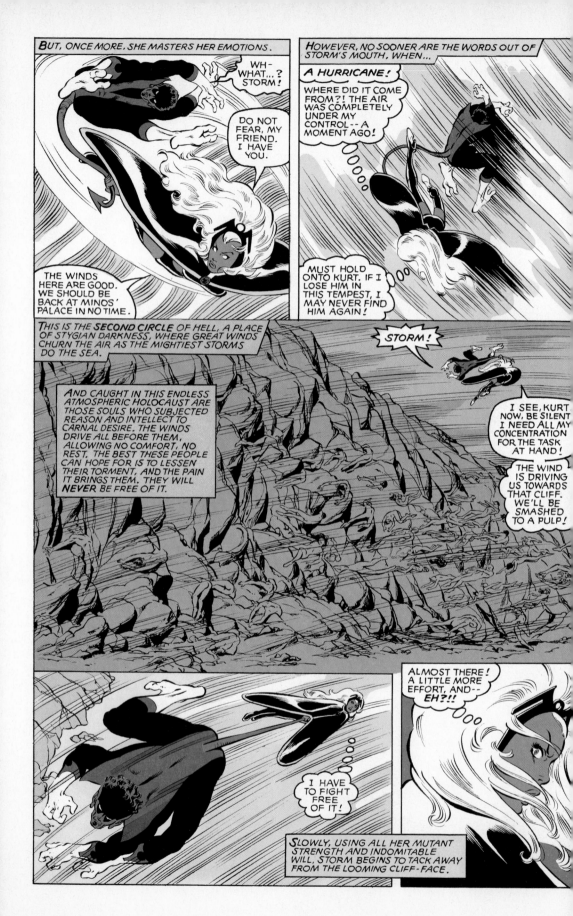

BUT, ONCE MORE, SHE MASTERS HER EMOTIONS.

WH-- WHAT...? STORM!

DO NOT FEAR, MY FRIEND. I HAVE YOU.

THE WINDS HERE ARE GOOD. WE SHOULD BE BACK AT MINOS' PALACE IN NO TIME.

HOWEVER, NO SOONER ARE THE WORDS OUT OF STORM'S MOUTH, WHEN...

A HURRICANE!

WHERE DID IT COME FROM?! THE AIR WAS COMPLETELY UNDER MY CONTROL-- A MOMENT AGO!

MUST HOLD ONTO KURT. IF I LOSE HIM IN THIS TEMPEST, I MAY NEVER FIND HIM AGAIN!

THIS IS THE SECOND CIRCLE OF HELL, A PLACE OF STYGIAN DARKNESS, WHERE GREAT WINDS CHURN THE AIR AS THE MIGHTIEST STORMS DO THE SEA.

AND CAUGHT IN THIS ENDLESS ATMOSPHERIC HOLOCAUST ARE THOSE SOULS WHO SUBJECTED REASON AND INTELLECT TO CARNAL DESIRE. THE WINDS DRIVE ALL BEFORE THEM, ALLOWING NO COMFORT, NO REST. THE BEST THESE PEOPLE CAN HOPE FOR IS TO LESSEN THEIR TORMENT, AND THE PAIN IT BRINGS THEM. THEY WILL NEVER BE FREE OF IT.

STORM!

I SEE, KURT. NOW, BE SILENT. I NEED ALL MY CONCENTRATION FOR THE TASK AT HAND!

THE WIND IS DRIVING US TOWARDS THAT CLIFF. WE'LL BE SMASHED TO A PULP!

I HAVE TO FIGHT FREE OF IT!

ALMOST THERE! A LITTLE MORE EFFORT, AND-- EH?!!

SLOWLY, USING ALL HER MUTANT STRENGTH AND INDOMITABLE WILL, STORM BEGINS TO TACK AWAY FROM THE LOOMING CLIFF-FACE.

40

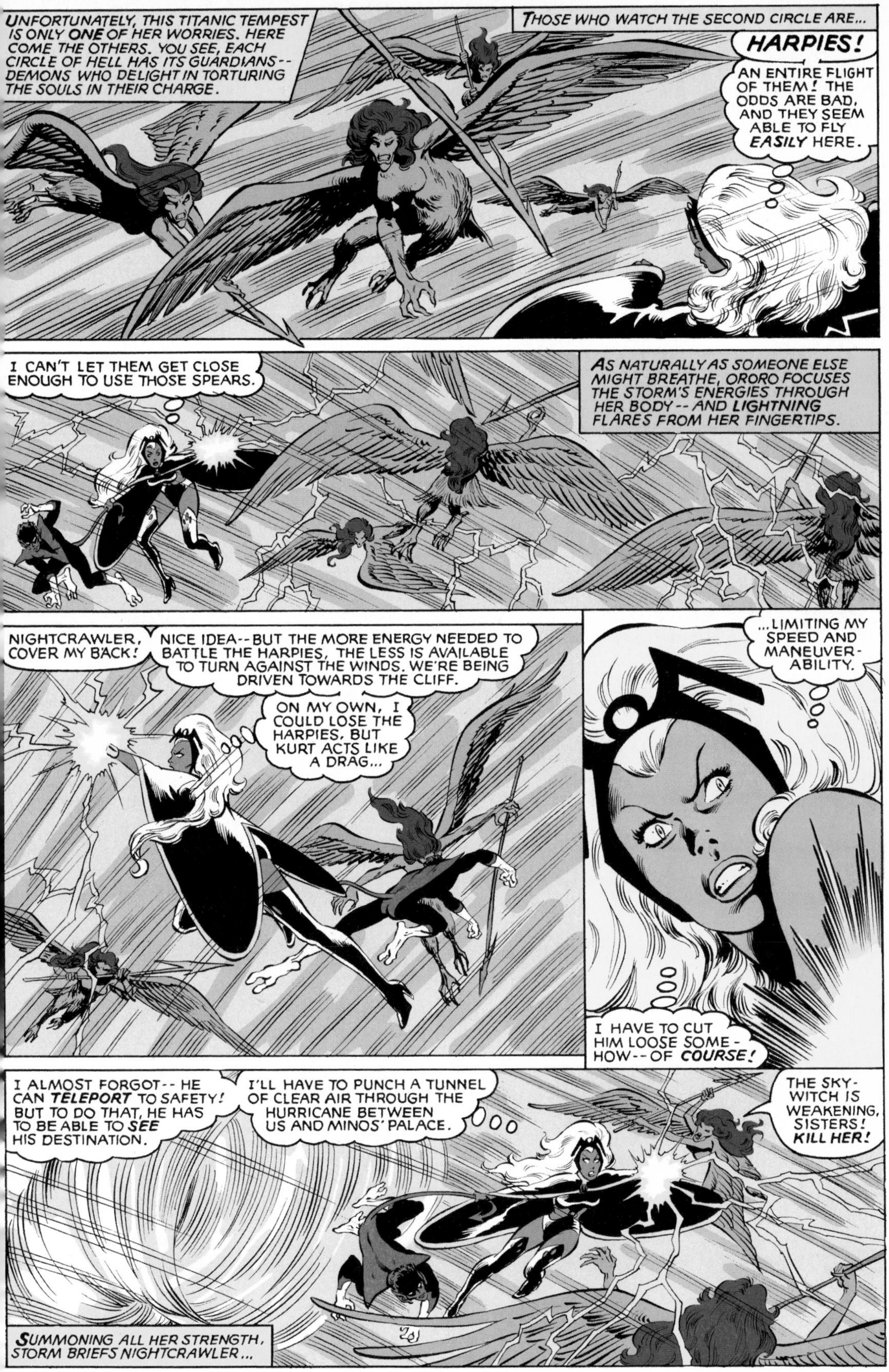
UNFORTUNATELY, THIS TITANIC TEMPEST IS ONLY ONE OF HER WORRIES. HERE COME THE OTHERS. YOU SEE, EACH CIRCLE OF HELL HAS ITS GUARDIANS-- DEMONS WHO DELIGHT IN TORTURING THE SOULS IN THEIR CHARGE.
THOSE WHO WATCH THE SECOND CIRCLE ARE...
HARPIES!
AN ENTIRE FLIGHT OF THEM! THE ODDS ARE BAD, AND THEY SEEM ABLE TO FLY EASILY HERE.
I CAN'T LET THEM GET CLOSE ENOUGH TO USE THOSE SPEARS.
AS NATURALLY AS SOMEONE ELSE MIGHT BREATHE, ORORO FOCUSES THE STORM'S ENERGIES THROUGH HER BODY -- AND LIGHTNING FLARES FROM HER FINGERTIPS.
NIGHTCRAWLER, COVER MY BACK!
NICE IDEA-- BUT THE MORE ENERGY NEEDED TO BATTLE THE HARPIES, THE LESS IS AVAILABLE TO TURN AGAINST THE WINDS. WE'RE BEING DRIVEN TOWARDS THE CLIFF.
ON MY OWN, I COULD LOSE THE HARPIES. BUT KURT ACTS LIKE A DRAG...
...LIMITING MY SPEED AND MANEUVER-ABILITY.
I HAVE TO CUT HIM LOOSE SOME-HOW-- OF COURSE!
I ALMOST FORGOT-- HE CAN TELEPORT TO SAFETY! BUT TO DO THAT, HE HAS TO BE ABLE TO SEE HIS DESTINATION.
I'LL HAVE TO PUNCH A TUNNEL OF CLEAR AIR THROUGH THE HURRICANE BETWEEN US AND MINOS' PALACE.
THE SKY-WITCH IS WEAKENING, SISTERS! KILL HER!
SUMMONING ALL HER STRENGTH, STORM BRIEFS NIGHTCRAWLER...

... AND THE INSTANT ALL IS READY, SENDS HIM ON HIS WAY.

THAT TAKES CARE OF KURT. NOW TO SAVE MYS--

AARRRGH!

THE SPEAR STABS DEEP...

BAMF

... FLOODING STORM WITH AN ICY AGONY THAT NUMBS MIND AND BODY. HELPLESS, NOW, SHE'S WHIRLED AWAY, SWEPT ROUND AND ROUND THE PIT, EACH CIRCUIT PULLING HER *DEEPER* INTO HELL.

THE LAST SOUNDS SHE HEARS ARE MINOS' LAUGHTER...

... AND HER OWN PRIMAL, NEVER-ENDING *SCREAM.*

MEANWHILE, IN MINOS' THRONE ROOM, A FRACTION OF A SECOND AFTER NIGHTCRAWLER DISAPPEARED FROM ORORO'S SIDE...

"VUOLSI COSÌ COLA DOVE SI PUOTE CIÒ CHE SI VUOLE, E PIÙ NON DIMANDARE!"

"IT IS SO WILLED WHERE WILL AND POWER ARE ONE; AND ASK NO MORE!"

IF YOU SAY SO, DOC!

WOLVERINE, DOCTOR-- *LOOK!*

NIGHT-CRAWLER!

NEVER... 'PORTED SO FAR... NON-STOP ALMOST... DIDN'T MAKE IT. FEEL... SO WEAK-- IT'S AN EFFORT JUST TO... BREATHE...

THAT INJUNCTION GOT *DANTE* THROUGH THE PIT WITH HIS HIDE INTACT. IT'LL DO THE SAME FOR YOU. MAYBE.

HE WAS INVITED BY UPSTAIRS. YOU *WEREN'T.*

STORM... WHERE IS SHE?

SHE SAID SHE'D *FOLLOW.*

SAYING IS ONE THING. *DOING* IS SOMETHING ELSE.

SHE'S BELOW, IN WHATEVER CIRCLE THAT'S APPROPRIATE FOR HER. SHE'LL BE THERE *FOREVER...*

... UNLESS SOMEONE GOES TO GET HER *OUT.*

WHEREVER STORM IS, GATEKEEPER, WE SHALL FIND HER. WHATEVER THE ODDS, WE WILL *FREE* HER!

BUT NOT STORM. NOT HERE. NOT BECAUSE OF ME. P-PLEASE.

THAT TEARS IT!

NEIN! DEAR, MERCIFUL LORD--*NO!*

I KNOW WHAT I DID. IF YOU WISH ME PUNISHED--MORE THAN I HAVE ALREADY PUNISHED MYSELF-- SO BE IT.

I'M *TIRED* O' YOU, BUB! AN' YER SMARMY VOICE AN' YER SLEAZEBALL ACT! LIKE MY PAL, PETEY, SAYS: WE'RE GOIN' AFTER 'RORO.

FOR YOUR SAKE, SHE BETTER BE *ALL RIGHT.*

'CAUSE IF SHE ISN'T, YOU AN' ME ARE GONNA MEET AGAIN. ONLY THEN, I'LL BE MAD-- *REAL* MAD. AN' WHAT'LL HAPPEN TO YOU JUST WON'T BEAR THINKIN' ABOUT.

ARE-- ARE YOU *THREATENING* ME, LITTLE MAN?

SNIKT!

YUP.

THIS AIN'T YOUR FIGHT, DOC. BUT... WE COULD SURE USE YOUR HELP. YOU SEEM TO KNOW YOUR WAY AROUND THIS PLACE.

WILL YOU JOIN US?

WANNA MAKE SOMETHIN OF IT?

MY DEAR WOLVERINE, I WOULDN'T MISS IT FOR THE WORLD.

SOMETHING DOESN'T FIT HERE. DESPITE APPEARANCES, I GET NO PSYCHIC SENSE OF FUNDAMENTAL *EVIL*-- AND OF ALL PLACES, HELL SHOULD REEK OF THAT.

BUT IF THIS ISN'T THE *TRUE* HELL, THEN WHERE ARE WE? WHAT POWER RULES HERE--THAT *MARGALI* WOMAN'S? AND WHY DOES IT-- SHE--*HATE* NIGHTCRAWLER SO?

FOR THE MOMENT, THE MAGE KEEPS HIS QUESTIONS TO HIMSELF -- AND THE HEROIC QUARTET BEGIN THEIR DESCENT FROM MINOS' PALACE INTO THE PIT, PAST THE SECOND CIRCLE AND INTO THE **THIRD**...

...A PLACE OF COLD, REMORSELESS, DRIVING RAIN. HERE RESIDE THE **GLUTTONS**.

I AIN'T SEEN WEATHER LIKE THIS SINCE ITALY -- THAT BLOODY WINTER BELOW MONTE CASSINO.

I HATED IT THEN. I HATE IT NOW.

I'M PICKIN' UP A FAINT TRACE O' STORM'S SCENT. IT SEEMS TA LEAD STRAIGHT ON. I DON'T THINK SHE'S AROUND HERE.

THIS CIRCLE IS PROTECTED BY THE THREE-HEADED DOG, **CERBERUS** -- WHOSE NATURE IS AS FOUL AS HIS APPEARANCE.

WOLVERINE -- **BEHIND YOU!**

Huh?!

BAD MOVE, POOCH!

I'VE BEEN ACHIN' FOR A CHANCE TA USE MY CLAWS SINCE WE HIT THIS BURG.

HERE'S WHERE YOU LEARN SOME **MANNERS**, BOWSER!

HE RAN AWAY.

CONSIDERING THE OPPOSITION, COLOSSUS...

...I'M HARDLY SURPRISED.

HE'LL THINK TWICE BEFORE HASSLIN' US AGAIN. LET'S HOPE HE SPREADS THE WORD.

WE'RE DOING WELL THUS FAR -- **TOO WELL.** I DON'T LIKE IT. ARE WE THAT GOOD...

OR ARE WE SIMPLY BEING LURED TO OUR DEATHS, LIKE LAMBS TO THE SLAUGHTER?

WITH MY TEMPER, I COULD END UP IN THAT SWAMP WHEN I DIE -- OR SOMEWHERE WORSE LOWER DOWN. SOMETHING TO THINK ABOUT.

I AIN'T ASHAMED OF WHAT I'VE DONE, THOUGH, OR WHAT I AM. WHATEVER COMES, I'LL HANDLE IT. I'LL SURVIVE.

TOVARISCH DOCTOR, IS THAT A...CITY?

IT IS *DIS*.

BEYOND LIES *NETHER HELL*.

PREPARE YOURSELVES, MY FRIENDS. WHAT WE'VE SEEN BEFORE IS *NOTHING* COMPARED TO WHAT LIES AHEAD.

NIGHTCRAWLER, I DO NOT MEAN TO PRY -- BUT THE TIME HAS COME FOR ANSWERS. WHO IS MARGALI? WHY DID SHE BRING YOU HERE?

WHAT BETTER PLACE TO PUNISH THE MAN WHO *KILLED* HER FIRST-BORN, HER ONLY *SON*...

..HIS OWN -- BELOVED -- *BROTHER*.

YOU DID SUCH A THING?

I DID WHAT HAD TO BE DONE, WHAT I HAD...PROMISED. IF I HAD TO DO IT OVER AGAIN, I WOULD.

THE MISFIT A *MURDERER*? NO FLAMIN' WAY!

HE AIN'T TELLIN' THE WHOLE STORY. IF HE KILLED MARGALI'S KID, THERE HAS TO BE A *REASON*.

WHERE DO WE GO FROM HERE, DOC? FEEL THE HEAT O' THOSE WALLS. I'D BE MORE COMFORTABLE STANDIN' IN FRONT OF AN OPEN *BLAST FURNACE*.

YOU FLEW ME DOWN THAT FIRST CLIFF. CAN'T YOU *CARRY* US OVER THE CITY?

POSSIBLY. IT DEPENDS ON...

X-MEN -- WE ARE *UNDER ATTACK!*

KANG!

"THAT'S WHAT I WAS AFRAID OF," STRANGE SAYS GRIMLY.

"A DEMON HORDE, DEFENDING THE WALLS. THEY WILL NOT VOLUNTARILY LET US PASS."

NO PROBLEM. WE'LL SIMPLY "PERSUADE" THE UGLY SUCKERS TO GET OUT OF OUR WAY.

'PORT UP THERE, 'CRAWLER!

BAMF

COLOSSUS-- "FASTBALL SPECIAL!" THROW ME AFTER HIM! LET'S GO, PEOPLE!

IT WON'T BE EASY, WOLVERINE.

WE FACE AN ARMY--

--FOES WITHOUT NUMBER! AND ALTHOUGH THEIR FLESH CAN ENDURE THESE RED-HOT WALLS, OURS CANNOT!

STILL, WE HAVE TO TRY.

THEY DO THEIR BEST...

...BUT IT ISN'T GOOD ENOUGH.

AFTER A BRUTAL FIGHT, THE X-MEN'S ASSAULT IS REPULSED.

MUST... TELEPORT TO THE GROUND -- BEFORE I BUILD UP TOO MUCH VELOCITY, OR... LANDING WILL INJURE, PERHAPS KILL, ME.

WE BARELY ESCAPED WITH OUR LIVES. THIS INFERNAL HEAT DRAINS STRENGTH -- AND LIFE -- FROM US, AND THE SLIGHTEST TOUCH OF THESE WALLS CAUSES SEVERE BURNS.

I HAVE YOU, WOLVERINE.

MUCH OBLIGED, DOC.

SO MUCH FOR THAT IDEA. ANYONE ELSE GOT SUGGESTIONS? I'M OUT.

WE CAN'T ATTACK THAT WALL AGAIN.

THAT'S SUICIDE!

WE WILL NOT HAVE TO.

I HAVE FOUND US A *GATE.*

I--DON'T UNDERSTAND. IT SHOULD BE *OPEN!*

BE PATIENT, COMRADE.

IT--

--WILL--

--BE!

SKRRRRRRR

PBOOM!

THE DEMONS-- THEY'RE FLEEING!

THEY SEEM *TERRIFIED* OF ME. I WONDER WHY?

BECAUSE, ACCORDING TO DANTE, ONLY *ONE* BEING COULD OPEN THESE UNHOLY GATES BY FORCE--

COLOSSUS MAY HAVE A PURE, NOBLE SPIRIT-- BUT HE IS STILL ONLY *HUMAN.* IN THE TRUE HELL, HE SHOULD NOT HAVE BEEN ABLE TO SMASH THESE GATES.

Part the Third

"THERE IS A PLACE IN HELL CALLED-- MALABOLGE."

IT IS THE EIGHTH CIRCLE OF HELL-- FAR, FAR BELOW DIS-- CAST IN THE SLATE GREY COLOR OF PENULTIMATE HOPELESSNESS. TEN CIRCULAR, DEEP, STEEP-SIDED RAVINES-- BOLGIAS-- CONNECTED BY NARROW, STONE BRIDGES, WATCHED BY HORNED DEMONS WHO MAKE THE HORDES OF DIS LOOK ANGELIC BY COMPARISON.

HERE ARE FOUND THOSE WHOSE LIVES WERE RULED BY FRAUD.

WILL IT NEVER END? SUCH HORROR, SUCH CRUELTY-- I NEVER DREAMED...

IF BELIEVING IN YOUR GOD, NIGHTCRAWLER, MEANS ACCEPTING THE EXISTENCE OF THIS PLACE, I AM NOW GLAD I WAS RAISED AN ATHIEST.

DO NOT BE SO HARSH, PETER, SO QUICK TO JUDGE. HELL IS BALANCED BY HEAVEN. AND THOSE WHO COME HERE DESERVE THEIR DAMNATION.

STORM'S HERE SOMEWHERE, BUB. YOU SAYIN' SHE DESERVES THIS?!

BLAST!

THIS PIT STINKS TOO MUCH. I CAN'T ISOLATE 'RORO'S SCENT.

I AM GLAD AS WELL...

...THAT I CANNOT CRY IN MY ARMORED FORM-- OR MY HEART WOULD CRACK FOR WEEPING.

TELL US ABOUT MALABOLGE, WILLYA, DOC? MAYBE THAT'LL GIVE US SOME KIND'A LEAD.

AS EVERYWHERE ELSE IN HELL, THE LOWER YOU ARE, THE MORE HEINOUS YOUR CRIMES, THE WORSE YOUR TORMENT.

HERE, YOU'LL FIND PANDERS AND SEDUCERS, FLATTERERS, SIMONISTS (CHURCHMEN WHO USE THEIR HOLY OFFICE FOR PERSONAL GAIN), DIVINERS (FALSE PROPHETS), FRAUDS AND CON-ARTISTS, HYPOCRITES, THIEVES...

48

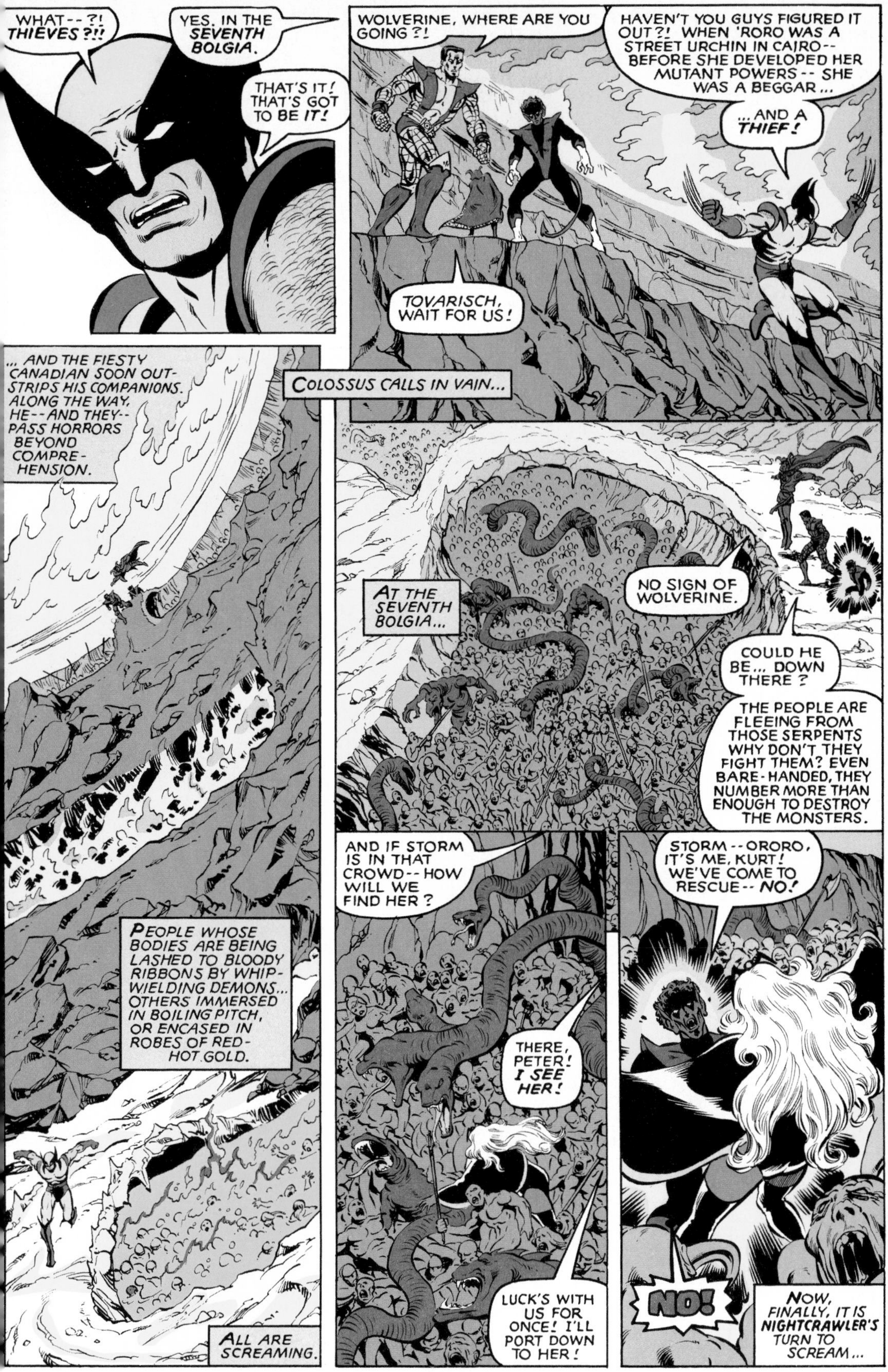
WHAT-- ?! THIEVES ?!!
YES. IN THE SEVENTH BOLGIA.
THAT'S IT! THAT'S GOT TO BE IT!
WOLVERINE, WHERE ARE YOU GOING ?!
HAVEN'T YOU GUYS FIGURED IT OUT ?! WHEN 'RORO WAS A STREET URCHIN IN CAIRO-- BEFORE SHE DEVELOPED HER MUTANT POWERS -- SHE WAS A BEGGAR ...
...AND A THIEF!
TOVARISCH, WAIT FOR US!
COLOSSUS CALLS IN VAIN...
... AND THE FIESTY CANADIAN SOON OUT-STRIPS HIS COMPANIONS. ALONG THE WAY, HE-- AND THEY-- PASS HORRORS BEYOND COMPRE-HENSION.
PEOPLE WHOSE BODIES ARE BEING LASHED TO BLOODY RIBBONS BY WHIP-WIELDING DEMONS... OTHERS IMMERSED IN BOILING PITCH, OR ENCASED IN ROBES OF RED-HOT GOLD.
ALL ARE SCREAMING.
AT THE SEVENTH BOLGIA...
NO SIGN OF WOLVERINE.
COULD HE BE... DOWN THERE ?
THE PEOPLE ARE FLEEING FROM THOSE SERPENTS WHY DON'T THEY FIGHT THEM? EVEN BARE-HANDED, THEY NUMBER MORE THAN ENOUGH TO DESTROY THE MONSTERS.
AND IF STORM IS IN THAT CROWD-- HOW WILL WE FIND HER ?
THERE, PETER! I SEE HER!
LUCK'S WITH US FOR ONCE! I'LL PORT DOWN TO HER!
STORM -- ORORO, IT'S ME, KURT! WE'VE COME TO RESCUE-- NO!
NO!
NOW, FINALLY, IT IS NIGHTCRAWLER'S TURN TO SCREAM ...

... AS HE FINDS HIS FELLOW X-MAN -- HIS FRIEND -- TRANSFORMED BEYOND RECOGNITION.

IT'S MORE THAN HE CAN STAND...

...AND SO, WHEN SHE LEAPS TO CLAW HIS EYES OUT...

...HE DOES NOT EVEN TRY TO DEFEND HIMSELF.

FORTUNATELY, HE DOES NOT HAVE TO.

WHA--?! BANDS OF CRIMSON ENERGY!

I CAN'T MOVE!

QUICKLY, THE TWO ARE BOUND BY THE CRIMSON BANDS OF CYTTORAK CONJURED BY DR. STRANGE...

... AND DRAWN OUT OF THE RAVINE.

OH, STORM -- WHAT HAS HAPPENED TO YOU?

WHAT I MOST FEARED, MY YOUNG FRIEND. THIS HARRIDAN IS *NOT* ORORO, THOUGH SHE WEARS HER CLOTHES.

NOT--?! WHERE IS SHE, WITCH?!

ANSWER ME!

TELL US WHAT YOU'VE DONE WITH STORM, OR BY ALL I HOLD DEAR, I'LL--!

LEAVE HER BE, PETEY.

SHE ONLY DID WHAT COMES *NATURALLY* IN THIS PLACE.

YOU WANT 'RORO?

HERE SHE IS.

SOME SERPENTS BURN THEIR VICTIMS TO ASHES. OTHERS *MERGE* WITH THEM, BECOMING PART-HUMAN, PART-MONSTER.

STILL OTHERS, WITH THEIR BITE, TRANSMUTE THEIR VICTIMS INTO SERPENTS, AND THEMSELVES INTO PEOPLE. SO IT MUST HAVE BEEN WITH STORM.

THAT IS WHY NO ONE FIGHTS THE SERPENTS, COLOSSUS. BECAUSE THEY CANNOT WIN.

HOW DO WE CHANGE HER BACK, DOC?

ARE YOU SURE THIS IS TRULY STORM?

SCENT'S RIGHT. FEEL'S RIGHT. I'LL *GUARANTEE* IT.

THEN... LET HER *BITE* THE WOMAN.

AND MAY THE VISHANTI HAVE MERCY ON BOTH THEIR SOULS.

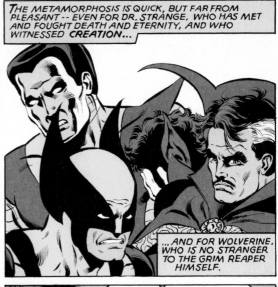

THE METAMORPHOSIS IS QUICK, BUT FAR FROM PLEASANT -- EVEN FOR DR. STRANGE, WHO HAS MET AND FOUGHT DEATH AND ETERNITY, AND WHO WITNESSED *CREATION*...

...AND FOR WOLVERINE, WHO IS NO STRANGER TO THE GRIM REAPER HIMSELF.

ALL ARE THANKFUL WHEN THE ORDEAL IS OVER.

THERE, THERE, MY CHILD. IT'S ALL RIGHT.

I... I... *MELTED!*

I... LANDED HARD -- WAS STUNNED. L-LIZARD BIT ME... AND I... *BECAME* A LIZARD! SMALL... UN-SPEAKABLY FOUL -- NO MIND. THINGS I DID... THINGS I SAW -- *HORRIBLE!*

I KNOW.

ARE YOU ALL RIGHT, ORORO?

GETTING THERE. SLOWLY...

...BUT... SURELY.

SHE TRIES A SMILE -- AND SURPRISES HERSELF BY SUCCEEDING.

WHEN SHE'S RESTED, THE DESCENT CONTINUES...

...OUT OF MALABOLGE...

... AND PAST THE GIANTS -- NIMROD, EPHIALTES, BRIAREUS AND ANTAEUS --

-- THE *TITANS* OF ANTIQUITY, SPIRITS OF THE EARTH WHO STAND SENTINAL OVER THE *NINTH,* AND LAST, CIRCLE OF HELL. AND OVER THE *RULER* OF THIS INFERNAL PIT:

SATAN!

THE X-MEN'S JOURNEY HAS NEARLY ENDED. THE HORROR HAS ONLY JUST BEGUN.

51

THIS IS THE BOTTOM OF THE ABYSS. COCYTUS IS ITS NAME, AND IT IS THE COLOR OF *DESPAIR*.

IT IS COLD AND BLEAK, WITHOUT LIFE, AND TOTALLY DEVOID OF HOPE.

IT IS DESOLATION.

THE *TREACHEROUS* ARE SENT HERE. THERE ARE FOUR LEVELS: *CAINA*, FOR THOSE WHO BETRAYED THEIR KINDRED; *ANTENORA*, FOR TRAITORS TO THEIR COUNTRY OF CAUSE; *PTOLOMEA*, FOR HOSTS WHO BETRAYED THEIR GUESTS.

AND *JUDECCA*, FOR ANY WHO BROKE FAITH WITH THEIR LORDS OR BENEFACTORS.

THEY PASS THROUGH THE FIRST THREE LEVELS WITHOUT INCIDENT, AND THEN...

AHHRRR--✳

NIGHTCRAWLER!

LOOK! THE MISFIT'S BURIED IN THE ICE-- AN' TWISTED UP LIKE SOME CRAZY PRETZEL!

WE GOTTA GET HIM OUT BEFORE HE SUFFOCATES, OR FREEZES!

THEY MAKE A VALIANT ATTEMPT...

... BUT NEITHER MYSTIC SPELLS, NOR MUTANT LIGHTNING BOLTS, NOR ADAMANTIUM CLAWS HAVE ANY EFFECT ON THE GERMAN-BORN X-MAN'S ICY PRISON.

LET ME TRY, MY FRIENDS.

PETEY--?!

IF THE STRENGTH, THE POWER OF COLOSSUS MEANS ANYTHING-- IF JUSTICE AND HONOR AND FRIENDSHIP MEAN ANYTHING--

--THEN NIGHTCRAWLER WILL BE *FREE!*

52

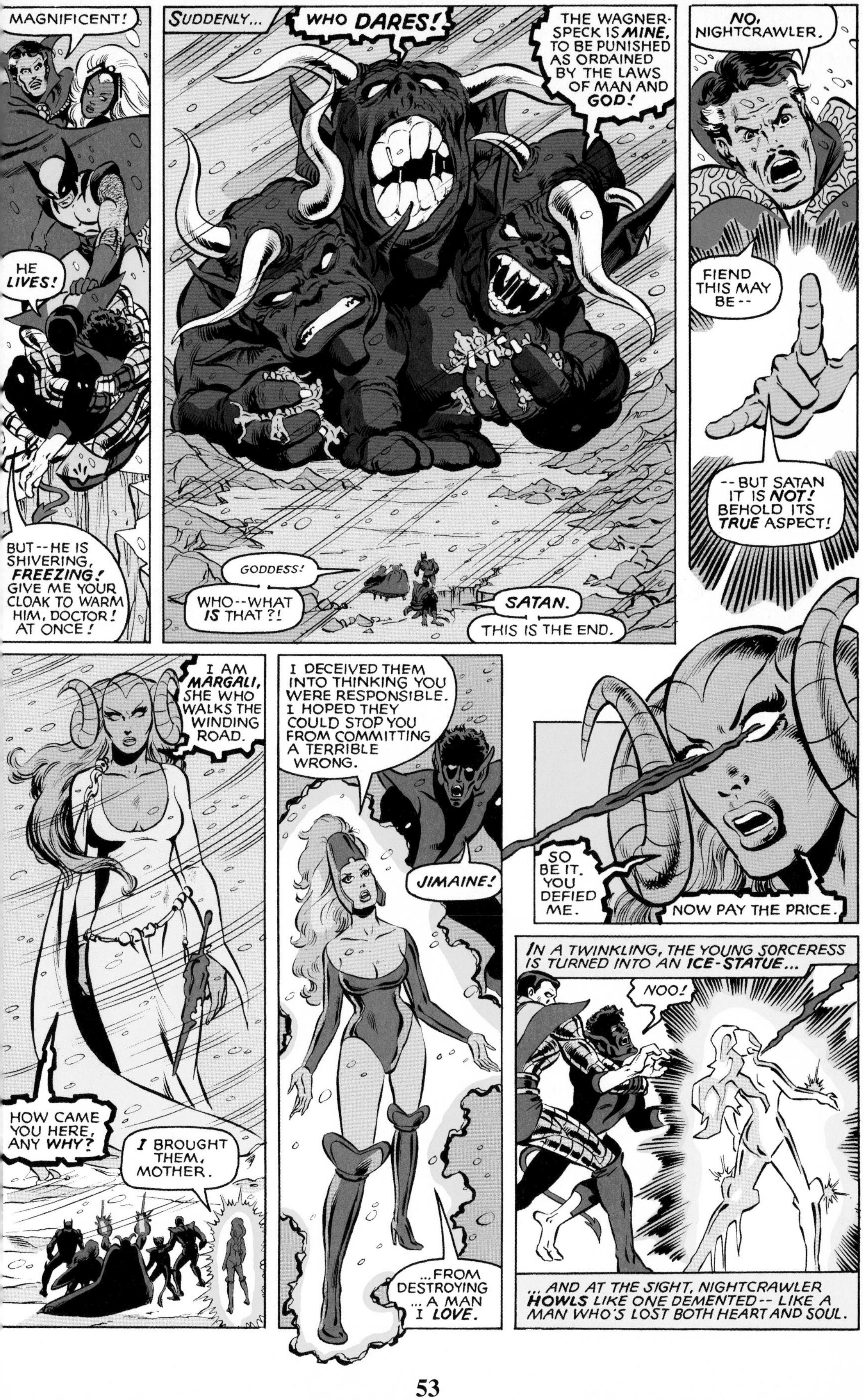
MAGNIFICENT!
HE LIVES!
BUT--HE IS SHIVERING, FREEZING! GIVE ME YOUR CLOAK TO WARM HIM, DOCTOR! AT ONCE!
SUDDENLY...
WHO DARES!
THE WAGNER-SPECK IS MINE, TO BE PUNISHED AS ORDAINED BY THE LAWS OF MAN AND GOD!
GODDESS!
WHO--WHAT IS THAT?!
SATAN.
THIS IS THE END.
NO, NIGHTCRAWLER.
FIEND THIS MAY BE--
--BUT SATAN IT IS NOT! BEHOLD ITS TRUE ASPECT!
I AM MARGALI, SHE WHO WALKS THE WINDING ROAD.
HOW CAME YOU HERE, ANY WHY?
I BROUGHT THEM, MOTHER.
I DECEIVED THEM INTO THINKING YOU WERE RESPONSIBLE. I HOPED THEY COULD STOP YOU FROM COMMITTING A TERRIBLE WRONG.
JIMAINE!
...FROM DESTROYING ...A MAN I LOVE.
SO BE IT. YOU DEFIED ME.
NOW PAY THE PRICE.
IN A TWINKLING, THE YOUNG SORCERESS IS TURNED INTO AN ICE-STATUE...
NOO!
...AND AT THE SIGHT, NIGHTCRAWLER HOWLS LIKE ONE DEMENTED-- LIKE A MAN WHO'S LOST BOTH HEART AND SOUL.

STAY BACK, X-MEN. THIS IS *MY* KIND OF FIGHT.

REGARDLESS, HER POWER IS AWESOME. I'LL NEED ALL MY WITS AND SKILL TO BEAT HER.

THE WOMAN IS NOT EVIL, I'LL STAKE MY LIFE ON THAT. WHY THEN IS SHE DOING THIS?!

IT'S A BATTLE OUT OF LEGEND -- ONE THAT ALL TO QUICKLY BECOMES A DRAW.

STOP IT! *STOP IT!*

NO MORE! *PLEASE!*

NO MORE BLOOD. NO MORE PAIN. NOT ON MY ACCOUNT.

YOU CAN END THIS, KURT. YIELD, AND YOUR FRIENDS ARE FREE TO GO. MY QUARREL WAS NEVER WITH THEM.

ONLY WITH *YOU.*

YOU NEED NOT DO THIS, NIGHT-CRAWLER. I AM PLEDGED TO PROTECT YOU.

I... I'M NOT WORTH IT.

I... YIELD, MARGALI.

DO WITH ME WHAT YOU WILL.

AN EYE FOR AN EYE, KURT.

YOUR LIFE--

--FOR THAT OF THE SON YOU FOULLY *MURDERED.*

HE TOLD YOU THAT, NO DOUBT, AND YOU BELIEVED HIM.

I KNOW DIFFERENTLY.

DO YOU SEEK JUSTICE, MARGALI -- OR VENGEANCE?

JUSTICE, MAGE.

HE MURDERED *NO ONE!*

YOU *TRY* MY PATIENCE, ARMORED ONE. STAND ASIDE.

I BRAVED *HELL* TO SAVE MY FRIEND.

YOUR THREATS -- DEATH ITSELF -- HOLD NO TERRORS FOR ME, WITCH!

HE IS *INNOCENT.* KURT WOULD NEVER DE-LIBERATELY *MURDER* ANYONE!

THEN THERE IS A SIMPLE WAY TO DETERMINE -- BEYOND ALL SHADOW OF A DOUBT -- NIGHTCRAWLER'S GUILT OR INNOCENCE.

AH! YOU REFER TO THE *EYE OF AGAMOTTO?*

YOU... KNOW OF THE ALL-SEEING EYE?

AMONG OTHER THINGS.

YOU ARE NOT THE FIRST CUSTODIAN OF THIS ANCIENT AMULET, DR. STRANGE, NOR WILL YOU BE THE LAST.

OSHTUR! SHE SUMMONED THE EYE...

...WITH JUST A GESTURE! I COULDN'T *PREVENT* IT!

WHO *IS* THIS WOMAN ?!?

LET THE *EYE OF TRUTH* PIERCE THE VEILS OF TIME AND SPACE. LET SHADOWS WALK AND MEMORIES SPEAK.

WOLVERINE. WHAT'S HAPPENING?

BEATS ME, BABE.

IMAGES UNFOLD...

... THE INFANT KURT WAGNER -- BARELY AN HOUR OLD -- FOUND BESIDE HIS DYING MOTHER, TAKEN IN BY THE GYPSY WITCH-QUEEN MARGALI SZARDOS, AND RAISED AS ONE OF HER OWN.

NEVER DID THREE CHILDREN LOVE EACH OTHER AS DID KURT, JEMAINE, AND MARGALI'S FIRST-BORN, *STEFAN.*

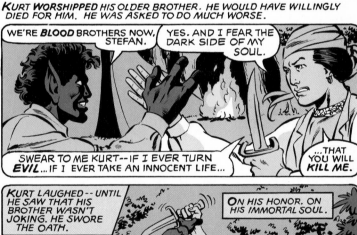

KURT *WORSHIPPED* HIS OLDER BROTHER. HE WOULD HAVE WILLINGLY DIED FOR HIM. HE WAS ASKED TO DO MUCH WORSE.

WE'RE *BLOOD* BROTHERS NOW, STEFAN.

YES. AND I FEAR THE DARK SIDE OF MY SOUL.

SWEAR TO ME KURT -- IF I EVER TURN *EVIL*... IF I EVER TAKE AN INNOCENT LIFE...

...THAT YOU WILL *KILL ME.*

KURT LAUGHED -- UNTIL HE SAW THAT HIS BROTHER WASN'T JOKING. HE SWORE THE OATH.

ON HIS HONOR. ON HIS IMMORTAL SOUL.

AND SO IT CAME TO PASS, YEARS LATER, OUTSIDE THE BAVARIAN VILLAGE OF *WINZELDORF,* THAT STEFAN KILLED -- CRUELLY, WANTONLY -- AND KURT FOUGHT TO STOP HIM FROM KILLING AGAIN.

KURT DID NOT WISH HIS BROTHER'S DEATH.

BUT STEFAN FOUGHT WITH ALL THE CONSIDERABLE WEAPONS -- PHYSICAL AND ARCANE -- AT HIS COMMAND.

AS KURT STRUGGLED WITH HIM STEFAN'S NECK SNAPPED.

KURT HADN'T MEANT TO KILL HIM...

BUT HE HAD SLAIN HIS BROTHER NONETHELESS, HE'D KEPT HIS VOW AND IT HAD BROKEN HIS HEART.

HE WAS RETURNING TO CAMP, TO TELL MARGALI WHAT HE'D DONE...

...WHEN THE VILLAGERS FOUND HIM, THEY ASSUMED HIM TO BE THE DEMON WHO'D SLAUGHTERED THEIR CHILDREN. PROFESSOR XAVIER SAVED HIM FROM A SUMMARY EXECUTION AND INVITED HIM TO JOIN THE X-MEN. KURT ACCEPTED.

MANY TIMES SINCE, HE'D TRIED TO FIND MARGALI AND FAILED.

BUT THAT SAME NIGHT, SHE DISAPPEARED, NEVER TO BE SEEN OR HEARD FROM AGAIN -- UNTIL NOW.

PROFESSOR -- THEY'RE BACK! NIGHTCRAWLER'S WITH THEM! HE LOOKS OKAY!

BUT -- WHO ARE THOSE TWO WEIRD WOMEN?!

STEFAN, MY SON -- MY POOR, PROUD, FOOLISH BOY -- WHY DIDN'T YOU CONFIDE IN ME? I COULD HAVE HELPED YOU -- SAVED YOU!

KURT, MY SON...

...I HATED YOU WITH ALL MY HEART. I WAS WRONG. I AM SORRY.

TO PUNISH YOU -- TO MAKE YOU SUFFER AS I HAD SUFFERED --

-- I CREATED A FACSIMILE OF DANTE'S HELL TO BE YOUR ETERNAL PRISON. WHAT A WASTE.

I CANNOT FORGET THAT YOU SLEW YOUR BROTHER.

BUT NOW THAT I UNDERSTAND WHY, I CAN -- AND DO -- FORGIVE.

FAREWELL, MY SON. WE WILL MEET AGAIN SOON. FOR WE HAVE MUCH CATCHING UP TO DO.

'BYE, MOM.

HI THERE, SEXY. REMEMBER ME?

I COULDN'T FORGET YOU IF I TRIED.

THAT'S NICE. SAME HERE.

LOOKS LIKE MY CRAZY GAMBLE PAID OFF, *huh?* EVERYTHING'S WORKED OUT FOR THE BEST.

WOLVERINE-- *HUSH!*

YOU ALMOST GOT US *KILLED*, KID!

HOW DID YOU FIND ME? I SEARCHED FOR YOU, BUT YOU'D VANISHED AS WELL.

I THOUGHT... YOU, TOO, HATED ME FOR WHAT I DID.

HATED YOU? FAR FROM IT.

I HAVE A CONFESSION, KURT. THESE LAST MONTHS, I'VE BEEN A LOT CLOSER THAN YOU THINK...

...AS *AMANDA SEFTON.*

AMANDA? KURT-- YOUR *GIRL FRIEND!*

OBOY!

THIS IS TOO FANTASTIC TO BE TRUE! NO WONDER MY REAL APPEARANCE NEVER STARTLED YOU! ALL THIS TIME-- THROUGH ALL WE'VE DONE TOGETHER-- AND I NEVER SUSPECTED!

ARE YOU ANGRY WITH ME?

I SUPPOSE I SHOULD BE, BUT I FEEL TOO *HAPPY!*

WHAT A *BIRTHDAY PRESENT!*

I NEVER ACCEPTED-- LIKE MOM DID-- THAT YOU KILLED STEFAN IN COLD BLOOD. I GOT CLOSE TO YOU-- AS AMANDA-- TO LEARN THE TRUTH.

BUT EVEN AFTER I BECAME CONVINCED, I COULDN'T SWAY MOTHER.

BOY, SHE CAN BE STUBBORN SOMETIMES!

I WAS DESPERATE. SO, WHEN SHE MADE HER MOVE, I MADE MINE. THE REST IS HISTORY. I REALLY AM SORRY, X-MEN -- IF THERE'D BEEN ANY OTHER WAY...

57

INCREDIBLE. A FAMILY OF GYPSY SORCERERS: THE SON EVIL, THE DAUGHTER GOOD, THE MOTHER AN ENIGMA...

...WHOSE POWER AND ABILITY RIVAL MY OWN.

I MUST LEARN MORE OF THIS!

I LOVE YOU, JIMAINE. ALWAYS HAVE. ALWAYS WILL.

I GET THAT IMPRESSION.

I'D BE MORE DEMONSTRA-TIVE ABOUT IT, BUT I DON'T WANT TO SET A BAD EXAMPLE FOR KITTY.

HAH!

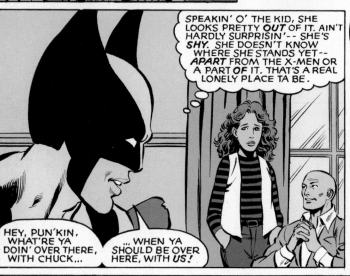

SPEAKIN' O' THE KID, SHE LOOKS PRETTY OUT OF IT. AIN'T HARDLY SURPRISIN'-- SHE'S SHY. SHE DOESN'T KNOW WHERE SHE STANDS YET-- APART FROM THE X-MEN OR A PART OF IT. THAT'S A REAL LONELY PLACE TA BE.

HEY, PUN'KIN, WHAT'RE YA DOIN' OVER THERE, WITH CHUCK...

...WHEN YA SHOULD BE OVER HERE, WITH US!

YOU'RE AN X-MAN, AIN'T'CHA?

Huh? AM I?

I MEAN, I GUESS I, I MEAN I SUPPOSE... I...

WOW!

SHE'S A NICE KID, BUT FER A GENIUS-- REAL SLOW ON THE UPTAKE, Y'KNOW?

HER TROUBLE, WOLVERINE, IS THAT, UNLIKE YOU, SHE SPEAKS ENGLISH.

WHAT A CUT! SCORE ONE FOR THE BIG GUY!

MADNESS, UTTER MADNESS. IT'S WONDERFUL.

YOUR STUDENTS HAVE A RIGHT TO CELEBRATE, CHARLES. IN MARGALI'S FACSIMILE HELL, THEY FACED THE ULTIMATE IN DESPAIR, AND EMERGED TRIUMPHANT.

PETER'S WONDERFUL.

THEY ARE HEROES.

THEY, MY DEAR STEPHEN, ARE THE X-MEN.

End!

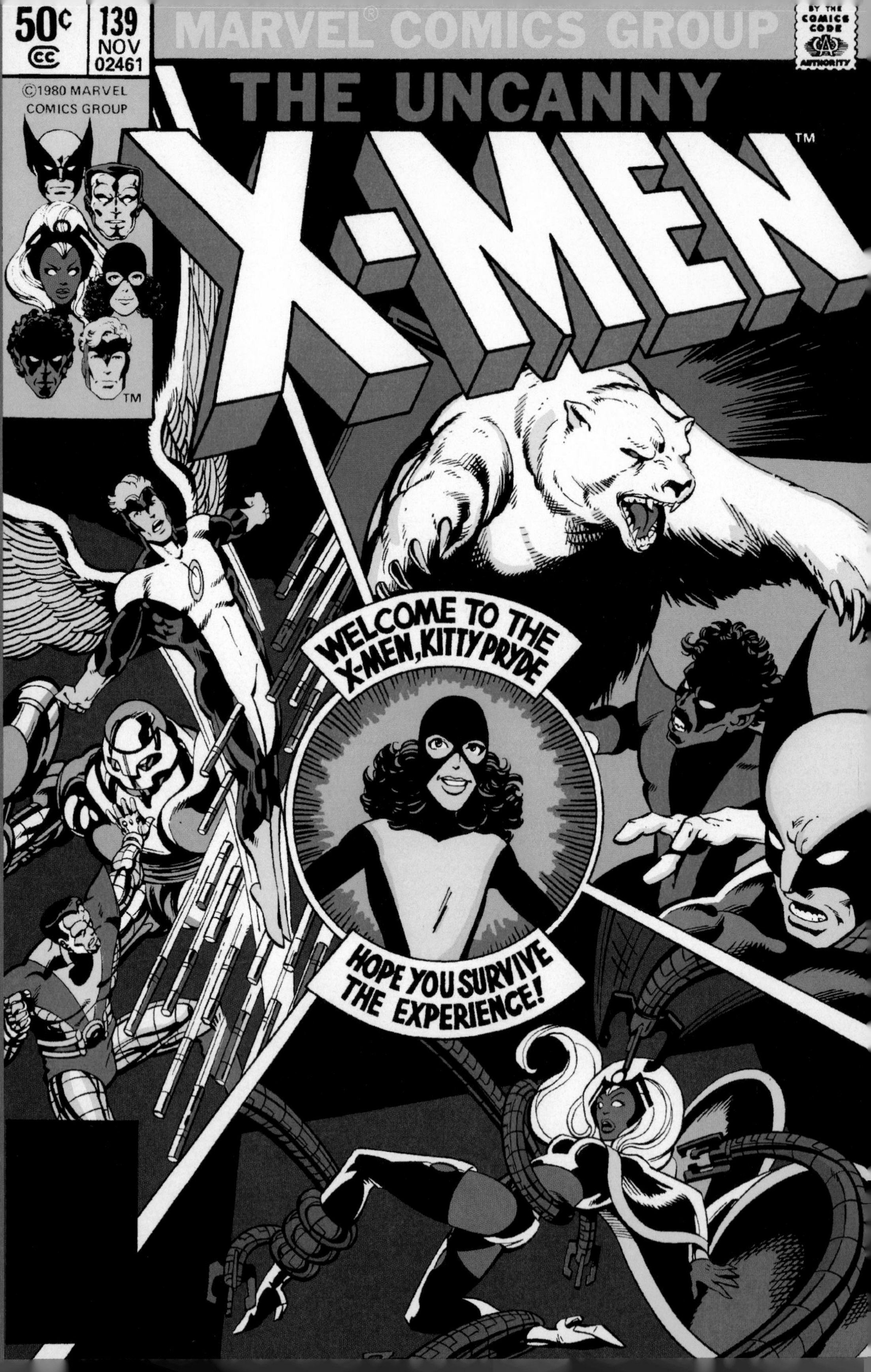
50¢
CC
139
NOV
02461
MARVEL® COMICS GROUP
APPROVED BY THE COMICS CODE AUTHORITY
©1980 MARVEL COMICS GROUP
THE UNCANNY
X-MEN™
WELCOME TO THE X-MEN, KITTY PRYDE
HOPE YOU SURVIVE THE EXPERIENCE!

Cyclops. Storm. Nightcrawler. Wolverine. Colossus. Children of the atom, students of Charles Xavier, MUTANTS — feared and hated by the world they have sworn to protect. These are the STRANGEST heroes of all!

STAN LEE PRESENTS: THE UNCANNY X-MEN!™

| CHRIS CLAREMONT WRITER | JOHN BYRNE PLOT-PENCILS | TERRY AUSTIN INKER | TOM ORZECHOWSKI, letterer GLYNIS WEIN, colorist | LOUISE JONES EDITOR | JIM SHOOTER Ed. in CHIEF |

...SOMETHING WICKED THIS WAY COMES!

ANGEL -- LOOK OUT!

HOLY CATS!

TO THE WORLD AT LARGE, PROFESSOR XAVIER'S **SCHOOL FOR GIFTED YOUNGSTERS** IS A SOMEWHAT RECLUSIVE, VERY EXCLUSIVE, WELL-RESPECTED PRIVATE ACADEMY FOR BUDDING YOUNG GENIUSES, LOCATED IN THE UPPER-MIDDLE CLASS, SUBURBAN ENVIRONS OF NEW YORK'S **WESTCHESTER COUNTY.** BUT TO THE STUDENTS ENROLLED IN XAVIER'S SCHOOL, IT IS THAT-- AND MUCH, MUCH **MORE.**

YOU SEE, THEY ARE ALL **MUTANTS,** EACH POSSESSING SUPER-POWERS THAT SET THEM APART FROM THE REST OF HUMANITY. TOGETHER, THEY COMPRISE THE UNCANNY **X-MEN.**

AND HERE, IN THE SCHOOL'S HUGE **DANGER ROOM,** THEIR MUTANT ABILITIES--BOTH AS INDIVIDUALS AND AS A FIGHTING TEAM-- ARE HONED TO A RAZOR-KEEN EDGE.

ANGEL, BE CAREFUL! YOU'RE HEADING STRAIGHT FOR **NIGHT-CRAWLER!**

I AM SORRY, MY MECHANICAL FRIEND. FOR ALL YOUR COMPUTER-IZED STRENGTH AND SPEED...

...YOU ARE STILL NO MATCH FOR THE ARMORED MIGHT OF **COLOSSUS.**

BWHAMK!

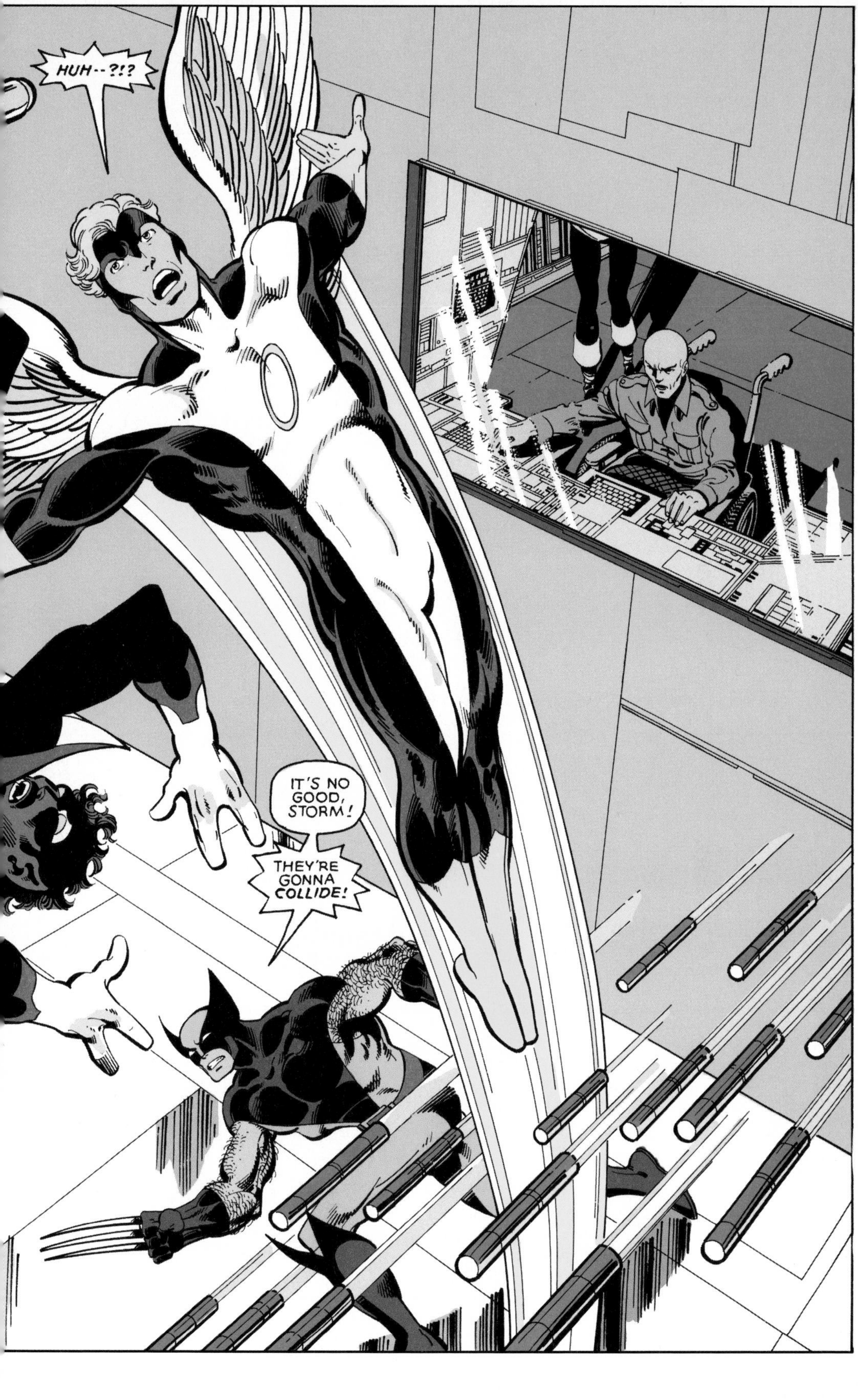
HUH--?!?
IT'S NO GOOD, STORM!
THEY'RE GONNA COLLIDE!

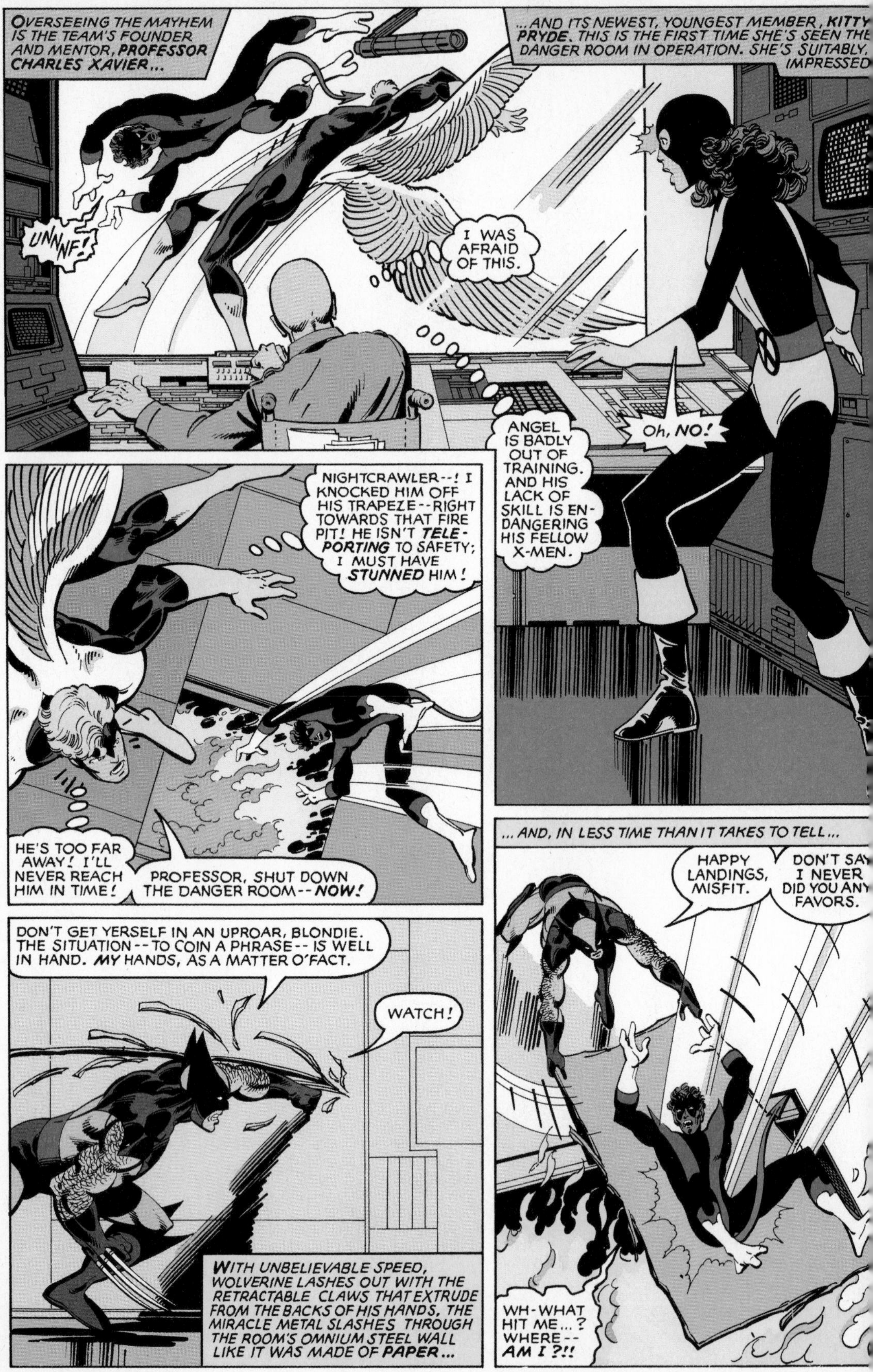
OVERSEEING THE MAYHEM IS THE TEAM'S FOUNDER AND MENTOR, PROFESSOR CHARLES XAVIER...
...AND ITS NEWEST, YOUNGEST MEMBER, KITTY PRYDE. THIS IS THE FIRST TIME SHE'S SEEN THE DANGER ROOM IN OPERATION. SHE'S SUITABLY, IMPRESSED
UNNNF!
I WAS AFRAID OF THIS.
ANGEL IS BADLY OUT OF TRAINING. AND HIS LACK OF SKILL IS ENDANGERING HIS FELLOW X-MEN.
Oh, NO!
NIGHTCRAWLER--! I KNOCKED HIM OFF HIS TRAPEZE--RIGHT TOWARDS THAT FIRE PIT! HE ISN'T TELEPORTING TO SAFETY; I MUST HAVE STUNNED HIM!
HE'S TOO FAR AWAY! I'LL NEVER REACH HIM IN TIME!
PROFESSOR, SHUT DOWN THE DANGER ROOM--NOW!
DON'T GET YERSELF IN AN UPROAR, BLONDIE. THE SITUATION--TO COIN A PHRASE--IS WELL IN HAND. MY HANDS, AS A MATTER O'FACT.
WATCH!
WITH UNBELIEVABLE SPEED, WOLVERINE LASHES OUT WITH THE RETRACTABLE CLAWS THAT EXTRUDE FROM THE BACKS OF HIS HANDS. THE MIRACLE METAL SLASHES THROUGH THE ROOM'S OMNIUM STEEL WALL LIKE IT WAS MADE OF PAPER...
...AND, IN LESS TIME THAN IT TAKES TO TELL...
HAPPY LANDINGS, MISFIT.
DON'T SAY I NEVER DID YOU ANY FAVORS.
WH-WHAT HIT ME...? WHERE--AM I?!!

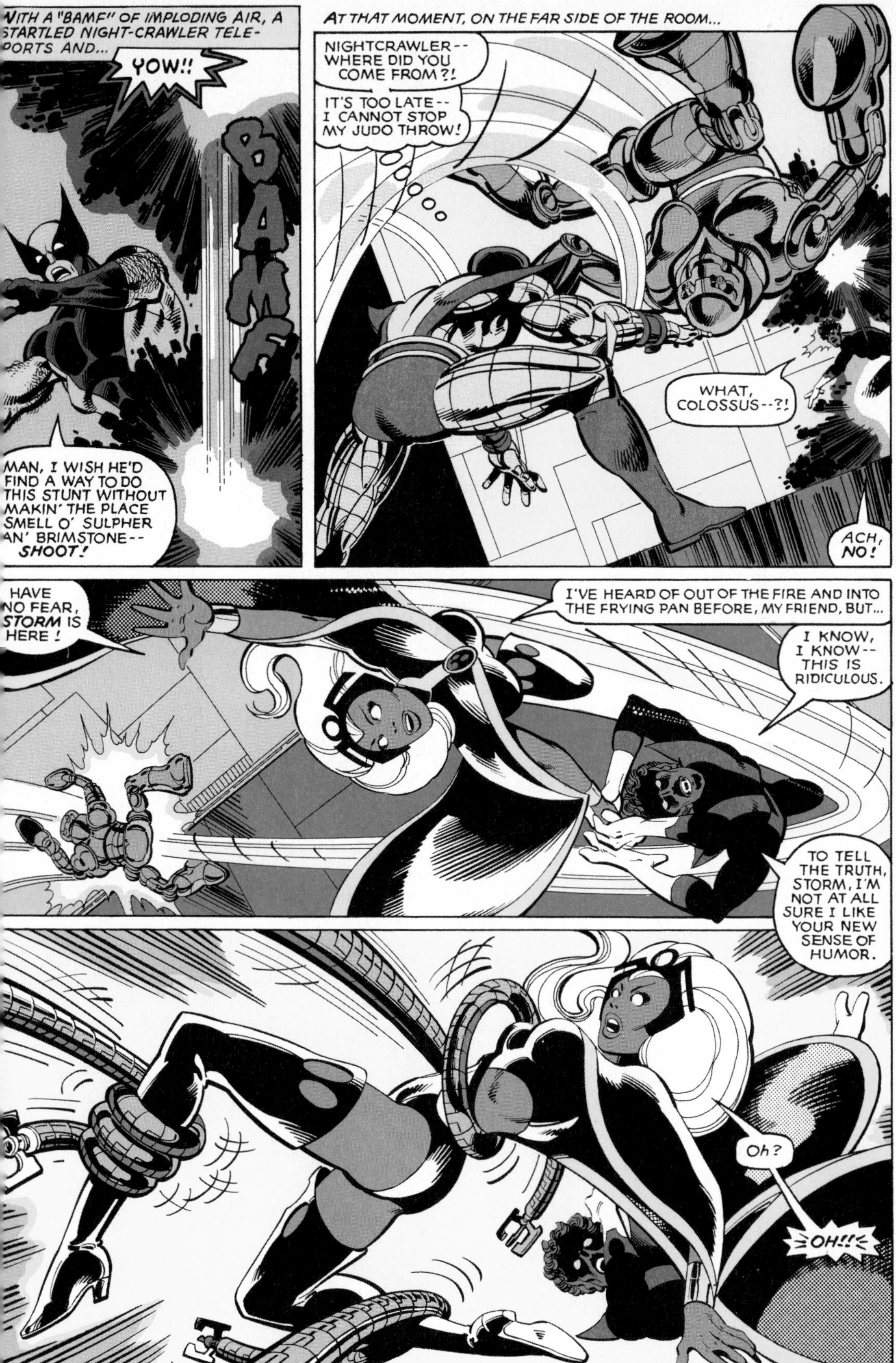
WITH A "BAMF" OF IMPLODING AIR, A STARTLED NIGHT-CRAWLER TELE-PORTS AND...
YOW!!
BAMF
MAN, I WISH HE'D FIND A WAY TO DO THIS STUNT WITHOUT MAKIN' THE PLACE SMELL O' SULPHER AN' BRIMSTONE-- SHOOT!
AT THAT MOMENT, ON THE FAR SIDE OF THE ROOM...
NIGHTCRAWLER-- WHERE DID YOU COME FROM?!
IT'S TOO LATE-- I CANNOT STOP MY JUDO THROW!
WHAT, COLOSSUS--?!
ACH, NO!
HAVE NO FEAR, STORM IS HERE!
I'VE HEARD OF OUT OF THE FIRE AND INTO THE FRYING PAN BEFORE, MY FRIEND, BUT...
I KNOW, I KNOW-- THIS IS RIDICULOUS.
TO TELL THE TRUTH, STORM, I'M NOT AT ALL SURE I LIKE YOUR NEW SENSE OF HUMOR.
Oh?
OH!!

COLOSSUS, CATCH NIGHTCRAWLER!

SORRY TO DROP YOU LIKE THIS, KURT...

...BUT I'LL HAVE A BETTER CHANCE OF DEALING WITH THESE TENTACLES IF I DON'T HAVE TO SPLIT MY CONCENTRATION BETWEEN THEM AND YOU.

I HAVE HIM, STORM.

I WILL EVEN BE GENTLE.

Hmm -- I'M NOT THE ONLY ONE DEVELOPING A STRANGE SENSE OF HUMOR. AFTER ALL WE'VE BEEN THROUGH LATELY, I WONDER IF I SHOULD EVEN BE SURPRISED.

THAT'S SOMETHING TO THINK ABOUT-- *AFTER* I'VE GOTTEN MYSELF OUT OF THIS TRAP. I'LL USE MY *ELEMENTAL* POWERS TO CREATE AN INSTANT MINI-THUNDERSHOWER.

THERE WE ARE.

THAT SHOULD SHORT-CIRCUIT THE TRAP'S CONTROL AND POWER CIRCUITS...

...AND, IN A MATTER OF SECONDS, SET ME FREE!

KOOM

WELL DONE, ORORO!

THANK YOU, PETER.

I GOTTA ADMIT, DARLIN'...

...I'M BEGINNING TA THINK CHARLEY MADE THE RIGHT DECISION WHEN HE NAMED YOU *TEAM LEADER* AFTER CYCLOPS LEFT. *

*ON A LEAVE OF ABSENCE, AT THE END OF LAST ISSUE.

WOLVERINE, CALL ME 'PROFESSOR,' 'PROFESSOR X', 'PROFESSOR XAVIER', OR EVEN, IF YOU MUST, 'CHARLES'. BUT NOT 'CHARLEY'. IS THAT UNDERSTOOD?

SURE, CHUCK.

Uh, GUYS, IS IT *SAFE* TO COME IN NOW?

I KNOW WHAT YOU'RE GOING TO SAY, PROFESSOR. MY DUMB MOVES NEARLY GOT NIGHT-CRAWLER BADLY HURT--OR WORSE.

I'M SORRY. IT WON'T HAPPEN AGAIN.

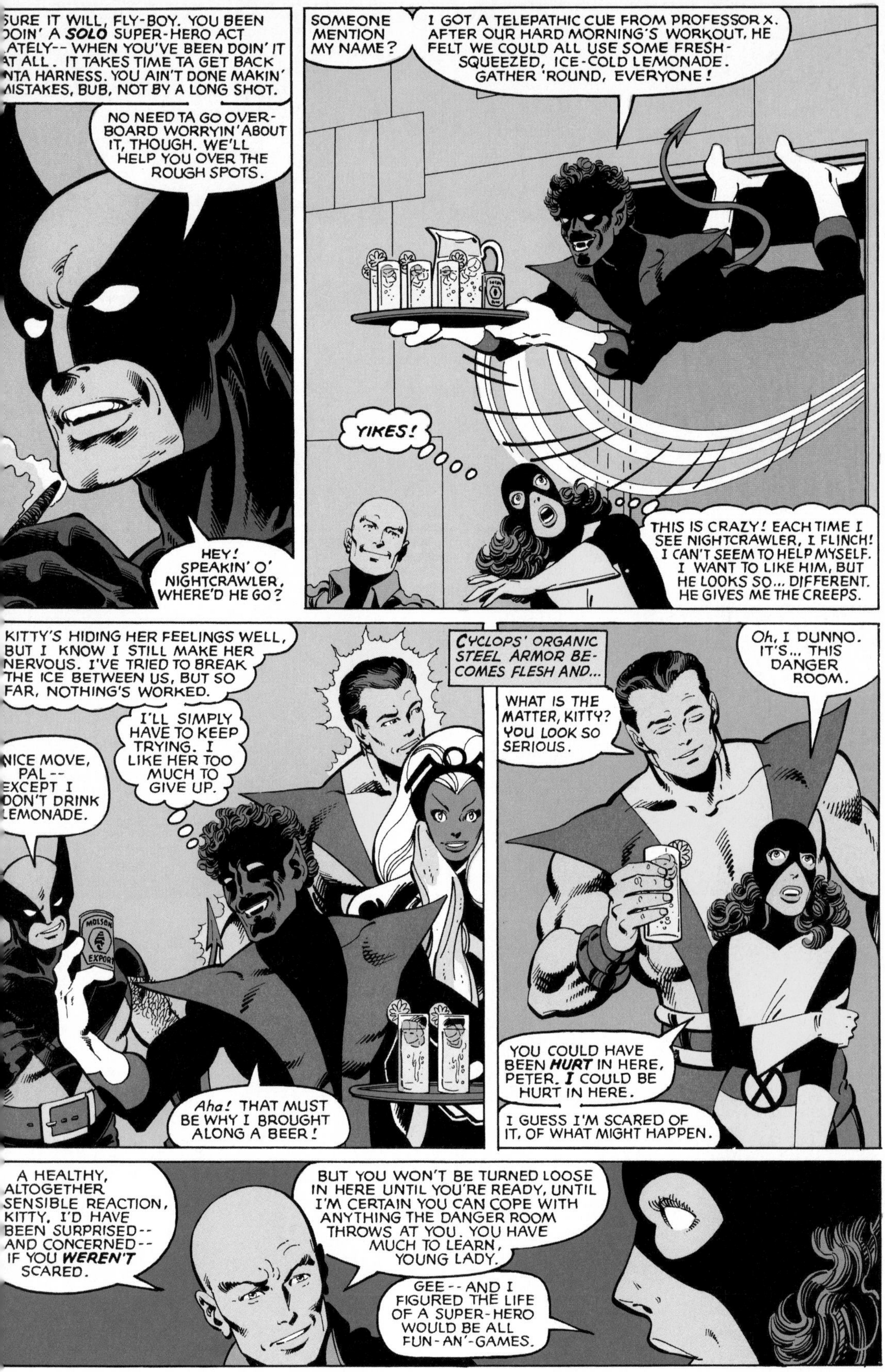
SURE IT WILL, FLY-BOY. YOU BEEN DOIN' A SOLO SUPER-HERO ACT LATELY-- WHEN YOU'VE BEEN DOIN' IT AT ALL. IT TAKES TIME TA GET BACK INTA HARNESS. YOU AIN'T DONE MAKIN' MISTAKES, BUB, NOT BY A LONG SHOT.
NO NEED TA GO OVERBOARD WORRYIN' ABOUT IT, THOUGH. WE'LL HELP YOU OVER THE ROUGH SPOTS.
HEY! SPEAKIN' O' NIGHTCRAWLER, WHERE'D HE GO?
SOMEONE MENTION MY NAME?
I GOT A TELEPATHIC CUE FROM PROFESSOR X. AFTER OUR HARD MORNING'S WORKOUT, HE FELT WE COULD ALL USE SOME FRESH-SQUEEZED, ICE-COLD LEMONADE. GATHER 'ROUND, EVERYONE!
YIKES!
THIS IS CRAZY! EACH TIME I SEE NIGHTCRAWLER, I FLINCH! I CAN'T SEEM TO HELP MYSELF. I WANT TO LIKE HIM, BUT HE LOOKS SO... DIFFERENT. HE GIVES ME THE CREEPS.
KITTY'S HIDING HER FEELINGS WELL, BUT I KNOW I STILL MAKE HER NERVOUS. I'VE TRIED TO BREAK THE ICE BETWEEN US, BUT SO FAR, NOTHING'S WORKED.
I'LL SIMPLY HAVE TO KEEP TRYING. I LIKE HER TOO MUCH TO GIVE UP.
NICE MOVE, PAL-- EXCEPT I DON'T DRINK LEMONADE.
Aha! THAT MUST BE WHY I BROUGHT ALONG A BEER!
CYCLOPS' ORGANIC STEEL ARMOR BECOMES FLESH AND...
WHAT IS THE MATTER, KITTY? YOU LOOK SO SERIOUS.
Oh, I DUNNO. IT'S... THIS DANGER ROOM.
YOU COULD HAVE BEEN HURT IN HERE, PETER. I COULD BE HURT IN HERE.
I GUESS I'M SCARED OF IT, OF WHAT MIGHT HAPPEN.
A HEALTHY, ALTOGETHER SENSIBLE REACTION, KITTY. I'D HAVE BEEN SURPRISED-- AND CONCERNED-- IF YOU WEREN'T SCARED.
BUT YOU WON'T BE TURNED LOOSE IN HERE UNTIL YOU'RE READY, UNTIL I'M CERTAIN YOU CAN COPE WITH ANYTHING THE DANGER ROOM THROWS AT YOU. YOU HAVE MUCH TO LEARN, YOUNG LADY.
GEE-- AND I FIGURED THE LIFE OF A SUPER-HERO WOULD BE ALL FUN-AN'-GAMES.

IF ONLY IT WERE.

AS AN X-MAN, KITTY, YOU'LL NEED A *CODE-NAME,* TO PROTECT YOUR TRUE IDENTITY. WHAT DO YOU THINK OF, *"ARIEL?"*

YUCK.

NO OFFENSE, PROFESSOR, BUT DO I HAVE TO TAKE IT?

I MEAN, IT'S ...OKAY, BUT IT DOESN'T REALLY SEND ME.

WELL NOW, LITTLE ONE, WE CERTAINLY WOULDN'T WAN' TO GIVE YOU A NAME YOU DON'T LIKE. LET'S SEE...

WHAT ABOUT *"SPRITE?"*

YEAH... *YEAH!*

BUT I BETTER NOT HEAR ANY CRACKS ABOUT PEOPLE PULLIN' MY *"TAB!"*

OUCH! X-MEN, I PROPOSE A TOAST-- TO OUR NEWEST MEMBER: *"SPRITE!"*

I HOPE YOU WILL BE HAPPY WITH US, KITTY. I PRAY YOU WILL NOT BE HURT, AS WE HAVE BEEN HURT. AND YET, I FEAR THAT, SOONER OR LATER, YOU *WILL.*

WOLVERINE, I'VE BEEN MEANING TO ASK YOU: *WHY* THE NEW COSTUME?

WHY *NOT?*

PROFESSOR, GOT A MINUTE?

I'VE BEEN THINKING ABOUT MY HASSLES WITH THE GOVERNMENT BACK HOME IN *CANADA.* YOU KNOW I WAS PART O' THEIR *SECRET SERVICE* 'TIL I RESIGNED TO JOIN THE X-MEN.

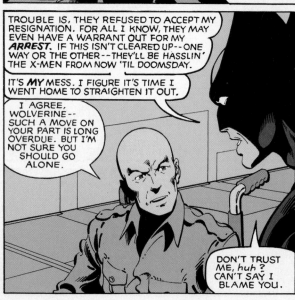

TROUBLE IS, THEY REFUSED TO ACCEPT MY RESIGNATION. FOR ALL I KNOW, THEY MAY EVEN HAVE A WARRANT OUT FOR MY *ARREST.* IF THIS ISN'T CLEARED UP-- ONE WAY OR THE OTHER-- THEY'LL BE HASSLIN' THE X-MEN FROM NOW 'TIL DOOMSDAY.

IT'S *MY* MESS. I FIGURE IT'S TIME I WENT HOME TO STRAIGHTEN IT OUT.

I AGREE, WOLVERINE-- SUCH A MOVE ON YOUR PART IS LONG OVERDUE. BUT I'M NOT SURE YOU SHOULD GO ALONE.

DON'T TRUST ME, *huh?* CAN'T SAY I BLAME YOU.

WANT'A PLAY *"CHAPERONE,"* MISFIT? KEEP ME OUT OF TROUBLE?

WHY *NOT?*

MY MOTHER ALWAYS SAID I LIKED TO LIVE DANGEROUSLY. BESIDES I'D LIKE TO SEE *AURORA* AGAIN; SHE'S A REAL *"FOXY LADY."*

I'LL MAKE THE NECESSARY TRAVEL ARRANGEMENTS.

IN THE MEANTIME, I'VE ONE MORE SURPRISE FOR SPRITE.

REALLY?! THAT'S GREAT-- I THINK.

WHAT IS IT?

GO WITH STORM. SHE'LL SHOW YOU.

AND SO, A BIT LATER THAT DAY, IN THE NEARBY TOWN OF *SALEM CENTER*...

I'VE RARELY SEEN YOU SO HAPPY, KITTEN.

I LOVE DANCING, ORORO. UP 'TIL NOW, I WAS AFRAID THAT BEING AN X-MAN MIGHT MEAN HAVING TO GIVE IT UP.

I'M SO GLAD I DON'T HAVE TO. LOOK! THERE'S THE ADDRESS PROFESSOR X GAVE US!

THIS IS THE ONLY ENTRANCE-- BUT THE DOOR WON'T OPEN. IT ISN'T LOCKED. SOMETHING MUST BE BLOCKING IT ON THE OTHER SIDE.

NO PROBLEM. I'LL CLEAR IT.

ALL RIGHT. BUT BE CAREFUL!

YOU BET! IT'S MY NECK, REMEMBER. I'M NOT ABOUT TO GET IT CHOPPED OFF AT MY TENDER AGE.

THE COAST IS CLEAR.

KEEP ME COVERED, ORORO. I'LL BE RIGHT BACK.

SHE CONCENTRATES...

...FEELING AN INCREASINGLY FAMILIAR BUZZ OF ENERGY AT THE BASE OF HER SKULL...

... AND-- WITH AN EASE THAT THRILLS AND EXCITES HER MORE THAN ALMOST ANYTHING SHE'S EVER KNOWN--

--KITTY PRYDE "PHASES" THROUGH THE DOOR.

MADE IT!

AND IT DIDN'T TAKE HARDLY ANY EFFORT AT ALL!

BOY, WHAT A MESS! WHOEVER TAKES CARE OF THIS BUILDING OUGHT TO BE ASHAMED OF HIMSELF. I'LL HAVE IT TIDIED UP IN A JIFFY.

HI, THERE! MISS ME?

TERRIBLY.

Awww-- I BET YOU SAY THAT TO ALL THE X-MEN.

... I'M A CERTIFIED *GENIUS*, Y'KNOW. MY PEERS ARE IN THE NINTH GRADE, AN' I'M TAKING COLLEGE-LEVEL COURSES. ACADEMICALLY, WE DON'T FIT.

DANCING IS HOW I BALANCE THE SCALES. I CAN'T MAKE MY BODY GROW ANY FASTER, AN' MY INTELLECT ISN'T MUCH GOOD AT HELPING ME PERFORM THE MOVES RIGHT.

HERE, I'M JUST LIKE EVERYBODY ELSE. I CAN RELATE TO KIDS MY OWN AGE AS *EQUALS*. BOY, IT'S NICE TO BE ABLE TO DO THAT.

INCREDIBLE. KITTY REASONS AS CALMLY, AS SENSIBLY, AS PROFESSOR X-- YET, FOR ALL OF THAT, SHE IS STILL A CHILD, STRUGGLING TO HOLD ONTO HER CHILDHOOD.

I, TOO, FACED SUCH A CONFLICT, IN CAIRO, AFTER MY PARENTS WERE KILLED. I HAD TO GROW UP VERY QUICKLY-- PERHAPS *TOO* QUICKLY. NOW, I REMEMBER ORORO THE GODDESS, AND ORORO THE GIRL-THIEF-- BUT NOT ORORO THE CHILD.

I WILL DO WHATEVER I CAN TO HELP KITTY WIN *HER* BATTLE, TO LIVE AS *NORMAL* A LIFE AS POSSIBLE.

MS. HUNTER DANCE ACADEMY

WELL, KITTEN, WE'VE ARRIVED.

I DON'T BELIEVE THIS. I'M SO... *NERVOUS!*

AFTERNOON, FOLKS! YOU'RE RIGHT ON TIME!

I'M *STEVIE HUNTER*. WELCOME TO MY STUDIO.

AND YOU MUST BE MS. MONROE AND MS. PRYDE, FROM PROFESSOR XAVIER'S SCHOOL, RIGHT?

I AM... ORORO.

I'M KITTY, KITTY PRYDE. I'M... I'M YOUR NEW STUDENT. I'M REAL PLEASED TO MEET YOU, MS. HUNTER. I SAW YOU DANCE IN CHICAGO, BEFORE YOUR ACCIDENT. YOU WERE WONDERFUL.

THANK YOU. AND THE NAME'S *STEVIE*.

SOME ICED TEA, ANYONE?

WITH THAT, AN EFFERVESCENT, ENTHUSIASTIC KITTY, AND SURPRISINGLY, A SLIGHTLY WARY STORM, GET TO KNOW KITTY'S NEW DANCE TEACHER OVER A POT OF ICED HERBAL TEA...

...AS WE SHIFT OUR SCENE AHEAD A DAY, AND SOME THREE HUNDRED MILES TO THE NORTH-WEST, FROM THE SUBURBS OF NEW YORK CITY TO THOSE OF OTTAWA, CAPITAL OF CANADA.

THIS IS LAURIER DRIVE, A PLEASANT, WHITE-COLLAR NEIGHBOR-HOOD. MOST OF THESE MODEST, SEMI-DETACHED HOUSES ARE OWNED BY PROFESSIONAL PEOPLE -- TEACHERS, DOCTORS, LAWYERS, GOVERNMENT WORKERS, ALL JUST GETTING STARTED IN THEIR VARIOUS FIELDS...

... AMONG THEM -- IN NUMBER 138A -- A BRILLIANT, MAVERICK RESEARCH PHYSICIST NAMED JAMES MacDONALD HUDSON...

... AND HIS WIFE, HEATHER, AN EXECUTIVE SECRETARY FOR YUKON OIL, ONE OF THE COUNTRY'S BIGGEST ENERGY CONGLOMERATES.

IT WAS NICE OF Mr. BERESFORD TO GIVE ME THE DAY OFF. BUT AFTER ALL THE HOURS I PUT IN HELPING HIM PREPARE FOR THIS MONTH'S BOARD MEETING...

... I DESERVE IT.

THAT OVERTIME MONEY WILL COME IN HANDY -- AND WITH JAMIE AWAY ON GOVERNMENT BUSINESS, MY EXTRA WORK DIDN'T CAUSE ANY HASSLES AT HOME.

HOME -- UGH! ALL I'VE DONE THIS PAST WEEK WAS TOUCH BASE LONG ENOUGH TO GRAB SOME SLEEP,...

...SHOWER, AND CHANGE MY CLOTHES. THE PLACE IS PROBABLY AN UNHOLY MESS.

FIGURES -- NOTHING BUT BILLS.

HOW CAN SO LITTLE COST SO MUCH?

BETWEEN US, JAMIE AND I MAKE A RESPECTABLE SALARY -- YET WE STILL HAVE TO STRAIN TO MAKE ENDS MEET. WE WANT CHILDREN, BUT HOW ARE WE GOING TO AFFORD THEM?

WHAT THE --?! OUR FRONT DOOR'S OPEN!

JAMIE? NOT LIKELY. WHEN I SPOKE TO HIM THIS MORNING, HE SAID HE'D BE UP NORTH FOR A FEW MORE DAYS, AT LEAST.

BURGLARS? NOTHING LOOKS TOUCHED.

I'M POSITIVE I LEFT THE DOOR LOCKED, BUT I WAS IN SUCH A RUSH--I OVERSLEPT-- MAYBE I FORGOT.

HOLD IT!

THAT SOUND-- SOMEONE... *BURPED!* IT CAME FROM THE KITCHEN!

I SHOULD GET OUT OF HERE WHILE I HAVE THE CHANCE, AND CALL THE POLICE FROM MRS. LaPIERRE'S APARTMENT DOWN-STAIRS, BUT IF THIS TURNS OUT TO BE A FALSE ALARM, I'LL FEEL SO FOOLISH.

VAS--?!

ALL RIGHT, WHOEVER YOU ARE -- DON'T MOVE OR--

YOU?!?

HIYA, SEXY. HOW YA BEEN?

WOLVERINE?!

LOGAN!!

Oh, IT'S SO GOOD TO SEE YOU! IT'S BEEN SO *LONG!*

YOU LOUSE! I NEARLY DIED OF FRIGHT JUST NOW.

SERVES YOU RIGHT.

ANYONE EVER TELL YOU YOU'RE BEAUTIFUL WHEN YOU'RE ANGRY?

YOU DID OFTEN.

WOLVERINE, SHE CALLED YOU..."*LOGAN?*"

YUP.

IS THAT YOUR NAME?

YUP.

YOU NEVER TOLD US.

YOU NEVER ASKED.

YOUR FRIEND IS ONE OF HE X-MEN, RIGHT? AMIE TOLD ME ABOUT THEM AFTER YOU HAD HAT SCRAP IN CALGARY.* THIS IS... *NIGHT-CREEPER?*

NIGHT-*CRAWLER.* TAKE A BOW, PAL, AN' MAKE NICE WITH THE LADY. 'TILL I MET YOU CLOWNS, SHE AN' MAC WERE THE ONLY TRUE FRIENDS I EVER HAD.

ENCHANTÉ, MADAME. WITH FRIENDS LIKE YOU, I CAN'T IMAGINE WHERE WOLVERINE DEVELOPED HIS *"DELIGHTFUL"* PERSONALITY.

*X-MEN #'s 120 & 121 -- LOUISE.

CAN IT, FUZZY. OR ELSE.

LOGAN, YOU'RE NOT HERE TO FIGHT MAC AGAIN, ARE YOU?

I CAME TO MAKE *PEACE,* HEATHER, IF I CAN.

GOOD. WE THREE HAVE BEEN APART TOO LONG.

HE'S IN THE NORTH COUNTRY-- *HUDSON BAY.* THERE'S SERIOUS TROUBLE UP THERE, SOMETHING SO DANGEROUS THAT THE MINISTER CALLED IN DEPARTMENT H, AND ALPHA FLIGHT.

TIME PASSES -- AND ALONG THE SHORELINE OF A BAY THAT'S BIGGER THAN MANY STATES, A BALL OF SCARLET FIRE STREAKS ACROSS THE EARLY EVENING SKY...

... SHATTERING THE SUMMERTIME SERENITY OF ONE OF THE MOST BEAUTIFUL WILDERNESS AREAS IN NORTH AMERICA.

IT IS A MAN -- JAMES MacDONALD HUDSON, BY NAME -- WHO, AS VINDICATOR, *FORMED AND NOW HEADS THE TEAM OF CANADIAN SUPER-HEROES KNOWN AS* ALPHA FLIGHT.

HE HADN'T WANTED THE JOB. THAT HONOR HAD BEEN INTENDED FOR HIS PROTEGE, WOLVERINE.

BUT THINGS HADN'T WORKED OUT THE WAY HE'D INTENDED. THAT FAILURE STILL RANKLES.

I'M BACK IN RECORD TIME. THIS BATTLE SUIT WORKS LIKE A DREAM. I DESIGNED IT AND ITS CAPABILITIES STILL CONTINUALLY AMAZE AND SURPRISE ME.

I ENJOY USING IT, TOO. IT'S BECOME LIKE AN EXTENSION OF MY OWN BODY.

IT'S PUTTING MY LIFE ON THE LINE, AS A MEMBER OF ALPHA FLIGHT, THAT GIVES ME THE WILLIES.

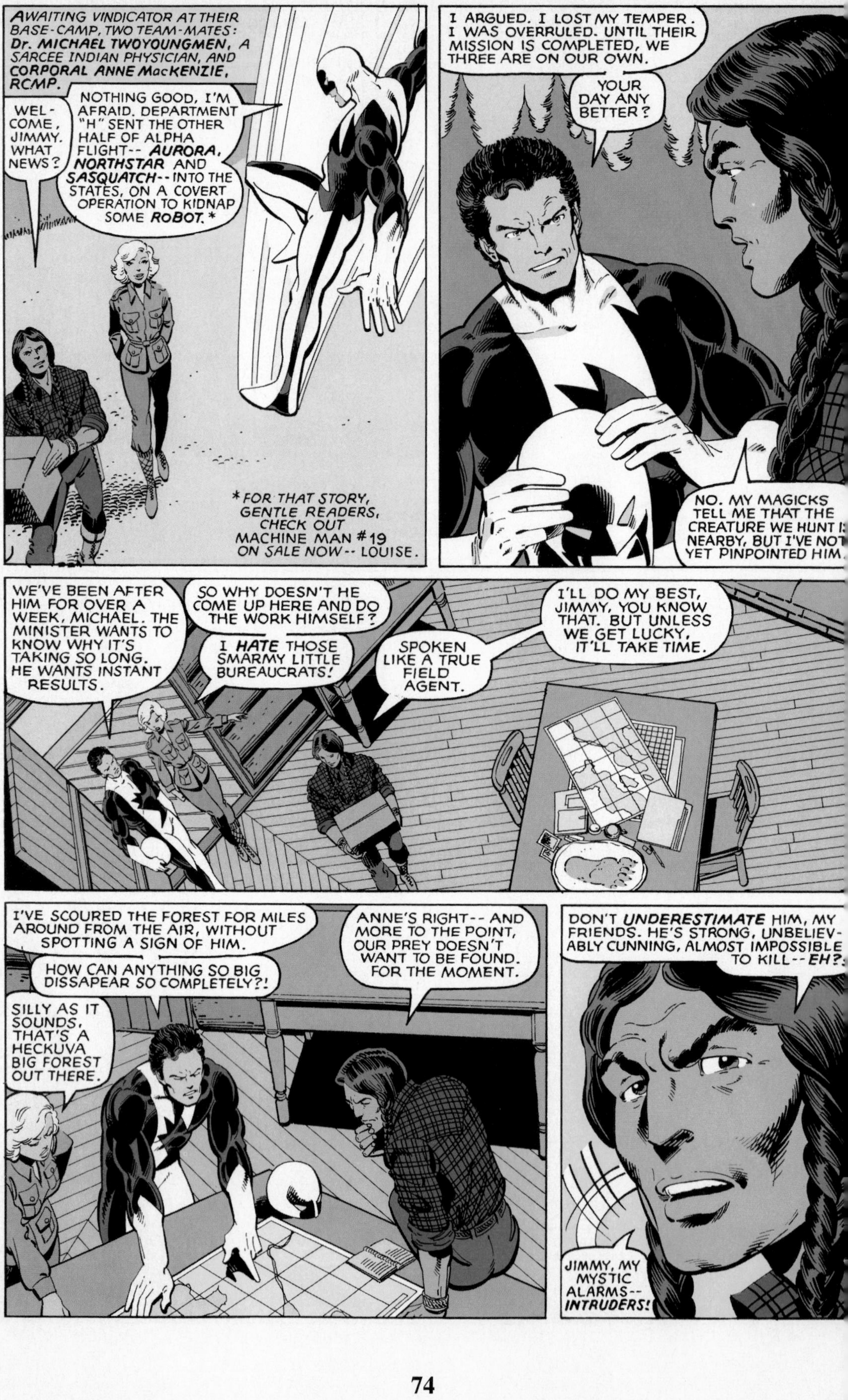

AWAITING VINDICATOR AT THEIR BASE-CAMP, TWO TEAM-MATES: Dr. MICHAEL TWOYOUNGMEN, A SARCEE INDIAN PHYSICIAN, AND CORPORAL ANNE MacKENZIE, RCMP.
WEL-COME, JIMMY. WHAT NEWS?
NOTHING GOOD, I'M AFRAID. DEPARTMENT "H" SENT THE OTHER HALF OF ALPHA FLIGHT-- AURORA, NORTHSTAR AND SASQUATCH--INTO THE STATES, ON A COVERT OPERATION TO KIDNAP SOME ROBOT.*
*FOR THAT STORY, GENTLE READERS, CHECK OUT MACHINE MAN #19 ON SALE NOW-- LOUISE.
I ARGUED. I LOST MY TEMPER. I WAS OVERRULED. UNTIL THEIR MISSION IS COMPLETED, WE THREE ARE ON OUR OWN.
YOUR DAY ANY BETTER?
NO. MY MAGICKS TELL ME THAT THE CREATURE WE HUNT IS NEARBY, BUT I'VE NOT YET PINPOINTED HIM.
WE'VE BEEN AFTER HIM FOR OVER A WEEK, MICHAEL. THE MINISTER WANTS TO KNOW WHY IT'S TAKING SO LONG. HE WANTS INSTANT RESULTS.
SO WHY DOESN'T HE COME UP HERE AND DO THE WORK HIMSELF?
I HATE THOSE SMARMY LITTLE BUREAUCRATS!
SPOKEN LIKE A TRUE FIELD AGENT.
I'LL DO MY BEST, JIMMY, YOU KNOW THAT. BUT UNLESS WE GET LUCKY, IT'LL TAKE TIME.
I'VE SCOURED THE FOREST FOR MILES AROUND FROM THE AIR, WITHOUT SPOTTING A SIGN OF HIM.
HOW CAN ANYTHING SO BIG DISSAPEAR SO COMPLETELY?!
SILLY AS IT SOUNDS, THAT'S A HECKUVA BIG FOREST OUT THERE.
ANNE'S RIGHT-- AND MORE TO THE POINT, OUR PREY DOESN'T WANT TO BE FOUND. FOR THE MOMENT.
DON'T UNDERESTIMATE HIM, MY FRIENDS. HE'S STRONG, UNBELIEVABLY CUNNING, ALMOST IMPOSSIBLE TO KILL-- EH?
JIMMY, MY MYSTIC ALARMS-- INTRUDERS!

THE THREE REACT IMMEDIATELY TO THE WARNING CRY. AS VINDICATOR DONS HIS HELMET, MICHAEL TWOYOUNG-MEN BRINGS A PAIR OF SACRED WRISTBANDS TOGETHER, MAGICALLY TRANSFORMING HIMSELF INTO THE SARCEE MEDICINE MAN KNOWN AS *SHAMAN*. AT THE SAME TIME, ANNE MacKENZIE'S FEATURES BLUR LIKE SMOKE; WHEN THEY SOLIDIFY ONCE MORE, THE YOUNG MOUNTIE IS GONE...

IN HER PLACE STANDS SNOW-BIRD, A SHAPE-CHANGER--A WOMAN OF HAUNTING, ELEMEN-TAL BEAUTY, YET ONE WHO IS NO LONGER QUITE... *HUMAN.*

SNOWBIRD-- *OUTSIDE!* FIND OUR VISITORS, BUT KEEP A LOW PROFILE. I WANT NO UNNECESSARY TROUBLE.

AFTER WHAT WE'VE SEEN HERE, JIM, I HOPE IT'S THE CREATURE WE'RE AFTER. I'D LIKE TO SEE HOW IMPRESS-IVE HE IS AGAINST SOMEONE WHO CAN FIGHT BACK!

DON'T FRET, BOSS. I'LL BE CAREFUL. BE SEEING YOU, GUYS.

I SHOULDN'T WORRY. SNOWBIRD CAN HANDLE HERSELF IN A SCRAP -- SHE'S PROVED THAT MORE THAN ONCE. BUT I'M STILL CONCERNED.

SHE SEEMS TO TAKE ON THE MENTAL CHARACTERISTICS OF THE ANIMALS SHE METAMOR-PHOSIZES INTO. IF SHE SHOULD EVER LOSE CONTROL, IF THE BEAST PART OF HER SHOULD EVER TAKE OVER...

HEY, MAC-- IF ALL THIS FUSS IS ON *OUR* ACCOUNT...

WHAT--?!

...DON'T BOTHER.

WOLVERINE, I HOPE-- I *PRAY*--YOU KNOW WHAT YOU'RE DOING.

BE COOL, PAL.

WOLVERINE! NIGHTCRAWLER!

WHAT ARE THE X-MEN DOING HERE ?!

I HAVEN'T THE FOGGIEST, SHAMAN. BUT IF IT'S TO SETTLE OLD SCORES, THEY'LL FIND US *READY* FOR THEM !

SHAME ON YOU, JAMIE. IS THIS ANY WAY TA TREAT THE *PRODIGAL SON?*

I'M NOT MAKIN' THE FIRST MOVE, FELLAS. BUT IF YOU START SOMETHIN', YOU SURE BETTER BE PREPARED TA *FINISH* IT.

STAY BACK, SHAMAN. IN THESE CLOSE QUARTERS, YOU'RE NO MATCH FOR WOLVERINE'S *ADAMANTIUM CLAWS.* LET MY BATTLE SUIT'S *FORCE FIELD* HANDLE THEM.

SHIKT

WOLVERINE, STOP THIS-- AT ONCE! WE CAME HERE TO *TALK,* NOT FIGHT-- REMEMBER?

DON'T TELL ME, PARTNER, TELL *THEM!*

'CRAWLER'S RIGHT, MAC. I WOULDN'T MIND A GOOD SCRAP, BUT THIS AIN'T THE TIME FER IT. I'M WILLIN' TO ABIDE BY A TRUCE.

THANK HEAVEN. I... *YIKES!!*

RRR!

DID I *STARTLE* YOU, X-MAN?

Oh, I AM SO TERRIBLY SORRY, REALLY I AM.

Uh... ah... *MY HEART...* oh my...

DO YOU *MIND?*

GET OFFA ME, WILLYA? BEFORE THESE BOZOS *LAUGH* THEMSELVES TO DEATH.

ONLY... IF IT'S *SAFE.*

RELAX, NIGHT-CRAWLER. YOU HAVE NOTHING TO FEAR-- FROM ALPHA FLIGHT, AT LEAST.

DÄNKE. HOW DOES SHE *DO* THAT?

YOU EMBARRASSED HIM, MAC. USUALLY, NIGHTCRAWLER'S THE SCARER, NOT THE SCARÉE.

YOU SAID WE HAVE NOTHING TO FEAR FROM *ALPHA FLIGHT.* THAT IMPLIES THERE'S SOMETHING LOOSE IN THESE PARTS THAT WE *SHOULD* FEAR? HEATHER TOLD ME THERE WAS TROUBLE.

THERE IS. BIG TROUBLE. FILL OUR... GUESTS IN ON THE GORY DETAILS, SHAMAN.

76

WOLVERINE, YOUR SENSE OF TIMING IS AS EXTRAORDINARY AS YOUR TEMPER. AT THE MOMENT, THOUGH, YOU'RE THE LEAST OF OUR CONCERNS.

WE'RE LOOKING FOR THE FAMILY OF A MOUNTIE NAMED *JOE PARNALL.* THEY WERE CAMPING ALONG BIG MOOSE CREEK, NEAR HUDSON BAY -- PARNALL, HIS WIFE, THEIR SIX-YEAR OLD SON AND INFANT DAUGHTER.

THEY WERE IN REMOTE, ROUGH COUNTRY-- BUT BOTH PARNALL AND HIS WIFE KNEW THE WOODS. THEY WERE WELL-SUPPLIED, ARMED, AND THEY HAD A PORTABLE, TWO-WAY, SHORTWAVE RADIO.

"THEY WERE CAREFUL PEOPLE. PARNALL CHECKED IN WITH UGALI STATION EVERY DAY.

"AT FIRST, EVERYTHING WAS NORMAL. THEY WERE HAVING A WONDERFUL TIME.

"THEN...

AARR

MOM? DAD?! SOMEONE'S SCREAMING--WHAT'S HAPPENING? *DAD?!*

RRIP

YOW!!

" TOMMY PARNALL RAN FOR HIS LIFE. HE DIDN'T STOP UNTIL A BUSH-PILOT FOUND HIM TWO DAYS LATER, WANDERING ALONG THE SHORE, HALF-DEAD FROM EXPOSURE.

"THE BOY'S STILL IN SHOCK, ALMOST CATATONIC. WHEN WE FOUND THE PARNALL CAMPSITE, AND WHAT WAS... LEFT OF HIS FATHER, WE UNDERSTOOD WHY."

PARNALL MUST HAVE LITERALLY BEEN *TORN APART* BEFORE THE BOY'S EYES. WE THINK, AS WELL, THAT WHATEVER KILLED HIM... *ATE* HIM.

WE SAW NO SIGN OF *EILEEN PARNALL,* OR THE BABY. OUR BEST GUESS IS THAT THEY WERE TAKEN AWAY BY THEIR ASSAILANT. WE DON'T KNOW IF THEY'RE STILL ALIVE. I KIND OF HOPE THEY AREN'T.

THIS MOLD OF THE BRUTE'S FOOT SHOULD GIVE YOU A GOOD IDEA *WHY.*

WE ASSUMED THAT A BEAR WAS RESPONSIBLE-- UNTIL WE STARTED SHOWING THIS AROUND. WE'VE CHECKED WITH GUIDES, TRAPPERS, NATURALISTS-- YOU NAME IT-- BUT NO ONE CAN IDENTIFY IT.

I CAN. IT AIN'T NO BEAR, JAMIE. IT'S SOMETHING A LOT WORSE.

HOW'S THIS FER ONE O' LIFE'S LITTLE IRONIES? I COME UP HERE TO TIE UP SOME OF THE LOOSE ENDS IN MY LIFE, AND WIND UP FACE-TO-FACE WITH THE BIGGEST LOOSE END OF 'EM ALL!

IT'D BE FUNNY IF IT WEREN'T SO FLAMIN' TRAGIC. WHAT YOU'RE CHASIN', JAMIE, IS A MYTH, A LEGEND COME LIFE CALLED--

--THE WENDIGO!

"I FOUGHT THAT MONSTER DURIN' MY FIRST MISSION, AS WOLVERINE, FOR DEPARTMENT 'H'. MY FIRST MISSION-- MY ONLY FAILURE.

"I'D BEEN SENT TO DEAL WITH THE HULK.

"I FOUND OL' GREEN-SKIN SLUGGIN' IT OUT WITH THE WENDIGO.

"I WAS A BIT... HEADSTRONG IN THOSE DAYS. I FIGURED TWO-TA-ONE ODDS MADE THIS A FAIR FIGHT.

IF YOU FREAKS WANT TO TANGLE WITH SOMEONE--

--WHY NOT TRY YOUR LUCK AGAINST -- ME!

"THE HULK AN' THE WENDIGO HAVE A LOT IN COMMON. BOTH ARE ORDINARY MEN, TRANSFORMED-- ONE BY SCIENCE, THE OTHER BY SORCERY. ACCORDING TO LEGEND, Y'SEE, THE WENDIGO IS A MAN WHO CONSUMES THE FLESH OF OTHER MEN.

"I LEARNED LATER, THAT'S EXACTLY WHAT HAD HAPPENED, TO A HUNTER NAMED PAUL CARTIER.

"HE AND SOME FRIENDS HAD BEEN TRAPPED BY WOLVES. ONE OF THE PARTY DIED. THEY HAD NO FOOD. FACED WITH STARVATION, CARTIER TURNED *CANNIBAL*-- AN' THE ANCIENT CURSE O' THE NORTH WOODS TRANSFORMED HIM INTO THE WENDIGO."

"WHAT I DIDN'T KNOW THEN WAS THAT CARTIER'S *SISTER* WAS TRYING TO SAVE HIM. WITH THE HELP OF HIS BEST FRIEND, *GEORGES BAPTISTE*, SHE INTENDED TO USE BLACK MAGIC TO SHIFT THE WENDIGO-CURSE FROM CARTIER TO THE HULK."

KROOM!

WEN-DI-GO!

"IT WAS A CRAZY FIGHT. I WAS HACKIN' AWAY LIKE A MAD-MAN, CONSUMED BY ONE O' MY *BERSERKER RAGES*."

"BY RIGHTS, I SHOULD HAVE BEATEN THOSE TWO FREAKS TO A PULP, OR CUT 'EM INTO SHISH-KEBAB. BUT NO MATTER HOW HARD I TRIED, I COULDN'T HURT EITHER OF 'EM. THEY WERE BOTH DARN NEAR *INVULNERABLE*."

"BETWEEN ME AN' THE HULK, WE MANAGED TO KNOCK WENDIGO UNCONSCIOUS. WITH HIM OUT OF THE WAY, I WAS FREE TO COMPLETE MY ORIGINAL MISSION: TO STOP THE HULK, ANY WAY I COULD."

"IN THE END, ALL I DID WAS MAKE HIM ANGRY."

"WE NEVER FINISHED THAT FIGHT. MARIE CARTIER HIT US WITH SOME SORT OF MAGIC WHAMMY-- INSTANT DREAMLAND. SHE NEVER GOT HER CHANCE TO ZAP THE HULK, THOUGH. BAPTISTE CAST THE BIG SPELL, INSTEAD OF HER, TAKING THE HULK'S PLACE FOR THE TRANSFORMATION."

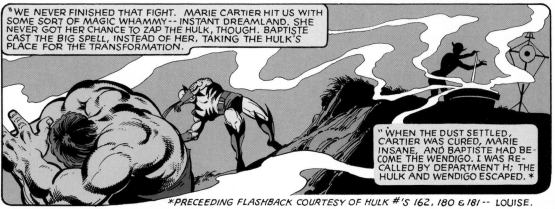

"WHEN THE DUST SETTLED, CARTIER WAS CURED, MARIE INSANE, AND BAPTISTE HAD BE-COME THE WENDIGO. I WAS RE-CALLED BY DEPARTMENT H; THE HULK AND WENDIGO ESCAPED. *

*PRECEEDING FLASHBACK COURTESY OF HULK #'S 162, 180 & 181-- LOUISE.

I WAS OUT OF CANADA A LOT AFTER THAT-- DOIN' MY "JAMES BOND" NUMBER-- I NEVER GOT ANOTHER CHANCE TO GO AFTER EITHER HULK OR WENDIGO.

THERE'S JUST ME AN' THE MISFIT HERE, MAC, BUT IF YOU WANT OUR HELP AGAINST WENDIGO, IT'S YOURS FOR THE ASKING. TRUTH T' TELL, IT'S YOURS WHETHER YOU WANT IT OR NOT.

SINCE YOU PUT IT THAT WAY, LOGAN, HOW CAN I REFUSE?

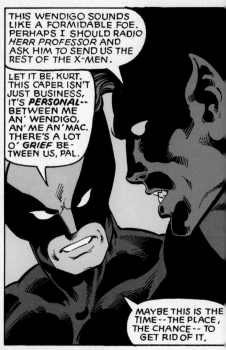

THIS WENDIGO SOUNDS LIKE A FORMIDABLE FOE. PERHAPS I SHOULD RADIO HERR PROFESSOR AND ASK HIM TO SEND US THE REST OF THE X-MEN.

LET IT BE, KURT. THIS CAPER ISN'T JUST BUSINESS, IT'S PERSONAL-- BETWEEN ME AN' WENDIGO, AN' ME AN' MAC. THERE'S A LOT O' GRIEF BE-TWEEN US, PAL.

MAYBE THIS IS THE TIME-- THE PLACE, THE CHANCE-- TO GET RID OF IT.

MEAN-WHILE, WE NEED OUR GEAR.

I'LL GET IT.

BAMF

OH!

NIGHTCRAWLER-- VANISHED!

HOW DOES HE DO THAT?

Y'KNOW, IF I REMEMBER RIGHT, WENDIGO'S PREFERENCE IS SUPPOSED TO BE FOR FRESH-KILLED MEAT. IF THAT HOLDS TRUE, EILEEN PARNALL AN' HER BABY MIGHT STILL BE ALIVE.

I MIGHT BE ABLE TO TRACK THEIR SCENT.

WE'VE TRIED. JUST ABOUT EVERYTHING ELSE.

FACE IT, JAMIE, IF ANY-ONE ON EARTH HAS A PRAYER O' FINDIN' 'EM, AN' BRINGIN' 'EM BACK WHOLE--

--IT'S ME.

I'M REALLY LOOKIN' FORWARD TO IT.

I NEVER REALIZED WOLVERINE FELT THINGS SO DEEPLY. HE'S A FAR MORE COMPLEX -- FAR MORE HUMAN -- PERSON THAN HE LETS ON.

UNGLAUBLICH! IT'S NEARLY MIDNIGHT, YET WE'RE SO FAR NORTH THAT THE SUN STILL HASN'T SET. AND THE SKY -- SO BEAUTIFUL -- LIKE IT'S ON FIRE.

THE COLORS... REMIND ME OF JEAN. IT'S BEEN MONTHS SINCE SHE DIED*, BUT IT FEELS LIKE IT HAPPENED ONLY YESTERDAY. AND IT STILL HURTS. FEW THINGS IN MY LIFE HAVE HURT AS MUCH.

*IN X-MEN #137 -- LOUISE.

PART OF ME WISHES THAT PAIN WOULD PASS; PART OF ME PRAYS IT NEVER WILL. FOR THAT WOULD MEAN I WOULD HAVE BEGUN TO FORGET, AND SUCH PEOPLE -- SUCH EVENTS SHOULD NOT BE FORGOTTEN.

ACH, LOOK AT ME -- I'M CRYING LIKE A BABY!

DEAR LORD IN HEAVEN -- WHY?! WHY DID JEAN HAVE TO DIE?! WHY DID YOU TRANSFORM HER INTO PHOENIX IN THE FIRST PLACE?! WHY?!?

U'rent
OTTOWA • TORONTO
WINNEPEG • SASKATOON
EDMONTON • CALGARY

HOW -- HOW COULD YOU HAVE BEEN SO... CRUEL?

NIGHTCRAWLER HEARS NO ANSWER TO HIS ANGUISHED CRY -- IN TRUTH, HE EXPECTED NONE -- AND SO, HE SITS, WATCHING THE BRILLIANT SUNSET...

... ALONE WITH A GRIEF TOO DEEP AND PERSONAL TO SHARE. HE KNOWS THE OTHER X-MEN FEEL -- AND HURT -- AS HE DOES, KNOWS AS WELL THAT JEAN GREY'S TRAGIC SACRIFICE HAS SCARRED THEM ALL FOR LIFE, BUT HE DOES NOT REACH OUT TO HIS FRIENDS.

THAT MUST -- AND WILL -- COME LATER. FOR THE MOMENT, HE'D RATHER BE ALONE.

WHEREVER JEAN'S SOUL IS, HE PRAYS THAT IT IS AT PEACE.

AND THEN, AS THE WORLD AROUND HIM GROWS AS DARK AS HIS INDIGO SKIN...

... HE PULLS HIMSELF TO-GETHER AND GETS TO WORK, THANKFUL THAT NO ONE FROM THE CABIN HAS COME LOOKING FOR HIM.

THAT'S THAT. TIME NOW TO GET WOLVERINE TO HELP ME LUG IT INSIDE.

WHAT'S THAT -- ? IS SOMEONE -- ?!

Oh!

NO.

81

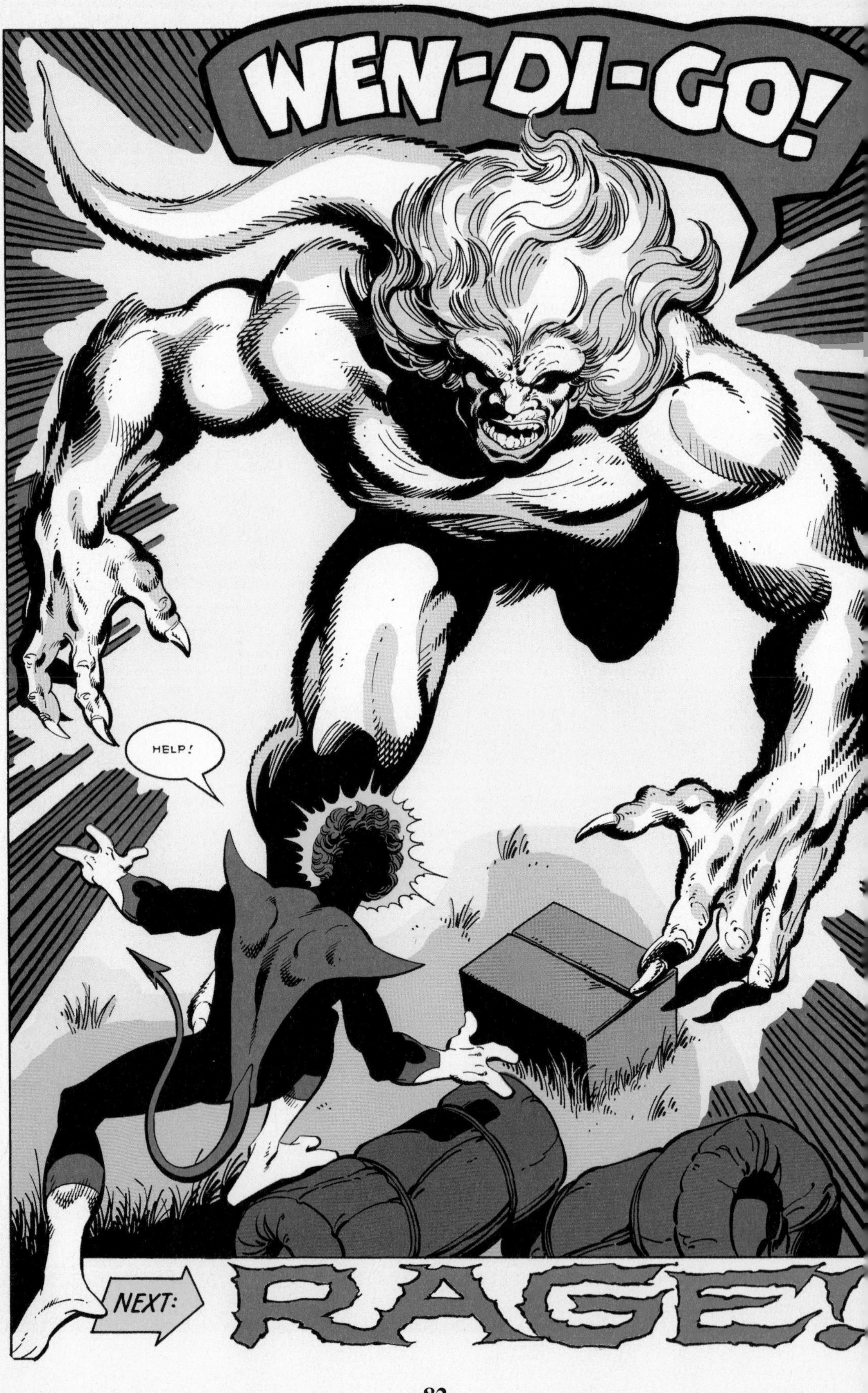
WEN-DI-GO!
HELP!
NEXT: RAGE!

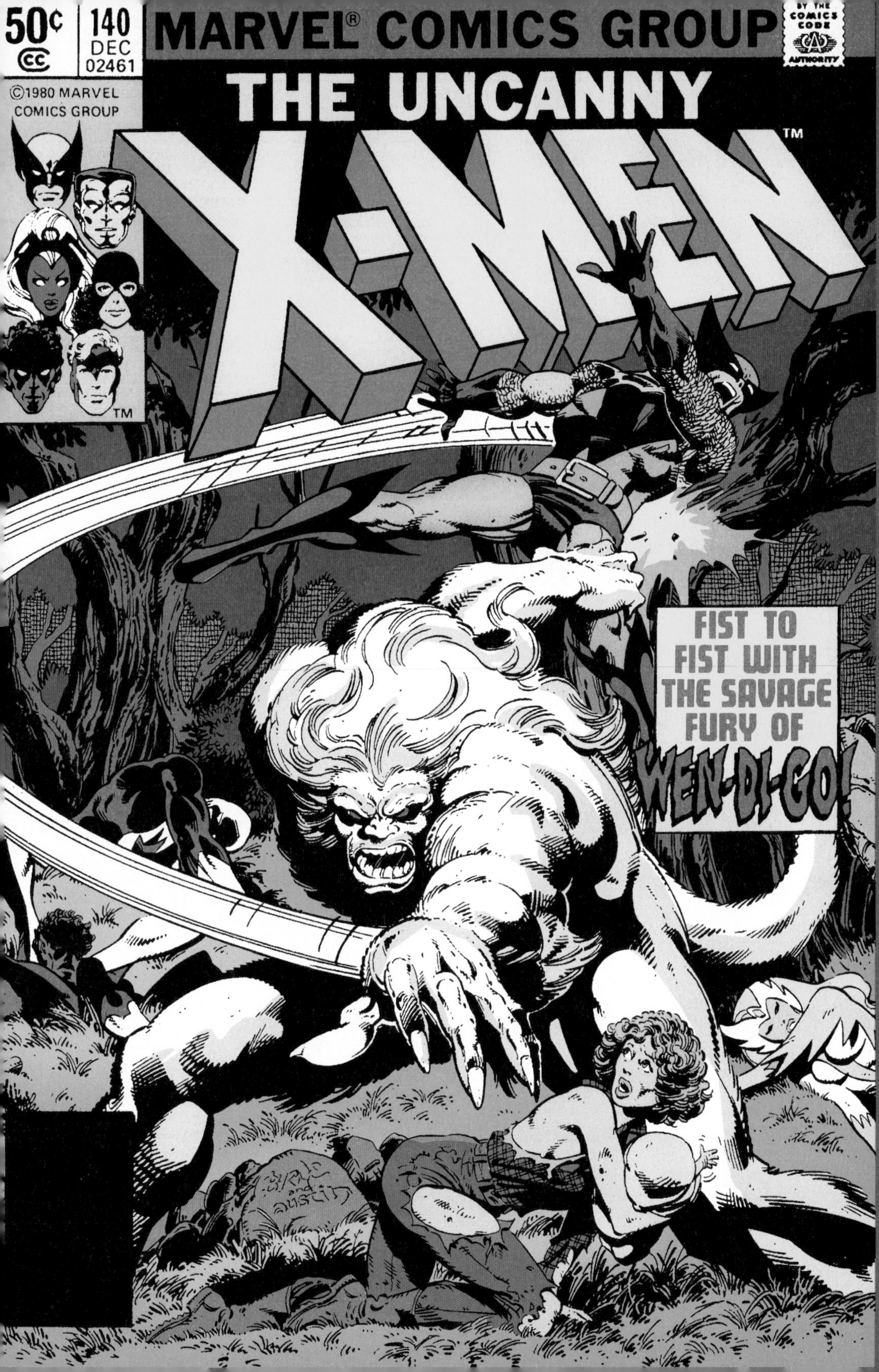
50¢
140
DEC
02461
MARVEL® COMICS GROUP
BY THE COMICS CODE AUTHORITY
THE UNCANNY
X-MEN™
©1980 MARVEL COMICS GROUP
FIST TO FIST WITH THE SAVAGE FURY OF
WEN-DI-GO!

Cyclops. Storm. Nightcrawler. Wolverine. Colossus. Children of the atom, students of Charles Xavier, MUTANTS — feared and hated by the world they have sworn to protect. These are the STRANGEST heroes of all!

STAN LEE PRESENTS: THE UNCANNY X-MEN! ™

CHRIS CLAREMONT
WRITER

JOHN BYRNE
PLOT-PENCILS

TERRY AUSTIN
INKER

TOM ORZECHOWSKI, letterer
GLYNIS WEIN, colorist

LOUISE JONES
EDITOR

JIM SHOOTI
Ed. IN CHIEF

RAGE!

OVERHEAD, THE GEESE ARE FLYING SOUTH, FIRST HINT THAT-- ALTHOUGH THE DAY IS WARM, THE LEAVES ON THE TREES STILL GREEN-- SUMMER IS ALMOST OVER.

ON THE SIBERIAN COLLECTIVE FARM THAT IS PETER RASPUTIN'S HOME, IT IS HARVEST TIME, THE STEPPES COVERED WITH HECTARE UPON HECTARE OF GOLDEN WHEAT. HE IS A CHILD OF THE LAND, HIS LIFE GOVERNED BY THE TIMELESS PROGRESSION OF THE SEASONS. FOR HIM, NATURE IS THE ONLY REALITY, AND HAD HE LIVED HIS ENTIRE LIFE A FARMER, HE WOULD HAVE BEEN CONTENT.

BUT FATE HAD OTHER PLANS FOR HIM, MOVING HIM FAR FROM HIS RUSSIAN BIRTHPLACE, AND TRANSFORMING THE FARM-BOY IRREVOCABLY INTO THE X-MAN, COLOSSUS.

BY LENIN, EITHER MY HEART WILL BURST AND MY STEEL BODY CRACK--

YET HE REFUSES TO ENTIRELY CUT HIS TIES WITH HIS FORMER LIFE-- WHICH EXPLAINS HIS PRESENCE IN THIS FIELD BEHIND PROFESSOR XAVIER'S SCHOOL FOR GIFTED YOUNGSTERS, AND HIS DUEL WITH AN OLD, WITHERED TREE STUMP.

LF 256

--OR I WILL PULL YOU *FREE!*

THERE ARE *EASIER* WAYS TO CLEAR A HECTARE OF LAND...

...BUT FEW MORE *SATISFYING.*

ENJOYING YOURSELF, PETER ?

ANGEL!

STRANGE AS IT SOUNDS, *TOVARISCH,* I AM.

IT HAS BEEN TOO LONG SINCE I GOT MY HANDS DIRTY DOING THE WORK I WAS BORN TO DO.

YOU SOUND HOMESICK. DO YOU WISH YOU'D STAYED A FARMER ?

OCCASIONALLY. BUT I KNOW I CANNOT GO BACK. AS AN X-MAN, I HAVE SEEN--EXPERIENCED --SO MUCH. *TOO* MUCH.

MY PARENTS-- MY... COMRADES-- WOULD NOT UNDERSTAND.

I KNOW THE FEELING.

BUT IF THAT'S SO, WHY ALL THIS WORK ?

IT... RELAXES ME. AND REMINDS ME THAT, FOR ALL THE VAUNTED POWER OF COLOSSUS I AM STILL *NOTHING* COMPARED TO THE POWER AND MAJESTY OF *NATURE.*

I HAVE BEHELD MANY WONDERS, WARREN, YET FEW COMPARE WITH THE SIMPLE BEAUTY OF A SEED GIVING BIRTH TO A FLOWER.

I AM SORRY. I AM NOT EXPRESSING MY THOUGHTS, MY FEELINGS, WELL. I HAVE NOT THE WORDS.

PAL, *SHAKESPEARE* COULDN'T HAVE SAID IT BETTER.

ANGEL...?

WHOOPS-- GOTTA FLY, PETE! I JUST GOT A TELE- PATHIC CALL FROM PROFESSOR XAVIER. BE SEEING YOU!

I'VE NEVER MET ANYONE QUITE LIKE PETER. AT FIRST, I THOUGHT HE WAS YOUR BASIC DUMB- CLUCK COUNTRY HICK.

BUT THERE'S A LOT MORE TO HIM THAN MEETS THE EYE. IN MANY WAYS, HE'S THE MOST HONEST--AND HONORABLE-- PERSON I KNOW.

YOU WANTED ME, PROFESSOR? ANYTHING IMPORTANT?

CURIOSITY, ANGEL. I WAS WONDERING ABOUT YOUR REACTIONS TO YOUR FELLOW X-MEN NOW THAT YOU'VE HAD A CHANCE TO WORK AND TRAIN BESIDE THEM?

NO PROBLEMS -- EXCEPT FOR *WOLVERINE*.

HE'S CRAZY, YOU KNOW -- AND DANGEROUS. SUPPOSE HE GOES BERSERK IN A FIGHT AND KILLS SOMEONE WITH THOSE FREAKY CLAWS OF HIS?

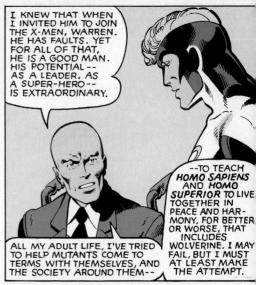

I KNEW THAT WHEN I INVITED HIM TO JOIN THE X-MEN, WARREN. HE HAS FAULTS. YET FOR ALL OF THAT, HE IS A GOOD MAN. HIS POTENTIAL -- AS A LEADER, AS A SUPER-HERO -- IS EXTRAORDINARY.

ALL MY ADULT LIFE, I'VE TRIED TO HELP MUTANTS COME TO TERMS WITH THEMSELVES, AND THE SOCIETY AROUND THEM --

-- TO TEACH *HOMO SAPIENS* AND *HOMO SUPERIOR* TO LIVE TOGETHER IN PEACE AND HARMONY, FOR BETTER OR WORSE, THAT INCLUDES WOLVERINE. I MAY FAIL, BUT I MUST AT LEAST MAKE THE ATTEMPT.

ON THAT THOUGHTFUL NOTE, LET'S SHIFT OUR SCENE TO THE NEARBY TOWN OF SALEM CENTER, WHERE WE FIND ANOTHER OF XAVIER'S STUDENTS: ORORO -- PERHAPS BETTER KNOWN AS STORM -- NEWLY APPOINTED LEADER OF THE X-MEN.

HEY, MAMA, *WAIT UP!*

OH, NO! NOT HIM AGAIN!

I BEG YOUR PARDON?

SWEET THING, I AM ONE FINE DUDE, YOU ARE ONE FINE FOX, THIS IS ONE FINE NIGHT. WHAT SAY WE MAKE BEAUTIFUL MUSIC TOGETHER ...

... AT STUDIO ONE, THE HOTTEST DISCO IN NEW YORK?

NOW, AS BEFORE, I THINK NOT.

WHY WON'T YOU TAKE "NO" FOR AN ANSWER?

'CAUSE I'M IN LOVE! WITH *YOU*, DARLIN'--

HEY!!

I'M SOAKIN' WET! WHERE'D THAT STORM COME FROM?!

OH, CALL IT... *MAGIC.*

SHE SMILES...

...AND, AS CASUALLY AS SHE CREATED THE MINIATURE THUNDERSHOWER, STORM MAKES IT GO AWAY.

THERE'S *KITTY,* AND HER NEW DANCE TEACHER, *STEVIE HUNTER.* THEY SEEM TO BE GETTING ALONG FAMOUSLY.

THAT SHOULDN'T BOTHER ME, BUT IT DOES. I'VE BEEN ON EDGE SINCE THE MOMENT WE MET. I KEEP TELLING MYSELF SUCH FEELINGS ARE ABSURD.

STEVIE IS ONE OF THE NICEST WOMEN *I'VE* EVER MET -- YET THE FEELINGS... REMAIN.

HIYA, 'RORO. BOY, YOU SHOULD HAVE STUCK AROUND TO WATCH THE CLASS. IT WAS *GREAT!*

OUR KITTEN HAS REAL TALENT, ORORO -- ONCE WE SMOOTH DOWN HER CONSIDERABLE ROUGH EDGES.

"OUR" KITTEN?

CAN I INTEREST YOU BOTH IN A BITE TO EAT? AFTER A DAY TEACHING BUDDING BARYSHNI-KOV'S AND MAKAROVA'S, I'M FAMISHED.

THANK YOU, STEVIE, BUT NO. WE MUST BE GETTING BACK TO THE SCHOOL.

SORRY, STEVIE. DUTY CALLS! SEEYA!

SOME OTHER TIME, PER-HAPS.

FOR *SURE!*

KITTY!

WHAT DO YOU THINK YOU'RE DOING, FLAUNTING YOUR POWER LIKE THAT?! SUPPOSE SOMEONE SEES YOU?!

I CHECKED BEFORE I DID IT, ORORO. NOBODY'S AROUND.

I'M SORRY. IT'S JUST THAT... USING MY POWER -- WALKING THROUGH SOLID OBJECTS -- IS *FUN!*

I KNOW, LITTLE ONE. BUT PLEASE BE MORE CAREFUL.

OKAY. ORORO, ARE YOU FEELING ALL RIGHT? YOU'RE ON AN AWFULLY SHORT FUSE ALL OF A SUDDEN. IS IT ME, OR...?

GODDESS, THE CHILD IS PERCEPTIVE!

N-NO, KITTEN. IT'S NOT YOU.

I'M, *ah,* CONCERNED FOR WOLVERINE AND NIGHTCRAWLER. WE'VE HEARD NOTHING FROM THEM SINCE THEY LEFT FOR CANADA THIS MORNING. I HOPE THEY HAVEN'T RUN INTO TROUBLE.

TO FIND OUT...

...LET'S TURN OUR ATTENTION AHEAD A FEW HOURS AND NORTH A THOUSAND MILES, FROM SALEM CENTER TO THE SHORES OF *HUDSON BAY*--

-- AND LET THE SITUATION SPEAK FOR ITSELF!

WEN-DI-GO!

YIKES!

THAT WAS TOO CLOSE FOR COMFORT!

THIS BEASTIE MAKES THE *JUGGERNAUT* LOOK PUNY BY COMPARISON. WHICH IS, I THINK, MY CUE TO LET DISCRETION PROVE THE BETTER PART OF VALOR--

--AND GET THE BLAZES OUT OF HERE!

TYPICAL. WOLVERINE DECIDES TO RETURN TO CANADA TO PERSUADE THE GOVERNMENT TO ACCEPT HIS RESIGNATION FROM THEIR SECRET SERVICE, AND TO MAKE PEACE BE-TWEEN THE X-MEN AND HIS FORMER COLLEAGUES IN *ALPHA FLIGHT*, CANADA'S OFFICIAL SUPER-HERO TEAM.

WOLVERINE ASKS ME ALONG AS CHAPERONE, TO KEEP HIM OUT OF TROUBLE...

... AND, IDIOT THAT I AM, I ACCEPT.

O, OF COURSE, WITH ALL EYES ON WOLVERINE, THE PROVERBIAL ROOF FALLS IN ON *ME!*

I'M NOT STAYING AHEAD OF THE MONSTER ON THE GROUND.

IT'S TOO RISKY TO TELEPORT UNLESS I ABSOLUTELY HAVE TO. PERHAPS I'LL HAVE BETTER LUCK IN THE TREETOPS. HE LOOKS TOO BULKY TO CLIMB AFTER ME.

WOLVERINE AND I FOUND HALF OF ALPHA FLIGHT -- *VINDICATOR, SHAMAN* AND *SNOWBIRD* -- UP HERE INVESTIGATING A SERIES OF MYSTERIOUS, HORRIBLE MURDERS AND DISAPPEARANCES.

WOLVERINE IDENTIFIED THEIR QUARRY AS A LEGENDARY WOODS-BEAST NAMED THE *WENDIGO.*

FROM THIS HULK'S BATTLE CRY, *HE* MUST BE IT!

MY *TREE* -- OH, NO!

SHAK!

WEN-DI-GO!

AARRRGH!

GRIP LIKE A VISE -- CRUSHING ME! CLAWS... CUTTING INTO ME!

WENDIGO... TOO STRONG. I CAN'T... BREAK FREE.

ONLY HOPE... FOCUS CONCENTRATION... IGNORE PAIN... BUT IT'S SO *HARD!* I HURT... SO MUCH! BUT -- I *MUST!*

A PSYCHIC SWITCH CLOSES IN NIGHTCRAWLER'S MIND -- AND WITH THE TRADITIONAL CRACK OF FLAME AND GUSTING STENCH OF BRIMSTONE...

BAMF

... HE *TELEPORTS* OUT OF WENDIGO'S GRASP.

THAT FEELS... SO MUCH BETTER!

I HAD TO TRY A *"BLIND"* 'PORT. I DON'T KNOW THE LAY OF THE LAND AROUND HERE. A WRONG MOVE -- EVEN A *SLIGHT* MIS-CALCULATION -- COULD HAVE HAD ME MATERIALIZING INSIDE A TREE.

AT BEST, I'D HAVE BEEN CRIPPLED OR MAIMED. AT WORST -- VERY MESSILY, AGONIZINGLY *KILLED.* LOVELY THOUGHT.

BAMF

AHA! THERE'S A CLEARING!

IT'S A FAR PIECE FROM WENDIGO, TOO. WITH LUCK, I'LL HAVE GIVEN HIM THE SLIP. I SHOULD BE ABLE TO GET BACK TO THE CABIN AND WARN THE OTHERS.

WEN-DI-GO!

ON THE OTHER HAND...

I CAN'T RUN AND IT'S TOO DARK -- TOO MANY TREES -- TO TRY ANOTHER 'PORT. I'LL HAVE TO *FIGHT.*

OH BOY!

WENDIGO HAS THE EDGE -- AND WHAT AN EDGE -- IN TERMS OF RAW STRENGTH, AND HIS TRACKING SKILL SEEM AS FORMIDABLE AS *WOLVERINE'S.*

IN *MY* FAVOR, I HAVE SPEED, AGILITY, MARTIAL ARTS TRAINING I'LL HIT-AND-RUN, TRY TO KEEP HIM CONFUSED AND OFF-BALANCE...

WHOULFFF!!

SO MUCH FOR *THAT* IDEA!

...AND TOWARDS THE CABIN...

HE TAKES OFF LIKE A **CANNONBALL**, CONSCIOUSNESS QUICKLY SLIPPING AWAY AS THE FORCE OF WENDIGO'S PUNCH HURLS HIM OUT OF THE FOREST...

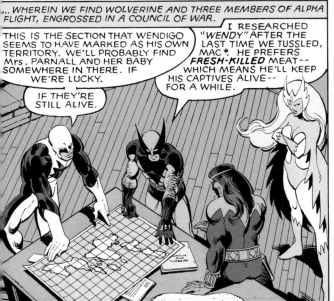

...WHEREIN WE FIND WOLVERINE AND THREE MEMBERS OF ALPHA FLIGHT, ENGROSSED IN A COUNCIL OF WAR.

THIS IS THE SECTION THAT WENDIGO SEEMS TO HAVE MARKED AS HIS OWN TERRITORY. WE'LL PROBABLY FIND Mrs. PARNALL AND HER BABY SOMEWHERE IN THERE. IF WE'RE LUCKY.

IF THEY'RE STILL ALIVE.

I RESEARCHED "**WENDY**" AFTER THE LAST TIME WE TUSSLED, MAC.* HE PREFERS **FRESH-KILLED** MEAT-- WHICH MEANS HE'LL KEEP HIS CAPTIVES ALIVE-- FOR A WHILE.

*HULK #'S 180-181--LOUISE.

THAT DOESN'T GIVE US -- OR Mrs. PARNALL -- THE **BEST** ODDS IN THE WORLD, BUT IT'S BETTER THAN **NOTHIN'**.

I'LL START HUNTING AT FIRST LIGHT.

WHAT THE --?!

THAT SOUND--!

THWUMP!

NIGHTCRAWLER!

HE'S OUT COLD-- AND HE LOOKS LIKE HE WAS JUST WORKED OVER BY A MACK TRUCK!

IMMEDIATELY, AT WOLVERINE'S MENTAL COMMAND, RETRACTABLE RAZOR-KEEN **ADAMANTIUM** CLAWS POP OUT OF THE BACKS OF HIS HANDS.

THEY'RE FORGED OF THE **STRONGEST** METAL KNOWN TO MAN AND ARE CAPABLE OF CUTTING SOLID STEEL AS EASILY AS PAPER.

TONIGHT, THIS SHORTEST, FEISTIEST X-MAN IS GOING TO **NEED** THEM.

MAC, I GOT THE FEELIN' THAT **FINDING** WENDIGO HAS JUST BECOME THE **LEAST** OF OUR PROBLEMS.

WEN-DI-GO!

GOOD GRIEF! HE'S HEFTING THAT PICK-UP LIKE IT WAS A **TOY!**

FAN OUT, PEOPLE! I'LL HANDLE THIS

FOR MONTHS, I'VE BEEN TELLING MYSELF HOW GOOD MY BATTLE SUIT WAS.

NOW COMES THE ACID TEST!

LORD, HELP ME. I'M... SCARED. I NEVER REALIZED WENDIGO WOULD BE SO-- BIG!

FOR ALL HIS UNSPOKEN FEAR, JAMES MacDONALD HUDSON--

--VINDICATOR, FOUNDER AND LEADER OF ALPHA FLIGHT-- STANDS HIS GROUND WITHOUT FLINCHING--

SPLOW!

...AND MEETS WENDIGO'S ATTACK WITH HIS SUIT'S BUILT-IN ENERGY BLASTERS LIKE A SUPER-HERO BORN!

BUT, WITH SURPRISING SPEED AND EVEN MORE SURPRISING -- ALMOST HUMAN -- CUNNING, WENDIGO GRABS FOR A NEARBY FIR TREE...

...AND DECIDES TO INDULGE IN SOME IMPROMPTU BATTING PRACTICE!

UNNNFFF!

SKRAM!

WEN-DI-GO!

REACTING WITH THE SPEED OF THOUGHT, *SNOWBIRD* (CORPORAL ANNE MacKENZIE, ROYAL CANADIAN MOUNTED POLICE)...

VINDICATOR!

...*SHAPE-SHIFTS* INTO A GREAT ARCTIC OWL AND RUSHES TO HIS AID.

HE'LL BE OKAY. MAC DESIGNED HIS BATTLE-SUIT TO PROTECT HIM FROM MY CLAWS. EVEN A ROUGH LANDING IN THOSE TREES SHOULDN'T DO MORE'N SHAKE HIM UP.

WENDIGO'S BEEN CONSIDERATE ENOUGH TO COME TO US, SHAMAN. LET'S FINISH OUR JOB RIGHT HERE 'N' NOW.

YOU GO AFTER HIM, WOLVERINE. I'LL FOLLOW WHEN I CAN.

HUH?!

THE EXPLOSION OF THE TRUCK'S FUEL HAS STARTED A FIRE. THESE WOODS ARE TINDER DRY. IF THIS BLAZE GETS OUT OF CONTROL, IT WILL BE ALMOST IMPOSSIBLE TO STOP!

SO SAYING, SHAMAN SCATTERS A HANDFUL OF SACRED POWDER ACROSS THE FACE OF THE FIRE, CREATING A WALL OF ICE TO SMOTHER IT. AND WHILE HE ACTS, HE LAUGHS INSIDE AT THE IRONY OF THE SITUATION --

*-- THAT HE, **DR. MICHAEL TWOYOUNGMEN,** WHO DELIBERATELY TURNED HIS BACK ON HIS SARCEE HERITAGE TO BECOME A PHYSICIAN, TO HELP HIS PEOPLE BY LEARNING THE **WHITE MAN'S** MEDICINE ...*

... SHOULD NOW USE THE MAGICAL SKILLS TAUGHT HIM BY HIS SHAMAN GRAND-FATHER TO HELP RED AND WHITE MEN BOTH!

WENDIGO, OF COURSE, IS AWARE OF NONE OF THIS. HE SIMPLY SENSES THAT IT'S TIME HE MADE HIS EXIT.

VINDICATOR -- JAMIE, ARE YOU --?!

I'M FINE, SNOWBIRD. THE ONLY THING HURT WAS MY *PRIDE.*

TAKE WOLVERINE AND FOLLOW THE WENDIGO.

SHAMAN AND I WILL BE ALONG AS SOON AS WE'VE EXTINGUISHED THE FIRE.

THAT SUCKER AIN'T AS DUMB AS HE LOOKS -- OR AS HE USED TO BE. IN THE OLD DAYS, WENDIGO WOULD GENERALLY LEAVE A *HULK*-SIZED TRAIL BEHIND HIM.

NOW, HE'S MOVIN' THROUGH THE FOREST LIKE HE WAS A *PART* OF IT.

AN' HE'S DOIN' A PRETTY GOOD JOB O' COVERIN' HIS TRACKS.

WOLVERINE, I CAN SEE NOTHING FROM THE AIR.

AIN'T SURPRISIN'. THE WOODS HERE-'BOUTS ARE AS THICK AS THEY CAN GET, AN' THERE ARE LOTS OF GULLIES AN' RAVINES FOR WENDY TO HIDE IN.

WE'RE GONNA HAVE'TA DO THIS THE HARD WAY, ON FOOT AN' ONE STEP AT A TIME.

WOLVERINE, I DO NOT LIKE YOU MUCH...

THANKS.

...BUT I CANNOT DENY THAT YOU ARE A GOOD LEADER. WHY DID YOU *RESIGN* FROM DEPARTMENT H?

I GOT A BETTER OFFER.

UNBIDDEN, HIS MIND FLASHES BACK ACROSS THE YEARS, REMEMBERING HOW JAMES AND HEATHER HUDSON FOUND HIM NEAR THEIR HOME IN THE CANADIAN ROCKIES -- SICK, FROZEN, STARVING, AS NEAR DEATH AS A BODY COULD BE.

THEY NURSED HIM BACK TO HEALTH, ACCEPTED HIM, LOVED HIM. AND HE LOVED THEM IN RETURN.

BUT, STILL, THERE WERE STRAINS.

YOU DON'T UNDERSTAND, MAC. YOU'VE *NEVER* UNDERSTOOD! I'VE ALWAYS BEEN A DANGEROUS MAN -- SCRAPPIN'S SECOND NATURE TO ME.

BUT THESE *CLAWS* -- THIS FLAMIN' *ADAMANTIUM SKELETON* I'VE GOT -- CHANGE EV'RYTHING!

AS FAR AS I'M CONCERNED, THERE'S NO SUCH THING AS A FAIR FIGHT ANY-MORE. I'M VIRTUALLY INVULNERABLE, MAC! I'VE BEEN TURNED INTO A *KILLING MACHINE* --

-- AN' I DON'T LIKE IT!

LOGAN!

TO THE CANADIAN *SECRET SERVICE*, HE WAS A GIFT FROM HEAVEN. THEY TURNED HIM LOOSE ON ALL THE DIRTY, BRUTAL, *NECESSARY* ASSIGNMENTS NO ONE ELSE WOULD TOUCH.

AND HE NEVER FORGAVE THEM FOR WHAT THEY DID TO HIM -- AND THEN MADE HIM DO -- AND WHEN *CHARLES XAVIER* OFFERED HIM A WAY OUT, HE TOOK IT...

... WITHOUT A SECOND THOUGHT, OR A REGRET.

ARE YOU SURE THE PARNALLS ARE STILL ALIVE?

PRINCESS, THE ONE THING I LEARNED EARLY IN LIFE WAS TO TELL THE DIFFERENCE BETWEEN THE SMELL OF A LIVE BODY AN' A DEAD ONE.

MAMA PARNALL IS SCARED STIFF, BUT SHE AN' HER BABY ARE BOTH BREATHIN'.

YOU BRING BACK MAC AN' THE OTHERS-- PRONTO. I'LL MAINTAIN SURVEILLANCE.

WHY SHOULD I GO?

BECAUSE I CAN'T FLY, DUMMY. AN' SPEED IS WHAT'S IMPORTANT. NOW SCOOT!

Uh-oh.

WENDY'S ACTIN' HUNGRY-- AN' I HAVE A HUNCH HE'S IN THE MOOD FOR SOMETHIN' MORE SUBSTANTIAL THAN DRIED-UP OLD BONES.

THE BOULDER BLOCKING THE SMALL CAVE WEIGHS A COUPLE OF TONS...

...YET WENDIGO ROLLS IT ASIDE WITH RIDICULOUS EASE, TO REVEAL...

OH, NO!

THE REENFORCEMENTS AIN'T GONNA ARRIVE IN TIME. IF MRS. PARNALL'S GONNA BE RESCUED, I'LL HAVETA DO THE JOB MYSELF. AN' THAT SUITS ME FINE.

I'VE BEEN ACHIN' FER A REMATCH WITH THE WENDIGO.

IT LOOKS LIKE-- THIS IS IT!

NNOOOOOOO!

Panel 1:

REMEMBER *ME*, BUB?

WOLVERINE'S THE NAME, *MAYHEM'S* THE GAME!

HE FEELS A *BERSERKER RAGE* BUILD WITHIN HIM ...

Panel 2:

... AND, THIS TIME, HE DOESN'T EVEN *TRY* TO DENY IT.

HE BECOMES *FURY* PERSONIFIED-- A GRIM, UNSTOPPABLE ENGINE OF DESTRUCTION. THE PACE IS INHUMAN ...

Panel 3:

... THE EQUIVALENT OF *DAYS* OF NON-STOP COMBAT COMPRESSED INTO A MATTER OF *MINUTES*. AND THROUGH IT ALL, WOLVERINE DENIES PAIN, DENIES FATIGUE, DENIES EVERYTHING BUT THE WILL TO *WIN*.

WENDY'S *REELING*! I'VE GOT HIM ON THE *ROPES*!

I'LL SETTLE FOR THAT. AS IF I REALLY HAD A CHOICE.

Panel 4:

ANY OTHER FOE WOULD HAVE BEEN SMASHED TO A PULP OR CUT INTO SHISH-KEBAB BY NOW. BUT WENDIGO'S THE NEXT BEST THING TO *INVULNERABLE*. I CAN HURT HIM -- TEMPORARILY -- AN' STUN HIM, BUT NO MORE THAN THAT, NO MATTER HOW HARD I TRY.

AN' I AM TRYIN' *REAL HARD*!!

whooo...

HE'S DOWN... AN' OUT. FINALLY. MY ADRENALIN SURGE -- MY PATENTED *"BERSERKER RAGE"* -- IS FADIN' FAST. BEEN... A LONG TIME SINCE I FELT THIS... *POOPED.*

CAN'T FOLD, THOUGH -- NOT 'TIL I GET THE LADY AN' HER KID OUT O' HARM'S WAY.

M- MRS. PARNALL...? NAME'S WOLVERINE. BE COOL, MA'AM, I'M ONE O' THE *GOOD* GUYS.

CAN YOU TRAVEL? THE SOONER WE'RE AWAY FROM HERE, THE BETTER. I CAN'T GUARANTEE HOW LONG SHAGGY'LL STAY IN SLUMBER-LAND.

I... CAN WALK.

THAT'S A START. WE'LL PICK UP SPEED AS WE GO ALONG, AS YOU GET YOUR STRENGTH BACK.

M-MY HUSBAND, JOE -- I HEARD HIM SCREAM. I... SAW--! IT WAS... HORRIBLE. AND... AND MY BOY, TOMMY...?

TOMMY'S FINE. HE'S IN THE HOSPITAL.

THANK GOD.

THAT'S ONLY *PART* O' THE TRUTH. BUT HOW DO I TELL HER THAT THE BOY'S IN *CATATONIC SHOCK* -- ALMOST A KIND OF LIVING DEATH?!

HUH?! THAT *SHADOW* --!

WHAM!

OF ALL ... THE DUMB... MISTAKES. I... DROPPED MY GUARD...

WENDY... HAS EDGE. ALL I CAN DO... IS RIDE THINGS OUT...

... AN' HOPE FOR ... THE BEST...

WEN-DI-GO!

HOPE, AS THE SAYING GOES, SPRINGS ETERNAL.

WOLVERINE'S UNBREAKABLE ADAMANTIUM SKELETON SAVES HIM FROM INSTANT DEATH...

THOOM

...BUT, EVEN SO, HE ENDURES A FRIGHTENING AMOUNT OF PUNISHMENT AT WENDIGO'S HANDS.

THAT... HURT!

GOTTA MAKE... SOME KIND'A MOVE. CAN'T TAKE... MUCH MORE... OF... THIS...

TAKE HEART, MEIN KLEIN FREUND! THE CAVALRY HAS ARRIVED!

AND IN THE PROVERBIAL NICK OF TIME, TOO. WOLVERINE LOOKS IN A BAD WAY.

NIGHTCRAWLER TELEPORTS TO THE ATTACK AND...

HERE, MONSTER! THIS IS FOR THE POUNDING YOU GAVE ME EARLIER TONIGHT!

KRAK!

NICE TRY, WENDIGO. BUT NO KEWPIE DOLL!

I LEARNED THE HARD WAY HOW FAST YOU MOVED. YOU'LL HAVE TO DO A LOT BETTER THAN THIS TO CATCH ME NOW!

VINDICATOR!

NO NEED TO PANIC, NIGHTCRAWLER. I'M HERE, JUST AS WE WORKED OUT.

PANIC, NO. WORRY-- WELL, MAYBE.

ZARK!

IT'S ONE THING TO **TALK** THROUGH A MANEUVER LIKE THIS. IT'S SOMETHING ELSE AGAIN TO DO IT FOR **REAL**.

I WAS AFRAID OF THIS. WE'RE STAGGERING WENDIGO, BUT NO MORE THAN THAT. THE ENCHANTMENT THAT CREATED HIM PROTECTS HIM FROM THE FULL FORCE OF OUR POWERS.

HE'S TOO STRONG. MY MAGICK CAN'T EVEN BIND HIM-- MUCH LESS **CURE** HIM-- WHILE HE'S CONSCIOUS.

PHYSICAL FORCE CAN OVERWHELM HIM. THE HULK AND WOLVERINE PROVED THAT.

...BUT PERHAPS I CAN SHAPE- CHANGE INTO THE NEXT BEST THING.

THERE IS GREAT **DANGER** IN THIS. I ASSUME THE PERSONA OF WHATEVER CREATURE I BECOME. IF I AM CONSUMED BY **BLOOD- LUST**, I COULD BECOME AS TERRIBLE A THREAT TO MY FRIENDS AS WENDIGO HIMSELF. BUT I CAN SEE NO ALTERNATIVE. THE RISK MUST BE TAKEN.

WOLVERINE'S OUT COLD, SNOWBIRD. AND THE HULK ISN'T AVAILABLE.

TRUE

OH, **HODIAK**-- SPIRIT OF THE NORTHERN LIGHTS-- GRANDFATHER--HELP ME! GIVE ME STRENGTH!

WITH THAT IMPASSIONED PRAYER, THE FORM OF THIS CHILD OF THE ICE AND SNOW BEGINS TO MELT AND FLOW LIKE MERCURY...

...TRANSFORMING A BEING WHO APPEARS HUMAN (BUT WHO, IN TRUTH, IS **NOT**)...

... FROM AN EXOTICALLY BEAUTIFUL YOUNG WOMAN INTO A **WHITE WOLVERINE**.

GRAM FOR GRAM, IT IS SAID THAT NO ANIMAL ON EARTH MATCHES A WOLVERINE'S FEROCITY OR INDOMITABLE WILL. *LOGAN* -- THE X-MAN, WOLVERINE-- IS THE CLOSEST AVATAR OF THIS SMALL, INCREDIBLY DEADLY WOODSBEAST.

RRAWR!

BUT SNOWBIRD HAS BECOME THE **REAL THING**-- AND BETWEEN THE TWO OF THEM, THERE IS NO COMPARISON.

WHAT FOLLOWS IS NOT SO MUCH A BATTLE AS A CLASH OF PRIMAL FORCES. A DUEL OF FANG AND CLAW, MUSCLE AND SINEW.

IT IS NOT PRETTY.

AND IT IS SOME-THING THAT ALL PRESENT WILL NEVER FORGET.

ANNIE...

...WHAT HAVE YOU DONE?!

WHEN IT IS OVER, WENDIGO LIES UNCONSCIOUS, THE DARKLING SPELL THAT CREATED HIM ALREADY HEALING HIS FEARSOME WOUNDS. IN A MATTER OF HOURS, HE WILL BE AS GOOD AS NEW. BUT, BY THEN, SHAMAN WILL HAVE HAD A CHANCE TO CAST HIS COUNTERSPELL.

HE STEPS FORWARD, ONLY TO FREEZE IN HIS TRACKS AS THE SNOWBIRD / WOLVERINE BARES HER TEETH AND WARNS HIM AWAY FROM HER PREY.

RRRR!

SHE'S STILL A **WOLVERINE!** THE ANIMAL-PERSONA MUST HAVE TAKEN OVER!

MY **CHANGELING** SPELL WILL WORK AS WELL ON SNOWBIRD AS ON WENDIGO...

NO! SHE'LL FIGHT YOU, PHYSICALLY AND PSYCHICALLY. YOU COULD BE LEFT SO WASTED YOU WON'T BE ABLE TO HELP WENDIGO, AN' THEN ALL THIS PAIN AN' GRIEF WOULD HAVE BEEN FOR NOTHING.

LEAVE ANNIE TO ME.

GRRR!

NO VIOLENCE. NO FEAR. I'VE GOTTA REACH ANNIE WITH WORDS-- AN' EMOTIONS-- JUST LIKE SCOTT REACHED JEAN GREY WHEN SHE'D BEEN CONSUMED BY **DARK PHOENIX.** *

* SEE X-MEN #136 -- LOUISE.

I AIN'T GOOD AT TALKIN'. EVERY INSTINCT IN ME WANTS TO FIGHT HER, TO PROVE MY OWN STRENGTH AN' SUPERIORITY BY SMASHIN' HER INTO SUBMISSION.

BUT THAT'S THE WRONG WAY. I CAN'T -- I WON'T DO THAT.

ANNIE, IT'S LOGAN.

HEAR ME, PRINCESS. **LISTEN** TO ME. REMEMBER WHO YOU ARE, WHAT YOU WERE...

HE ISN'T AWARE OF HOW LONG HE TALKS, OR INDEED OF PRECISELY WHAT HE SAYS. IN A SENSE, HE BARES HIS **SOUL** TO HER, REACHING OUT WITH AS WILD AND FREE A PASSION AS HER OWN.

RRAWR!

AND THEN, WITH A BLOOD-CURDLING SCREAM, THE SNOWBIRD / WOLVERINE RESPONDS.

LOGAN... OH, LOGAN ...

...THANK YOU...

HUSH, DARLIN', HUSH. I KNOW HOW YOU FEEL. YOU'LL BE OKAY NOW, THOUGH. YOU'VE GONE THROUGH THE VALLEY, FACED THE WORST PARTS OF YOURSELF, AND **TRIUMPHED.** IT'LL NEVER BE AS ROUGH AGAIN.

THEY MOVE APART FROM THE OTHERS, THEIR WORDS AS PRIVATE AS THE EMOTIONS THEY STRUGGLE TO EXPRESS.

FOR THEM, IN THAT BRIEF SPACE OF TIME, THE WORLD HAS CHANGED, AND NEITHER OF THEM IS QUITE SURE HOW TO DEAL WITH IT.

NOW, THOUGH, THE FOCUS SHIFTS TO SHAMAN.

HE SPENDS THE REST OF THE NIGHT PREPARING HIMSELF FOR THE ORDEAL TO COME. BY DAWN, HE IS READY.

THE OTHERS STAND GUARD, ALERT SHOULD ANYTHING GO WRONG. AROUND THEM, THE FOREST HAS GONE DEATHLY STILL -- NO SOUND OF MAN OR BEAST, NOT EVEN A WAYWARD BREATH OF WIND, DISTURBS THE EERIE SILENCE.

HIS VOICE LOW, SHAMAN BEGINS TO SPEAK--

-- SEEMINGLY RANDOM, GUTTERAL SOUNDS AT FIRST, THAT GRADUALLY RESOLVE THEMSELVES INTO WORDS...

... THE WORDS INTO A SING-SONG RHYTHMIC CHANT. THE LANGUAGE IS OLDER THAN RECORDED HISTORY, AND BESIDES SHAMAN, ONLY SNOWBIRD KNOWS THE WORDS' MEANING. ALL, HOWEVER, RESPOND TO THE SPELL AS SHAMAN DRAWS ON THE POWER OF THEIR COMBINED WILL...

... RELEASING IT ON THE ENCHANTED WOODSBEAST.

AND, BEFORE THEIR EYES, MONSTER BECOMES MAN.

IT... IS DONE.

AND DONE **WELL**, MY FRIEND.

REST NOW, MICHAEL. YOU HAVE EARNED IT.

GEORGES BAPTISTE?

Y-YES.

AM... AM I TRULY FREE OF MY CURSE? IS MY NIGHTMARE AT LAST ENDED?!

I'M AFRAID NOT.

YOU'RE **UNDER ARREST.**

WHAT--?!?

LATER... I KNOW ARRESTING BAPTISTE SOUNDS CRUEL AND HEARTLESS, BUT I HAD NO CHOICE. HE BECAME WENDIGO OF HIS OWN FREE WILL. UNDER CANADIAN LAW, THAT RENDERS HIM CULPABLE FOR ANY CRIMES HE COMMITTED AS WENDIGO.

THE COURTS SHOULDN'T BE TOO HARD ON HIM, THOUGH. HIS ACTS WERE THOSE OF AN INSANE MAN, AND HIS MEMORIES OF WHAT HE DID ARE A FAR WORSE PUNISH-MENT THAN A LIFETIME STRETCH IN PRISON.

THANKS FOR YOUR HELP, LOGAN. WE COULDN'T HAVE STOPPED HIM WITHOUT YOU. I'LL SPEAK TO THE MINISTER ABOUT YOUR RESIGNATION. THERE'LL BE NO MORE HASSLES, OF YOU OR THE X-MEN.

AND NOW THAT YOU'RE A FREE MAN, COME VISIT ME AND HEATHER MORE OFTEN. WE'RE YOUR FRIENDS, LOGAN. WE CARE ABOUT YOU. WE MISS YOU.

I KNOW, MAC. AND... I WILL.

WILL I SEE WOLVERINE AGAIN? WHO CAN SAY? DO I *WISH* TO?

YES.

LOOKING AT GEORGES BAPTISTE, *MEIN FREUND*, I CAN'T HELP THINKING, *"THERE BUT FOR THE GRACE OF GOD GOES YOU."*

HOW SO?

BAPTISTE, AS WENDIGO, KILLED. NOW HE MUST PAY THE PRICE. AND YOU, WOLVERINE? SHOULD YOU NOT PAY A PRICE AS WELL?

KURT, IN MY LIFE, I'VE BEEN TWO THINGS: A WARTIME *SOLDIER* AND A *SECRET AGENT.* AS ONE, MY GOVERNMENT *PAID* ME TO KILL; AS THE OTHER, THEY *LICENSED* ME TO KILL. I WAS VERY GOOD AT BOTH JOBS. THEY LIKED THAT-- AN' I GOT THE MEDALS AND COMMENDATIONS TO PROVE IT.

PERHAPS, BUT...

I AIN'T FINISHED YET, BUB.

A MAN COMES AT ME WITH HIS FISTS, I'LL MEET HIM WITH FISTS. BUT IF HE PULLS A GUN -- OR THREATENS PEOPLE I'M PROTECTIN'-- THEN I GOT NO SYMPATHY FOR HIM. HE MADE HIS CHOICE. HE'LL HAVE TO LIVE-- OR DIE-- WITH IT.

I NEVER USED MY CLAWS ON SOME-ONE WHO HADN'T TRIED TO KILL ME FIRST. I CALL THAT *SELF-DEFENSE.*

I UNDERSTAND, LOGAN. WHAT YOU SAY IS REASONABLE, LOGICAL, JUSTIFIABLE.

BUT DOES THAT MAKE IT *RIGHT?*

WOLVERINE DOES NOT REPLY AND, FOR A LONG WHILE, THERE IS SILENCE BETWEEN THE TWO MEN...

... AND THE FEW TIMES HE DOES SPEAK, DURING THEIR LEISURELY MEANDER -- A VACATION BY ANY OTHER NAME -- HOME, HIS TONE IS THOUGHTFUL. NIGHTCRAWLER'S WORDS -- HIS FINAL QUESTION -- STRUCK DEEP.

NOW -- LIKE IT OR NOT, FOR BETTER OR WORSE -- WOLVERINE MUST DEAL WITH THEM.

MEANWHILE, IN THE PARLIAMENT BUILDING IN OTTAWA ...

YOU WANTED TO SEE ME, PRIME MINISTER?

YES, Dr. HUDSON. FIRSTLY, I'D LIKE TO CONGRATULATE ALPHA FLIGHT FOR YOUR HANDLING OF THIS "WENDIGO" BUSINESS. YOU DID WELL. I WISH I HAD A ... BETTER REWARD.

SIR?

THERE'S NO EASY WAY TO SAY THIS. I'M AFRAID DEPARTMENT H AND ALPHA FLIGHT ARE BEING DISBANDED.

TIMES ARE HARD. MONEY IS IN SHORT SUPPLY. THE HOUSE FELT THAT SUPER-HEROES WERE A LUXURY THE FEDERAL GOVERNMENT COULD NO LONGER AFFORD.

MANY MEMBERS -- LIKE THEIR CONSTITUENTS -- HAVE NEVER FELT ENTIRELY ... COMFORTABLE WITH THE IDEA OF SUPER-BEINGS. THE CURRENT ANTI-MUTANT SENTIMENT IN THE UNITED STATES IS A GOOD EXAMPLE OF THAT.

REGRETTABLY, IGNORING YOUR EXISTENCE -- AS MANY ARE TRYING TO DO -- WILL NOT MAKE YOU DISAPPEAR.

THE GENIE IS OUT OF THE BOTTLE. PANDORA'S BOX IS OPEN. WE MUST LIVE WITH THIS REALITY AS BEST WE CAN. IF FOR NO OTHER REASON THAN THAT WE HAVE NO OTHER CHOICE.

I'M SORRY, JAMES. I WILL GIVE YOU AND ALPHA FLIGHT WHAT AID I CAN. YOU CAN KEEP YOUR SECURITY CLEARANCES AND YOUR STATUS AS R.C.M.P. AUXILIARIES. I WISH I COULD DO MORE.

I KNOW, SIR. DON'T WORRY, THOUGH. WE'LL MANAGE. SOMEHOW. WE'VE WORKED AND FOUGHT TOO HARD TO CHUCK EVERY-THING NOW.

THAT'S THE SPIRIT.

VINDICATOR -- WHATEVER HAPPENS, I PRAY YOU'LL KEEP THE WELFARE OF CANADA AND HER PEOPLE FOREMOST IN YOUR THOUGHTS AND ACTIONS.

I WILL, PRIME MINISTER. AND I HOPE YOU'RE RIGHT. GOOD-BYE.

IN TIME, THEY WILL COME TO RESPECT -- AND HONOR -- YOU AND ALPHA FLIGHT, AS I DO.

AN ENDING OF SORTS, YET ALSO A BEGINNING -- OF A NEW, POSSIBLY BRIGHTER CHAP-TER IN THE LIFE OF ALPHA FLIGHT.

104

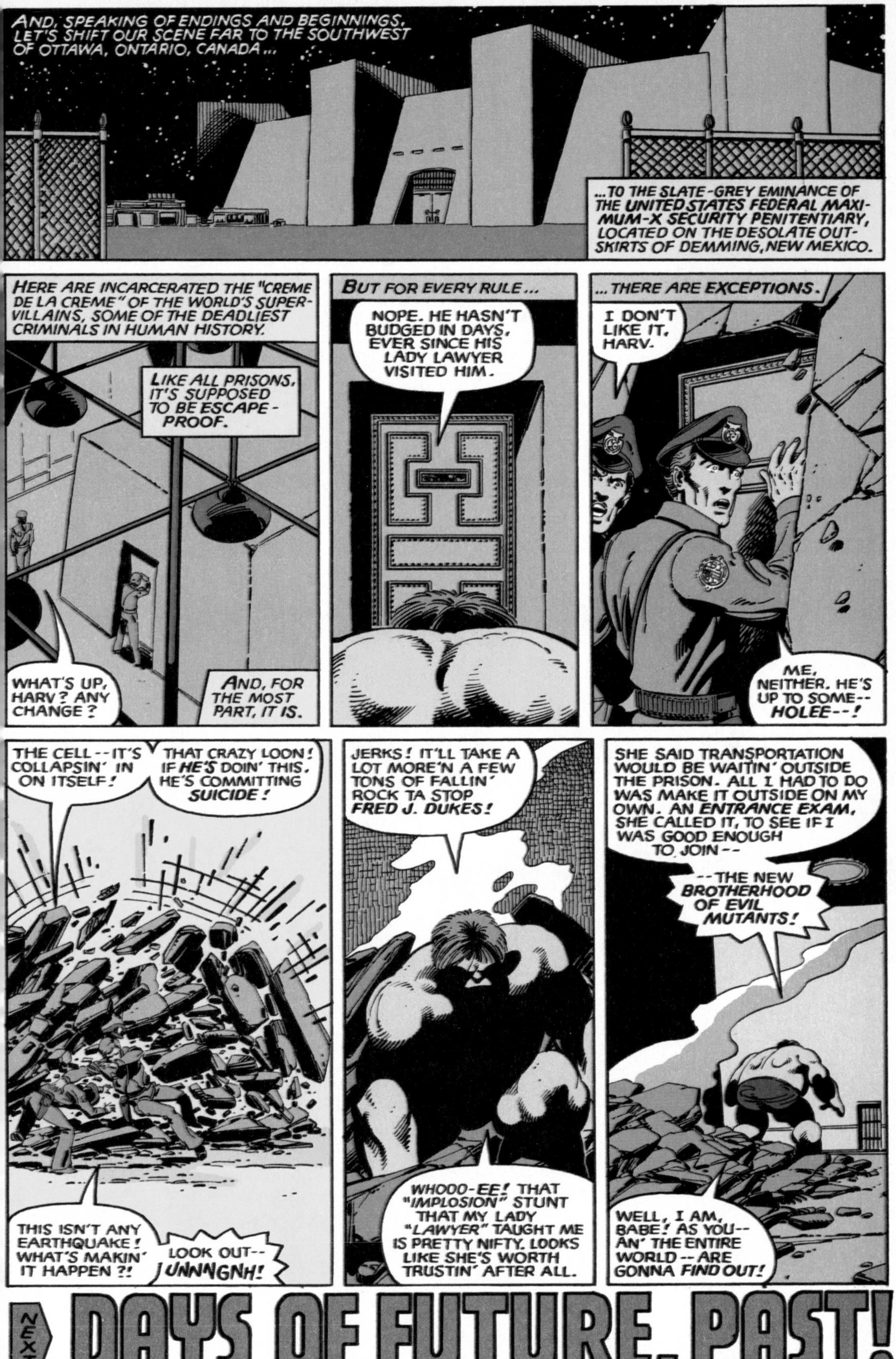
AND, SPEAKING OF ENDINGS AND BEGINNINGS, LET'S SHIFT OUR SCENE FAR TO THE SOUTHWEST OF OTTAWA, ONTARIO, CANADA...
...TO THE SLATE-GREY EMINANCE OF THE UNITED STATES FEDERAL MAXIMUM-X SECURITY PENITENTIARY, LOCATED ON THE DESOLATE OUTSKIRTS OF DEMMING, NEW MEXICO.
HERE ARE INCARCERATED THE "CREME DE LA CREME" OF THE WORLD'S SUPER-VILLAINS, SOME OF THE DEADLIEST CRIMINALS IN HUMAN HISTORY.
LIKE ALL PRISONS, IT'S SUPPOSED TO BE ESCAPE-PROOF.
WHAT'S UP, HARV? ANY CHANGE?
AND, FOR THE MOST PART, IT IS.
BUT FOR EVERY RULE...
NOPE. HE HASN'T BUDGED IN DAYS, EVER SINCE HIS LADY LAWYER VISITED HIM.
...THERE ARE EXCEPTIONS.
I DON'T LIKE IT, HARV.
ME, NEITHER. HE'S UP TO SOME-- HOLEE--!
THE CELL--IT'S COLLAPSIN' IN ON ITSELF!
THAT CRAZY LOON! IF HE'S DOIN' THIS, HE'S COMMITTING SUICIDE!
THIS ISN'T ANY EARTHQUAKE! WHAT'S MAKIN' IT HAPPEN?!
LOOK OUT-- UNNNGNH!
JERKS! IT'LL TAKE A LOT MORE'N A FEW TONS OF FALLIN' ROCK TA STOP FRED J. DUKES!
WHOOO-EE! THAT "IMPLOSION" STUNT THAT MY LADY "LAWYER" TAUGHT ME IS PRETTY NIFTY. LOOKS LIKE SHE'S WORTH TRUSTIN' AFTER ALL.
SHE SAID TRANSPORTATION WOULD BE WAITIN' OUTSIDE THE PRISON. ALL I HAD TO DO WAS MAKE IT OUTSIDE ON MY OWN. AN ENTRANCE EXAM, SHE CALLED IT, TO SEE IF I WAS GOOD ENOUGH TO JOIN--
--THE NEW BROTHERHOOD OF EVIL MUTANTS!
WELL, I AM, BABE! AS YOU-- AN' THE ENTIRE WORLD--ARE GONNA FIND OUT!
NEXT
DAYS OF FUTURE, PAST!

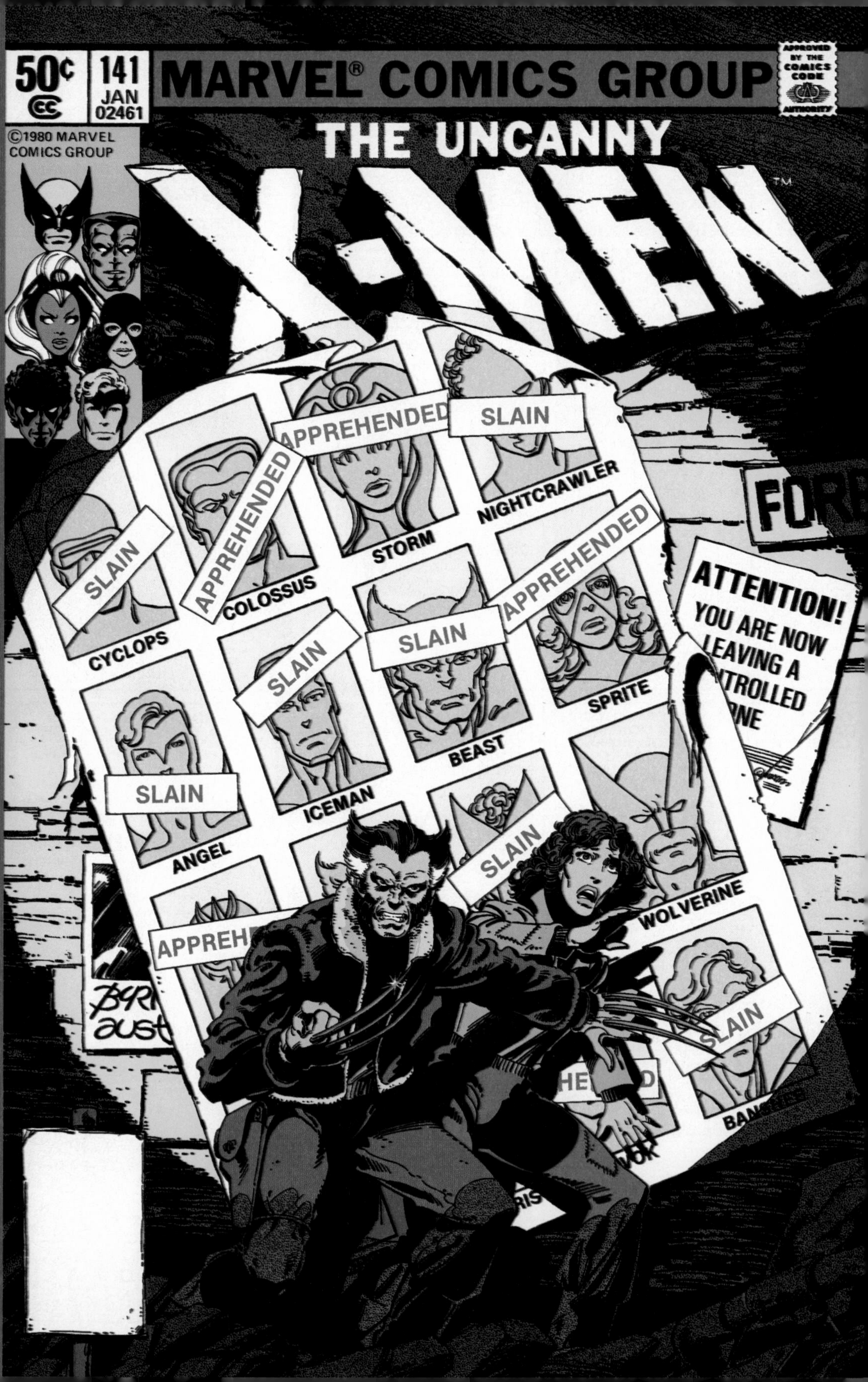

50¢
CC
141
JAN
02461
MARVEL® COMICS GROUP
APPROVED BY THE COMICS CODE AUTHORITY
©1980 MARVEL COMICS GROUP
THE UNCANNY
X-MEN™
SLAIN
CYCLOPS
APPREHENDED
COLOSSUS
APPREHENDED
STORM
SLAIN
NIGHTCRAWLER
SLAIN
ANGEL
SLAIN
ICEMAN
SLAIN
BEAST
APPREHENDED
SPRITE
SLAIN
WOLVERINE
SLAIN
ATTENTION!
YOU ARE NOW
LEAVING A

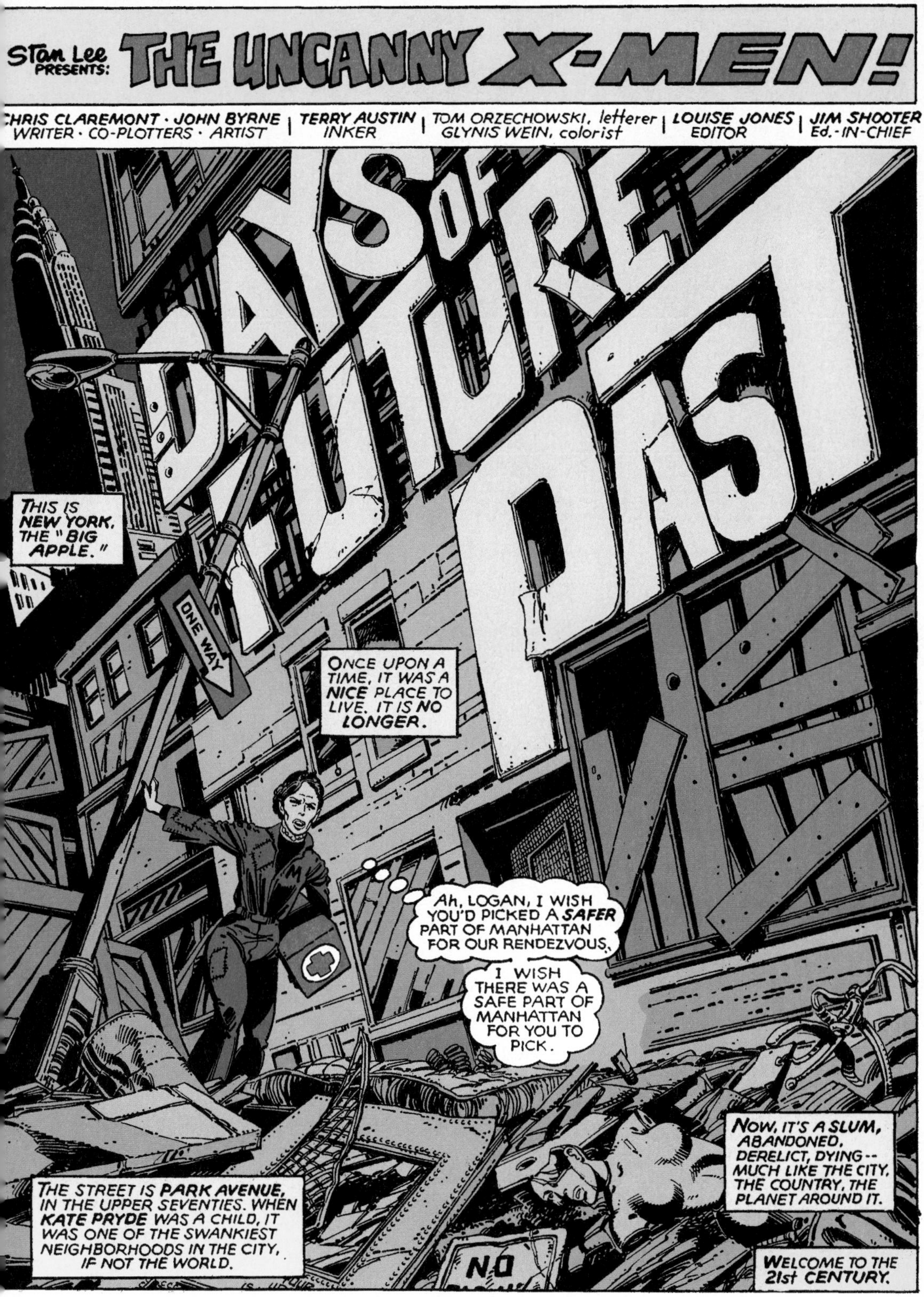
Stan Lee PRESENTS: THE UNCANNY X-MEN!
CHRIS CLAREMONT · JOHN BYRNE WRITER · CO-PLOTTERS · ARTIST
TERRY AUSTIN INKER
TOM ORZECHOWSKI, letterer GLYNIS WEIN, colorist
LOUISE JONES EDITOR
JIM SHOOTER Ed.-IN-CHIEF
DAYS OF FUTURE PAST
THIS IS NEW YORK, THE "BIG APPLE."
ONE WAY
ONCE UPON A TIME, IT WAS A NICE PLACE TO LIVE. IT IS NO LONGER.
Ah, LOGAN, I WISH YOU'D PICKED A SAFER PART OF MANHATTAN FOR OUR RENDEZVOUS.
I WISH THERE WAS A SAFE PART OF MANHATTAN FOR YOU TO PICK.
NOW, IT'S A SLUM, ABANDONED, DERELICT, DYING-- MUCH LIKE THE CITY, THE COUNTRY, THE PLANET AROUND IT.
THE STREET IS PARK AVENUE, IN THE UPPER SEVENTIES. WHEN KATE PRYDE WAS A CHILD, IT WAS ONE OF THE SWANKIEST NEIGHBORHOODS IN THE CITY, IF NOT THE WORLD.
NO
WELCOME TO THE 21st CENTURY.

THIS IS *ROGUE* TERRITORY, THE LAST PLACE ON EARTH THE SENTINELS WOULD EXPECT A MUTANT-- ESPECIALLY AN X-MAN TO BE, WHICH IS WHY WOLVERINE CHOSE IT.

I WISH HE'D MAKE HIS ENTRANCE, THOUGH.

EVERYTHING *LOOKS* PEACEFUL ENOUGH...

...BUT IT FEELS-- *HEY!*

A *TRAP-DOOR!*

NO! THIS CAN'T BE HAPPENING NOW! NOT WHEN WE'RE SO CLOSE!

NOT WITH SO MUCH DEPENDING ON US!

ROGUES!

HOW PERCEPTIVE OF YOU, MUTIE. AND HOW *KIND* OF YOU TO, SHALL WE SAY, DROP IN.

YOU'D BE ADVISED TO LET ME GO. I'M ON OFFICIAL *SENTINAL* BUSINESS.

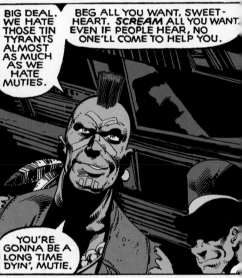

BIG DEAL. WE HATE THOSE TIN TYRANTS ALMOST AS MUCH AS WE HATE MUTIES.

BEG ALL YOU WANT, SWEETHEART. *SCREAM* ALL YOU WANT. EVEN IF PEOPLE HEAR, NO ONE'LL COME TO HELP YOU.

YOU'RE GONNA BE A LONG TIME DYIN', MUTIE.

NOT IF *I* HAVE ANYTHING TO SAY ABOUT IT, ROGUE!

WHUNFFF!

LET'S HEAR IT FOR KATE'S LAST STAND! THIS INHIBITOR COLLAR I'M FORCED TO WEAR NEUTRALIZES MY POWER TO PHASE THROUGH SOLID OBJECTS. I'M JUST A NORMAL WOMAN.

AGAINST THESE ODDS...!

ROBBO, GEORGE -- *GRAB HER!* I'M GONNA FLAY THIS MUTIE WITCH ALIVE!

NO YOU'RE NOT, BUB.

YOU'RE GONNA *RELEASE* THE LADY, JUST LIKE SHE ASKED.

WHO'S GONNA MAKE ME, SHORT STUFF-- YOU?!

NOBODY GIVES "BIG ALEX" ORDERS ON HIS TURF. YOU WANT THE WOMAN, OLD MAN--

--THEN YOU COME SAVE HER!

IF YOU INSIST. BUT DON'T SAY I DIDN'T WARN YOU.

IN THE OLD DAYS, I'D HAVE SIMPLY CUT THE PUNK IN TWO WITH MY RETRACTABLE CLAWS. BUT DOIN' THAT WOULD TELL THE SENTINELS--

URRRGH!

--THAT WOLVERINE'S BACK IN TOWN--

--AND THAT WOULD JEOPARDIZE THE MISSION.

YOU OKAY, KATE?

I'M FINE, LOGAN-- BUT CALLS THIS CLOSE, I CAN LIVE WITHOUT.

I KNOW WHAT YOU MEAN. C'MON, LET'S ROLL.

SO TELL ME, COLONEL LOGAN, HOW'S LIFE IN THE CANADIAN RESISTANCE ARMY?

A THRILL A MINUTE, DARLIN'.

THE WORD FROM LONDON IS THAT EVERYTHING'S ON AUTOMATIC. THE MOMENT THE SENTINELS MOVE OUT OF NORTH AMERICA, THE OTHER GREAT POWERS WILL LAUNCH A FULL-SCALE NUCLEAR STRIKE.

THEN... IT'S UP TO THE X-MEN.

ATTENTION! YOU ARE LEAVING A CONTROLLED ZONE

AS ALWAYS, WHEN THERE'S A WORLD TO SAVE.

HERE'S THE LAST COMPONENT OF THE "JAMMER."

LIKE THE OTHER MODULES, IT'S INVISIBLE TO THE SENTINELS' SENSORS. YOU SHOULDN'T HAVE ANY PROBLEM SMUGGLIN' IT INTO CAMP.

THAT'S EASY FOR YOU TO SAY.

YOU GOT A POINT. PHASE TWO BEGINS AT MIDNIGHT, WHEN I BUST YOU GUYS OUT. BE READY, KATE. GOOD LUCK.

WE'LL BE WAITING, LOGAN. AND THANKS.

AT FIRST AVENUE, KATE CATCHES THE UPTOWN EXPRESS TRAM TO THE BRONX.

EN ROUTE, SHE DOESN'T BOTHER TO HIDE THE **SORROW** IN HER EYES AS SHE CONTRASTS WHAT IS WITH WHAT ONCE WAS AND WONDERS HOW SO MUCH COULD CHANGE SO QUICKLY.

IN NORTH AMERICA, IN THE YEAR 2013, THERE ARE **THREE** CLASSES OF PEOPLE:

"H," FOR BASELINE HUMAN -- CLEAN OF MUTANT GENES, ALLOWED TO BREED.

"A," FOR ANAMOLOUS HUMAN -- A NORMAL PERSON POSSESSING MUTANT GENETIC POTENTIAL...

...FORBIDDEN TO BREED.

"M," FOR MUTANT. THE BOTTOM OF THE HEAP, MADE PARIAHS AND OUTCASTS BY THE MUTANT CONTROL ACT OF 1988. HUNTED DOWN AND -- WITH A FEW RARE EXCEPTIONS -- KILLED WITHOUT MERCY.

IN THE QUARTER-CENTURY SINCE THE ACT'S PASSAGE, MILLIONS HAVE DIED.

SOUTH BRONX MUTANT INTERNMENT CENTER

THEY WERE THE LUCKY ONES.

MUTANT 187, YOU ARE BEHIND SCHEDULE. EXPLAIN.

I WAS ATTACKED BY ROGUES, SENTINAL ALPHA 3. I ESCAPED. THAT CAUSED THE DELAY.

ENCEPHALO-SCAN INDICATES TRUTHFUL REPLY. YOU MAY PASS.

AFTER AN EXHAUSTIVE -- AND INTENTIONALLY HUMILIATING -- SECURITY EXAMINATION, TO ENSURE THAT SHE CARRYING NO CONTRABAND, KATE IS ALLOWED TO RE-ENTER THE CAMP THAT HAS BEEN HER HOME SINCE THE TURN OF THE CENTURY.

AS ALWAYS, THE FIRST THING SHE SEES IS THE CEMETARY. AS ALWAYS, THERE'S A FRESH GRAVE.

INTERRED HERE ARE ALL THE VICTIMS OF THE SENTINELS. SOME I KNEW, MOST I DIDN'T -- BUT, IN A WAY, WE'RE ALL FAMILY.

FORGIVE US, MY FRIENDS. WE CANNOT AVENGE YOU -- FOR WHAT POINT IS VENGEANCE AGAINST AN UNFEELING MACHINE? BUT AT LEAST, WE CAN TRY TO ENSURE THAT THIS NIGHTMARE NEVER HAPPENS, NEVER EVEN BEGINS!

KURT WAGNER

SCOTT SUMMERS

WARREN WORTHI

CHARLES XAVIER

BEN GRIMM

REED RICHA

JOHNNY STORM

OF ALL THE X-MEN WHO EVER WERE, ONLY *FOUR* REMAIN: *LOGAN (WOLVERINE), KATE (SPRITE), ORORO MONROE (STORM),* AND *PETER RASPUTIN (COLOSSUS).* THEY, ALONG WITH *FRANKLIN RICHARDS (LAST SURVIVOR OF THE FABLED FANTASTIC FOUR)...*

...AND HIS LADY, *RACHEL,* A TELEPATH/ TELEKINETIC, COMPRISE THE CORE CADRE OF THE ANTI-SENTINEL RESISTANCE...

I'M HOME!

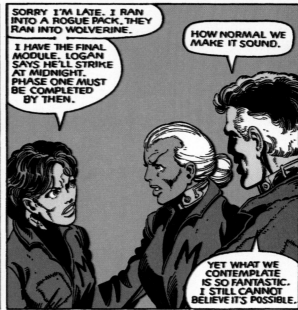

SORRY I'M LATE. I RAN INTO A ROGUE PACK. THEY RAN INTO WOLVERINE.

HOW NORMAL WE MAKE IT SOUND.

I HAVE THE FINAL MODULE. LOGAN SAYS HE'LL STRIKE AT MIDNIGHT. PHASE ONE MUST BE COMPLETED BY THEN.

YET WHAT WE CONTEMPLATE IS SO FANTASTIC. I STILL CANNOT BELIEVE IT'S POSSIBLE.

THAT'S STRANGE TALK, PIOTR ALEXANDREIVITCH, COMING FROM ONE WHO'S SEEN AND DONE WHAT YOU HAVE.

I HAVE EVER BEEN A... SIMPLE MAN, OLD FRIEND, MORE FARMER IN MY SOUL THAN SUPER-HERO.

MAGNETO!

I CANNOT SHAKE MY DOUBTS.

IF THERE WERE AN ALTERNATIVE, PETER-- *ANY* ALTERNATIVE--WE WOULD TAKE IT. BUT IF WE DO NOTHING, BY TOMORROW, THE WORLD WILL BE AT WAR. AND BY THE DAY AFTER TOMORROW--

...THE WORLD WILL BE *DEAD.*

OUR ACTIONS MAY NOT MAKE THINGS BETTER--FOR HUMANITY OR MUTANTKIND--BUT THEY CERTAINLY CANNOT MAKE THEM WORSE.

RACHEL-- CHILD. SO MUCH DEPENDS ON YOU...

I WON'T FAIL, MAGNETO. I'VE BEEN MEDITATING ALL DAY. ONCE THE JAMMER'S OPERATIONAL...

...WE CAN START ANYTIME.

THEN WHAT ARE WE WAITING FOR?!

A MOMENT, MY WIFE.

Hm?

AS I SAID, I HAVE DOUBTS. CAN OUR MAD, DESPERATE PLAN WORK? MORE IMPORTANTLY, *SHOULD* IT? WE ARE TOYING WITH THE BASIC FABRIC OF REALITY.

AND IF WE SUCCEED, WHAT WILL HAPPEN TO US, TO OUR LOVE? IT MIGHT CEASE TO EXIST, ALONG WITH THE SENTINELS.

THAT'S A RISK WE HAVE TO TAKE. WHAT DOES THE LOVE OF TWO PEOPLE MATTER AGAINST THE LIVES OF BILLIONS?

I AM SELFISH. IT MATTERS TO ME.

PETER, IF OUR LOVE WAS MEANT TO BE, IT *WILL* BE. ONLY THIS TIME IN A WORLD WHERE OUR CHILDREN CAN GROW UP *FREE* AND *UNAFRAID!*

THE SENTINELS KILLED MY FRIENDS AND THEY KILLED MY... MY BABIES.

IF CHANGING THE PAST HOLDS OUT EVEN THE SLIGHTEST HOPE OF SAVING THEM, I'LL DO IT. WHATEVER THE COST.

I LOVE YOU, KATE.

AND I, YOU, PETER...

...FROM THE MOMENT WE FIRST MET.

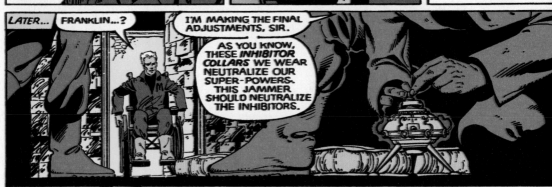

LATER... FRANKLIN...?

I'M MAKING THE FINAL ADJUSTMENTS, SIR.

AS YOU KNOW, THESE *INHIBITOR COLLARS* WE WEAR NEUTRALIZE OUR SUPER-POWERS. THIS JAMMER SHOULD NEUTRALIZE THE INHIBITORS.

INSIDE THIS ROOM, WE'LL BE AS STRONG AS WE EVER WERE, FOR AS LONG AS THE UNIT'S POWER CELLS FUNCTION.

BY THEN, WE'LL BE FREE OF THE COLLARS.

LAY BACK AND RELAX, KATE.

THIS IS CRAZY. I'VE GOT BUTTERFLIES IN MY STOMACH.

HUSH!

SORRY.

BREATHE WITH ME.

"LET YOUR MIND BECOME *ONE* WITH MINE, AND OUR MINDS ONE WITH *ALL.*"

ETERNITY. WHAT HAPPENS NEXT IS ANYBODY'S GUESS.

112

FRIDAY, OCTOBER 31, 1980-- IT'S THE FINAL FRIDAY OF ONE OF THE CLOSEST, HARDEST-FOUGHT PRESIDENTIAL ELECTIONS IN RECENT MEMORY. FOR THE *UNCANNY X-MEN*, STORM, ANGEL, COLOSSUS, WOLVERINE AND NIGHT-CRAWLER--HOWEVER, IT'S A DAY LIKE ANY OTHER--WHICH BEGINS WITH A STRENUOUS COMBAT WORKOUT IN THE *DANGER ROOM* OF THEIR WESTCHESTER COUNTY, NEW YORK MANSION HEADQUARTERS. THIS IS WHERE THEY HONE THEIR MUTANT ABILITIES TO A RAZOR-KEEN EDGE, UNDER THE TUTELAGE OF THEIR MENTOR, *PROFESSOR CHARLES XAVIER.*

IT'S NO PLACE FOR THE UNINITIATED, AS *KITTY PRYDE*-- THE NEWEST, YOUNGEST MEMBER OF THE TEAM -- IS ABOUT TO DISCOVER.

KITTY! WHAT ARE YOU DOING IN HERE?!

UH... NIGHT-CRAWLER SENT ME TO TELL YOU THAT HE GOT HELD UP IN THE KITCHEN.

BUT STORM, THE DOOR WAS *UNLOCKED!* I FIGURED THAT YOU HADN'T STARTED YOUR TRAIN-ING SESSION.

KID, THAT FLAMIN' STUPID DOOR IS *ALWAYS* UNLOCKED!

113

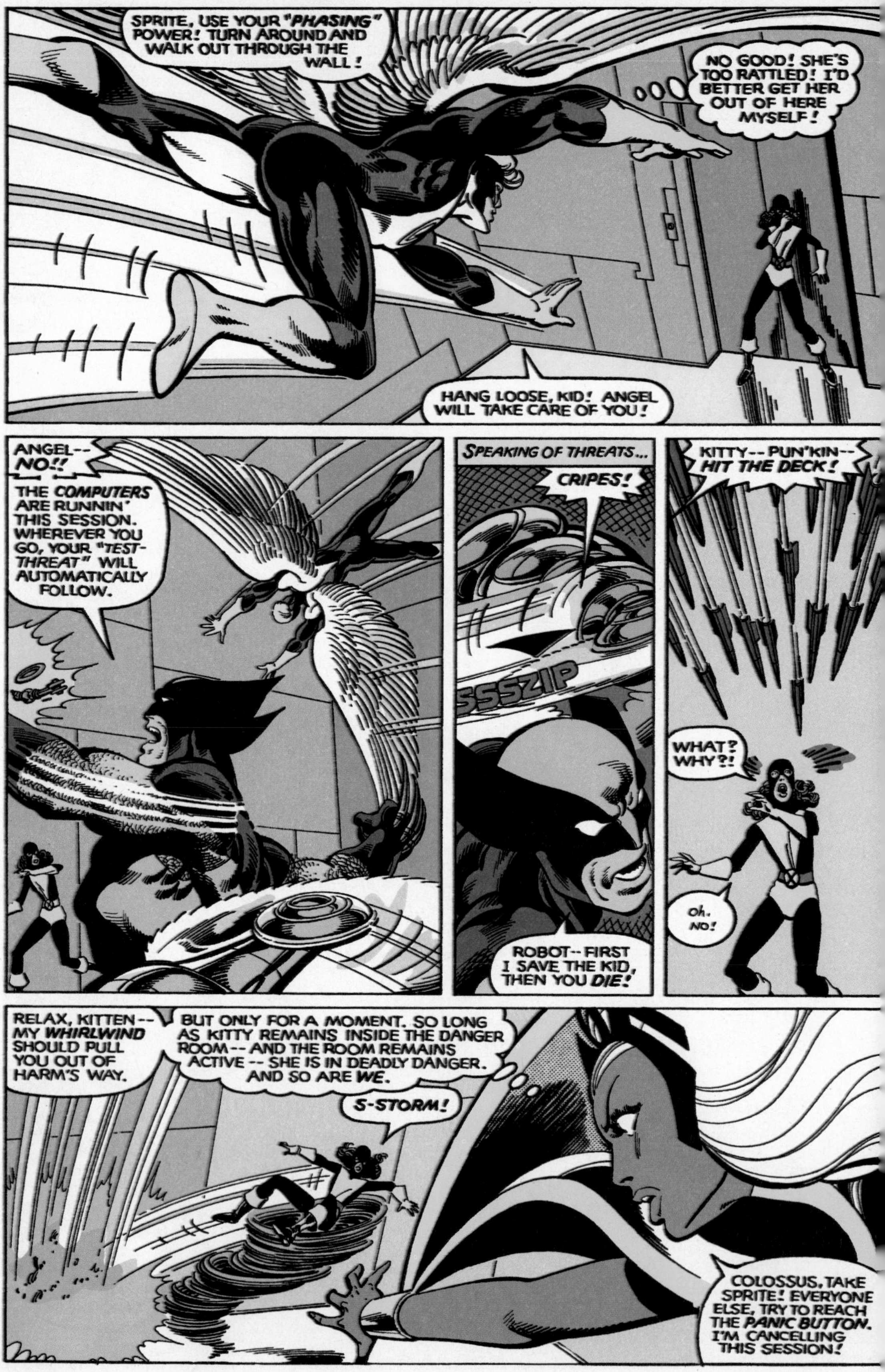
SPRITE, USE YOUR "PHASING" POWER! TURN AROUND AND WALK OUT THROUGH THE WALL!
NO GOOD! SHE'S TOO RATTLED! I'D BETTER GET HER OUT OF HERE MYSELF!
HANG LOOSE, KID! ANGEL WILL TAKE CARE OF YOU!
ANGEL-- NO!!
THE COMPUTERS ARE RUNNIN' THIS SESSION. WHEREVER YOU GO, YOUR "TEST-THREAT" WILL AUTOMATICALLY FOLLOW.
SPEAKING OF THREATS...
CRIPES!
SSSZIP
ROBOT-- FIRST I SAVE THE KID, THEN YOU DIE!
KITTY-- PUN'KIN-- HIT THE DECK!
WHAT? WHY?!
Oh. NO!
RELAX, KITTEN-- MY WHIRLWIND SHOULD PULL YOU OUT OF HARM'S WAY.
BUT ONLY FOR A MOMENT. SO LONG AS KITTY REMAINS INSIDE THE DANGER ROOM-- AND THE ROOM REMAINS ACTIVE -- SHE IS IN DEADLY DANGER. AND SO ARE WE.
S-STORM!
COLOSSUS, TAKE SPRITE! EVERYONE ELSE, TRY TO REACH THE PANIC BUTTON. I'M CANCELLING THIS SESSION!

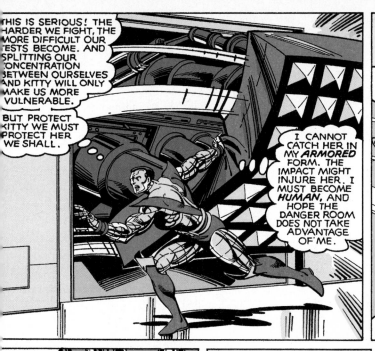

THIS IS SERIOUS! THE HARDER WE FIGHT, THE MORE DIFFICULT OUR TESTS BECOME. AND SPLITTING OUR CONCENTRATION BETWEEN OURSELVES AND KITTY WILL ONLY MAKE US MORE VULNERABLE.

BUT PROTECT KITTY WE MUST PROTECT HER WE SHALL.

I CANNOT CATCH HER IN MY *ARMORED* FORM. THE IMPACT MIGHT INJURE HER. I MUST BECOME *HUMAN*, AND HOPE THE DANGER ROOM DOES NOT TAKE ADVANTAGE OF ME.

THE YOUNG RUSSIAN CONCEN-TRATES AND, WITH A BURST OF ENERGY, HIS ORGANIC STEEL BODY ONCE MORE BECOMES FLESH AND BLOOD.

AM I IN TROUBLE, PETER? AM I GONNA GET YELLED AT?

PROBABLY. IF YOU SURVIVE.

IF I ... SURVIVE--?!?

PETER-- *LOOK!!*

THE *PILE-DRIVER!*

HE HAS SPLIT-SECONDS TO ACT...

... BUT BEFORE COLOSSUS EVEN BEGINS TO MOVE, A BURST OF FLAME COUPLED WITH THE STENCH OF BRIMSTONE HERALDS THE ARRIVAL OF *NIGHTCRAWLER!*

PANIC BUTTON

TALK ABOUT YOUR DRAMATIC ENTRANCES!

IT SEEMS I *TELEPORTED* HERE IN THE PROVERBIAL NICK OF TIME.

YOU COULD SAY THAT, FRIEND KURT. ARE YOU ALL RIGHT, KITTY?

Uh-huh.

WERE YOU FRIGHTENED?

Uh-HUH!

I, ALSO.

WHERE WERE YOU, KURT? I KNOW IT WAS YOUR TURN TO CLEAN THE BREAKFAST DISHES, BUT THAT SHOULDN'T HAVE MADE YOU LATE FOR THIS TRAINING SESSION.

I'M SORRY, ORORO. THE MORNING NEWS HAD AN INTER-VIEW WITH PROFESSOR XAVIER ABOUT TODAY'S "MUTANT HEARINGS" IN WASHINGTON. I GUESS I LOST TRACK OF TIME.

115

DON'T DO IT AGAIN.

AND YOU, YOUNG LADY, ARE *NEVER* TO COME THROUGH THAT DOOR WHEN THE WARNING LIGHT IS ON.

DON'T BE HARSH, STORM. KITTY'S FIRST TRAINING SESSION IS SCHEDULED FOR THIS MORNING. I'M SURE HER EAGERNESS GOT THE BETTER OF HER. *NICHT WAHR,* KITTY?

UH, YEAH, NIGHTCRAWLER, SURE.

SHE'S STILL ANTSY AROUND YOU, KURT.

JA, WOLVERINE. I'VE TRIED TO BREAK THE ICE BETWEEN US, BUT NOTHING WORKS. FROM STRANGERS, I DON'T MIND THAT REACTION. FROM A FRIEND -- A FELLOW X-MAN -- IT HURTS.

BE PATIENT, KURT. SHE HAS SO MUCH TO LEARN.

SPRITE, THIS IS STORM. BEGIN WHENEVER YOU WISH. ALL YOU HAVE TO DO IS WALK ACROSS THE ROOM.

DON'T SWEAT IT, PUN'KIN. IT WON'T HURT. MUCH.

THANKS, WOLVERINE. I REALLY NEEDED THAT.

I KNOW THE ROOM IS SET ON LOW POWER. IT REALLY *CAN'T* HURT BUT I'M STILL NERVOUS-- I'M *SCARED!*

BUT ORORO BELIEVES IN ME. THEY ALL BELIEVE IN ME. I CAN'T LET 'EM DOWN.

SHE'S SHAKING AS SHE TAKES HER FIRST, HESITANT, STEP.

BUT AS SHE MOVES FURTHER INTO THE ROOM -- AND NOTHING NASTY SEEMS TO HAPPEN TO HER --

-- HER CONFIDENCE SLOWLY INCREASES.

UNSURE OF HOW TO COPE WITH ALL THE MYRIAD THREATS THROWN HER WAY, KITTY RESPONDS IN-STINCTIVELY-- BY SIMPLY USING HER MUTANT ABILITY TO PHASE *THROUGH* SOLID OBJECTS. SHE DOESN'T HAVE TO. NOTHING CAN TOUCH HER.

SIMULTANEOUSLY, AS SHE DOESN'T SO MUCH WALK ON THE FLOOR AS ON THE MOLECULES OF AIR ABOVE THE FLOOR, WHEN TRAP DOORS OPEN, SHE DOES NOT FALL.

THE DANGER ROOM DOES ITS LEVEL BEST TO STOP HER ...

.. BUT IT'S A **WASTED** EFFORT.

AND IN THE OBSERVATION BOOTH...

I THOUGHT I'D SEEN IT ALL! CHARLEY SPENDS WEEKS PROGRAMMING THE ROOM FOR KITTY, AN' SHE BEATS IT WITH HER *EYES CLOSED!*

MAN, OH MAN, I WISH XAVIER WERE HERE. I'D GIVE ANYTHING TO SEE HIS REACTION!

BACK TO THE DRAWING BOARD, I THINK.

I MADE IT! HOW'D I DO, STORM?

YOU WERE SPLENDID, KITTEN.

GEE.

SUDDENLY, REALITY TWISTS INSIDE-OUT FOR KITTY. SHE COMES FACE-TO-FACE WITH HERSELF -- AN OLDER, SADDER, WISER, STRONGER SELF --

--AND THEN HER SOUL, TOO, IS FLUNG OUT OVER THE ABYSS OF ETERNITY.

IN HER MIND, SHE SCREAMS.

IN REALITY, SHE DROPS WITHOUT A SOUND.

KITTY!!

KURT, GET DOWN THERE!

HOW IS SHE?!

BREATHING, THANK HEAVEN. HER PULSE IS STRONG AND STEADY. THERE'S NO SIGN OF ANY GROSS INJURY.

SHE LOOKS... STUNNED, ORORO.

IMPOSSIBLE. WE'D HAVE SEEN THE STUN BEAM. AND, BESIDES, I SHUT DOWN THE ROOM'S SYSTEMS THE MOMENT SHE REACHED THE DOOR.

TAKE HER TO THE INFIRMARY FOR AN IN-DEPTH EXAMINATION. PERHAPS THIS IS A DELAYED REACTION TO SOMETHING THAT HAPPENED DURING HER TEST.

AND IF IT IS? IF MY KITTEN IS HURT, OR CRIPPLED, OR... WORSE? NO, I DARE NOT THINK OF THAT. SHE'S ALL RIGHT. SHE *HAS* TO BE.

SOON... ACCORDING TO THE BIO-SENSORS, KITTY'S FINE.

THEN WHY DID SHE COLLAPSE?! WHY IS SHE STILL UNCONSCIOUS?!

EASY, STORM. 'CRAWLER SAID THE KID'S OKAY.

OKAY, PHYSICALLY, FLY-BOY. BUT I'M GETTIN' SOME WEIRD READINGS FROM THE *ELECTRO-ENCEPHELOGRAM.*

I RAN COMPARISONS BETWEEN THESE AND THE ONES IN KITTY'S MEDIFILE. THE BASIC PATTERN IS THE SAME, BUT THESE ARE MORE COMPLEX.

MAYBE CHARLEY OR MOIRA MacTAGGERT CAN PUZZLE IT OUT. THIS IS SURE WAY BEYOND ME.

ONE THING IS CERTAIN: *SOMETHING* HAPPENED TO KITTY. BUT WAS IT AN ATTACK, AND IF SO, FROM WHOM? OR ARE WE SIMPLY LETTING OUR IMAGINATIONS RUN AWAY WITH US?

MMMMHHH...

WHO...? KURT...?

AHA! OUR *KLEINE FRAULEIN* IS...

... AWAKE?!?

KURT! IT'S YOU!! REALLY YOU!! ALIVE!!

OF... COURSE, I'M ALIVE. WHAT ELSE WOULD I BE?

I'M IN THE MEDILAB. IN THE MANSION. IN WESTCHESTER.

THEN... I MADE IT!

KITTY, YOU AREN'T MAKING SENSE. LIE DOWN, LITTLE ONE. REST NOW.

I CAN'T. THERE'S NO TIME.

ANGEL! ORORO! *PETER!*

THIS IS INCREDIBLE! RACHEL SAID SHE COULD DO IT, BUT IN MY HEART OF HEARTS, I DIDN'T BELIEVE SHE COULD PULL IT OFF.

WHO IS RACHEL?

PULL *WHAT* OFF, KITTEN?

"KITTEN." IT'S BEEN YEARS SINCE YOU CALLED ME THAT.

KITTY, CHILD, ARE YOU ALL RIGHT?

I'M FINE, ORORO. BUT I'M NOT KITTY. I'M *KATE*. THIS BODY IS INHABITED BY THE MIND, THE PERSONA, THE SOUL, OF THE WOMAN I'LL BE IN THIRTY YEARS.

I'M FROM THE *FUTURE*.

ARE YOU INDEED?

I THINK YOU'RE TIRED. YOU'VE HAD A ROUGH MORNING AND A HARD SHOCK.

I'M CONCUSSED AND HALLUCINATING, IS THAT IT?

IT'S FUNNY. I REMEMBER YOU TELLING ME THAT THE HARDEST PART OF THIS OPERATION WOULD BE CONVINCING YOU OF THE TRUTH.

THE FACT REMAINS THAT ON HALLOWE'EN, 1980 -- *TODAY* -- THE BROTHERHOOD OF EVIL MUTANTS WILL MURDER PRESIDENTIAL CANDIDATE *ROBERT KELLY*, ALONG WITH CHARLES XAVIER AND MOIRA MacTAGGERT.

KELLY'S ASSASSINATION WILL SET IN MOTION A SEQUENCE OF EVENTS THAT-- 30 YEARS FROM NOW-- WILL CULMINATE IN THE DESTRUCTION OF THE WORLD IN A NUCLEAR HOLOCAUST. I'M HERE TO PREVENT THAT.

ORORO, WHAT I SAY MAY BE A FANTASY, BUT SUPPOSE IT ISN'T? CAN YOU AFFORD TO STAND IDLY BY WHILE SENATOR KELLY-- NOT TO MENTION CHARLES AND MOIRA-- ARE MURDERED?

NO. I CAN'T.

WE'LL TAKE YOU TO WASHINGTON, KITTEN.

SHE LOOKS LIKE A KID. BUT SHE STANDS, TALKS, MOVES-- SMELLS-- LIKE A WOMAN.

CRAZY AS IT SOUNDS, 'RORO, MY INSTINCTS SAY SHE *IS* TALKING TRUTH.

"THERE, PROFESSOR X CAN TELEPATHICALLY MINDSCAN YOU, TO DETERMINE YOUR BONAFIDES FAR MORE EFFECTIVELY THAN ANY OF US COULD...

"... AND ALSO DETERMINE THE VERACITY OF YOUR STORY."

AND SO, AS SOON AS ANGEL-- IN HIS ALTER EGO AS *WARREN WORTHINGTON III*, MASTER OF ONE OF AMERICA'S LARGER PRIVATE FORTUNES--WHISTLES UP HIS PRIVATE JET, THE X-MEN ARE ON THEIR WAY.

YOU SAY KELLY'S DEATH INITIATES A SEQUENCE OF EVENTS, KITTY. WHAT EVENTS?

KELLY IS A DECENT MAN, WITH WHAT HE FEELS ARE LEGITIMATE CONCERNS ABOUT THE INCREASING NUMBERS OF SUPER-POWERED MUTANTS IN THE WORLD.

"THE BROTHERHOOD KILLED HIM TO TEACH HUMANITY TO FEAR AND RESPECT THE POWER OF *HOMO SUPERIOR*. THEIR PLAN BACKFIRED. MUTANTS BECAME OBJECTS OF FEAR AND *HATRED*.

"WE THOUGHT THE MOOD OF HYSTERICAL PARANOIA WOULD PASS. IT DIDN'T.

"IN 1984, A RABID ANTI-MUTANT CANDIDATE WAS ELECTED PRESIDENT. WITHIN A YEAR, THE FIRST *MUTANT CONTROL ACT* WAS PASSED. THE SUPREME COURT, BLESS 'EM, STRUCK IT DOWN AS UNCONSTITUTIONAL.

AMERICA! IT'S 1984! DO YOU KNOW WHAT YOUR CHILDREN ARE?

"THE ADMINISTRATION RESPONDED BY REACTIVATING THE *SENTINELS*. THE ROBOTS WERE GIVEN AN OPEN-ENDED PROGRAM, WITH FATALLY BROAD PARAMETERS, TO 'ELIMINATE' THE MUTANT MENACE ONCE AND FOR ALL.

"THE SENTINELS CONCLUDED THAT THE BEST WAY TO DO THAT WOULD BE TO TAKE OVER THE COUNTRY.

"IN THE PROCESS, THEY DESTROYED NOT ONLY MUTANTS, BUT NON-MUTANT SUPER-BEINGS-- BOTH HEROES AND VILLAINS. BY THE TURN OF THE CENTURY...

"...THE NORTH AMERICAN CONTINENT WAS UNDER THEIR COMPLETE CONTROL.

WE FOUGHT. WE LOST. WE D-DIED. AND NOW... SEEING YOU ALL ALIVE-- OH GOD, I DIDN'T THINK IT WOULD HURT SO MUCH.

FOR A WHILE, THERE ARE NO SOUNDS IN THE JET'S CABIN...

...SAVE THIS CHILD-WOMAN'S ANGUISHED SOBS.

THEN, HER VOICE LOW AND CHOKED, KATE FORCES HERSELF TO FINISH HER STORY...

THE REST OF THE WORLD BECAME MORE FRIGHTENED OF THE SENTINELS THAN OF MUTANTKIND. THEY THREATENED WAR IF THE SENTINELS MOVED AGAINST THEM. THE SENTINELS, DRIVEN BY THEIR PRIME DIRECTIVE, ARE ABOUT TO MAKE THAT MOVE.

ONE OF THE SURVIVING X-MEN IS A *TELEPATH*. SHE DEVISED A PLAN TO PSYCHICALLY EXCHANGE THE MIND OF ONE OF US IN THE FUTURE WITH OUR COUNTER-PART IN THE PAST.

I WAS CHOSEN BECAUSE, AT THIS TIME, AS KITTY, I HADN'T YET BEEN TRAINED TO DEFEND MYSELF AGAINST A PSYCHIC ATTACK.

WOLVERINE SHOULD HAVE FREED THE OTHERS BY NOW--WHENEVER/ WHEREVER "NOW" IS. I WONDER HOW THEY'RE DOING?

2013--NEW YORK CITY...

THIS OLD SUBWAY TUNNEL'S WORKIN' LIKE A CHARM. IT'LL TAKE US INTO THE HEART O' MANHATTAN.

HOW'S KATE?

UNCONSCIOUS. I HOPE SHE REMAINS SO. THE LESS KITTY KNOWS OF WHAT HAS HAPPENED TO HER-- AND WHAT MAY HAPPEN TO HER-- THE BETTER.

I WISH WE COULD HAVE BROUGHT MAGNUS -- I MEAN, MAGNETO.

HE KNEW WHAT HE WAS DOIN' WHEN HE VOLUNTEERED TO COVER OUR ESCAPE. HIS WHEELCHAIR WOULD HAVE SLOWED US UP TOO MUCH.

A NOBLE DEATH IS STILL A DEATH, LOGAN. AND I AM SO SICK OF DEATH -- eh?!

ABOVE US! THAT SOUND!

SENTINELS!!

AARRRGH!!

FRANKLIN!!

ALL UNITS, ALERT! PATROL 3L-40 HAS CONTACTED MUTANT ESCAPEES FROM SOUTH BRONX INTERNMENT FACILITY.

MUTANTS, YOU ARE ADVISED TO SURRENDER OR FACE IMMEDIATE TERMINATION. THIS IS YOUR ONLY WARNING.

F-FRANKLIN, HE... HE... OH, STORM, HELP ME! WHEN HE DIED, I FELT IT, IN MY MIND!

I KNOW, RACHEL. BUT YOU MUSTN'T YIELD TO YOUR PAIN, YOUR GRIEF. WE NEED YOU!

121

I WON'T BREAK, STORM.

THOSE BLOODY ROBOTS KILLED MY MAN. THE LEAST I CAN DO IN RETURN IS -- *KILL THEM!!*

WARNING! *WARNING!* THIS UNIT UNDER TELEKINETIC ATTACK --

SKWAURGGHH!

CENTRAL CONTROL. ALL CITY ALERT! MUTANT CONTACTS NOT WEARING INHIBITOR COLLARS. PATROL 3L-40 REQUESTING IMMEDIATE REENFORCEMENT.

IDENTIFICATION: THIS UNIT FACING THE X-MAN, STORM.

THE FORCE OF MY LIGHTNING BOLTS IS STAGGERING THE SENTINAL, BUT I'M NOT DOING HIM ANY REAL DAMAGE. HE'S TOO WELL INSULATED.

RACHEL, GUARD KATE -- WITH YOUR LIFE!

HOLA, WOLVERINE! IT'S BEEN A LONG WHILE SINCE WE'VE PRACTICED A "*FAST-BALL SPECIAL,*" HAS IT NOT?

TOO LONG, PAL.

AS NIGHTCRAWLER USED TO SAY: "*UP, UP, AND AWAY!*"

MUSCLES CLENCH, SYNAPSES CLOSE, AND GLEAMING *ADAMANTIUM CLAWS* POP OUT OF THE BACKS OF WOLVERINE'S HANDS. THESE RETRACTABLE CLAWS ARE FORGED OF THE *STRONGEST METAL KNOWN* -- ONE FAR STRONGER THAN THE SENTINAL'S OMNIUM STEEL BODIES.

LIKEWISE, HIS ENTIRE SKELETON IS LACED WITH THAT SAME MIRACLE METAL, MAKING HIS BONES VIRTUALLY UNBREAKABLE. ADD TO THAT A *BERSERKER FURY* THAT GIVES HIM THE FIGHTING PROWESS OF A SCORE OF HEROES...

SQUAWRRRRKK!

...AND IT'S NO WONDER THAT EVEN THESE EMOTION- LESS ROBOTS RESPECT -- AND ALMOST *FEAR* -- HIM

THIS UNIT CRITICALLY DAMAGED, BUT STILL FUNCTIONAL. MUTANT ASSAILANT IDENTIFIED AS WOLVERINE HAS BEEN CAPTURED. TERMINATION IMMINENT.

STORM, I'VE GIVEN YOU AN OPENING! FINISH THIS SUCKER!

AS GOOD AS DONE, WOLVERINE.

THIS LIGHTNING BOLT SHOULD REDUCE THE SENTINEL'S COMPUTER BRAIN TO SO MUCH SLAG.

WAY TA GO, DARLIN'! COLOSSUS AN' RACHEL ZAPPED THE LAST ONE!

THREE DOWN. HOW MANY MILLION TO GO?

COMPANY IS COMING, MY FRIENDS.

ANOTHER TRIAD PATROL.

THE LONGER WE STAY IN ONE PLACE, THE MORE VULNERABLE WE BECOME. NO MATTER HOW HARD-- OR WELL-- WE FIGHT, THE SENTINELS CAN OVERWHELM US THROUGH SHEER WEIGHT OF NUMBERS.

OUR ONLY HOPE IS TO HIT AND RUN, AND NEVER LET OURSELVES BE BACKED INTO A CORNER.

ALERT! CONTACT ESTABLISHED WITH MUTANT X-MAN, COLOSSUS!

IF I HIT THE BASE OF THIS DERELICT HOTEL PRECISELY RIGHT...

...I THINK I CAN GIVE OUR WOULD-BE PURSUERS A HEADACHE THEY'LL NEVER FORGET.

THE ROBOTS' SCREAMS ARE FRIGHTENINGLY HUMAN...

...BUT COLOSSUS DOES NOT CARE.

HE WAS THE GENTLEST OF SOULS, UNTIL THE SENTINELS SLEW HIS FRIENDS, AND HIS CHILDREN-- AND THEREBY TAUGHT HIM HOW TO HATE.

WE MUST PUSH ON. THE BAXTER BUILDING IS THE SENTINELS' CONTINENTAL NERVE CENTER. DESTROY IT AND WE CAN CRIPPLE THEM.

I WISH KATE LUCK, WHEREVER SHE IS. I DO NOT KNOW WHO WILL NEED IT MORE...

...HER-- OR US.

OCTOBER 31, 1980 -- *WASHINGTON, D.C.*

THIS IS THE PENTAGON, THE LARGEST BUILDING OF ITS TYPE IN THE WORLD, COMMAND HEADQUARTERS OF THE MIGHTIEST MILITARY MACHINE THAT WORLD HAS EVER KNOWN.

TO MANY PEOPLE, IT IS MORE TRULY REPRESENTATIVE -- FOR GOOD OR ILL -- OF THE *REALITY OF AMERICA* THAN THE WHITE HOUSE OR CONGRESS JUST ACROSS THE *POTOMIC RIVER.*

DEEP WITHIN THIS MAN-MADE LABYRINTH, WE FIND A YOUNG WOMAN NAMED *RAVEN DARKHOLME.*

COLONEL, I'LL EXPECT THE LATEST *"STEALTH"* TEST RESULTS ON MY DESK MONDAY MORNING.

YOU'LL HAVE 'EM, MA'AM.

SHE WORKS OUT OF THE OFFICE OF THE ASSISTANT SECRETARY OF DEFENSE FOR RESEARCH AND DEVELOPMENT AND, AS SUCH, HAS ACCESS TO THE MOST SECRET AND SOPHISTICATED WEAPONRY IN AMERICA'S ARSENAL.

SHE'S EARNED HER POSITION, AND THE COMPLETE TRUST OF HER SUPERIORS.

UNFORTUNATELY, THAT LOYALTY IS AS MUCH AN *ILLUSION* AS HER APPEARANCE.

FOR RAVEN DARKHOLME IS A *METAMORPH,* A *SHAPE-SHIFTER* --

-- A *MUTANT,* BETTER KNOWN TO HER COMRADES AS *MYSTIQUE*...

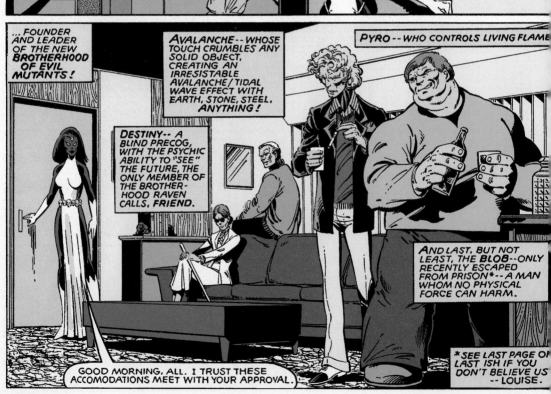

... FOUNDER AND LEADER OF THE NEW *BROTHERHOOD OF EVIL MUTANTS!*

AVALANCHE -- WHOSE TOUCH CRUMBLES ANY SOLID OBJECT, CREATING AN IRRESISTABLE AVALANCHE/TIDAL WAVE EFFECT WITH EARTH, STONE, STEEL, ANYTHING!

PYRO -- WHO CONTROLS LIVING FLAME

DESTINY -- A BLIND PRECOG, WITH THE PSYCHIC ABILITY TO *"SEE"* THE FUTURE, THE ONLY MEMBER OF THE BROTHERHOOD RAVEN CALLS, *FRIEND.*

AND LAST, BUT NOT LEAST, THE *BLOB* -- ONLY RECENTLY ESCAPED FROM PRISON* -- A MAN WHOM NO PHYSICAL FORCE CAN HARM.

*SEE LAST PAGE OF LAST ISH IF YOU DON'T BELIEVE US -- LOUISE.

GOOD MORNING, ALL. I TRUST THESE ACCOMODATIONS MEET WITH YOUR APPROVAL.

NO COMPLAINTS? HOW NICE.

DESTINY, WHAT DOES THE FUTURE HOLD?

IT'S HARD TO BE CERTAIN, RAVEN. I SENSE A VARIABLE-- A NEW RANDOM ELEMENT THAT COULD SERIOUSLY AFFECT OUR PLAN. I'VE BEEN UN-ABEL TO FOCUS ON IT.

ALSO, THE BLOB IS... UNCOMFORTABLE... WITH YOUR LEADERSHIP. THERE IS A POTENTIAL FOR TROUBLE.

BLOB?

HEY, RAY, YOU HELPED ME BUST OUTTA THE JOINT, YA GOT ME THREADS, BREAD, A CLASSY PAD-- FER THAT I'M GRATEFUL.

WELL, LAH-DEE-DAH, CHUNKY. YOU THINK *YOU* CAN DO BETTER?

I JUST DON'T TAKE ORDERS FROM A BROAD.

BLOW IT OUT YOUR UNION JACK, LIMEY.

THIS IS BETWEEN ME AN'--

YEEOWW!

WATCH YOUR MOUTH, AND REMEMBER YOUR PLACE, OR THE NEXT TIME YOU LIGHT A MATCH...

...I'LL CREATE A DEMON THAT WILL *PAR-BROIL*, INSTEAD OF SCARE, YOU.

I'VE TAKEN ALL THE LIP FROM YOU I'M GONNA, ENGLISHMAN! *FRED J. DUKES* AIN'T NO TWO-BIT AMATEUR!

I WAS PART O' THE *ORIGINAL* BROTHERHOOD. I WORKED FER *MAGNETO!*

IF THAT WAS SUCH AN HONOR, BLOB, HOW COME YOU SPENT THE LAST FEW YEARS IN PRISON?

THAT SCULPTURE-- AVALANCHE, YOU *DISINTEGRATED* IT!

A MINOR DEMONSTRATION OF MY POWER.

WELL, I DON'T NEED NO HUNK'A ROCK TA PULVERIZE THIS PUNK.

THAT'S *ENOUGH,* ALL OF YOU!

YOU'RE CORRECT, BLOB. I'M NOT MAGNETO. BUT CROSS ME-- IN *ANY* WAY-- AND YOU'LL FIND I CAN BE AS IMPLACABLE AND *DEADLY* A FOE AS THE MASTER OF MAGNETISM EVER WAS.

NOW, PREPARE YOURSELVES, MUTANTS. THE TIME HAS COME-- TO *STRIKE!*

THE UNITED STATES SENATE HAS BEEN DESCRIBED AS THE GREATEST DELIBERATIVE BODY ON EARTH. IT HAS SEEN NOBLE TIMES AND SHAMEFUL ONES. IT HAS EPITOMIZED THE HIGHEST IDEALS OF HUMANITY...

...AND THE WORST REALITIES.

TODAY, ONCE AGAIN, IT-- AND THE PEOPLE IT REPRESENTS-- ARE BEING PUT TO THE TEST.

WE ARE GATHERED HERE TO ADDRESS AN ISSUE OF CRITICAL NATIONAL AND INTERNATIONAL IMPORTANCE. THIS IS NOT A WITCH HUNT BUT, WE HOPE AND PRAY, A SEARCH FOR TRUTH.

MUCH ABOUT OUR WORLD HAS CHANGED IN RECENT YEARS. WE FACE SITUATIONS-- AND THREATS-- UN-DREAMED OF BY EARLIER GENERATIONS.

ONE SUCH IS THE APPEARANCE OF HOMO SUPERIOR -- MUTANTS! FLESH OF OUR FLESH, BLOOD OF OUR BLOOD, YET POSSESSING POWERS AND ABILITIES WHICH SET THEM APART-- SOME WOULD SAY ABOVE-- THE REST OF HUMANITY.

KELLY'S LAYING IT ON A BIT THICK.

SO WHAT ELSE IS NEW?

AMONG OUR WITNESSES ARE PROFESSOR CHARLES XAVIER, WORLD-RENOWNED EXPERT ON GENETICS, AND Dr. MOIRA MacTAGGERT OF EDINBURGH UNIVERSITY, WHOSE WORK IN THE FIELD HAS WON HER A NOBEL PRIZE.

IF YOU ASK ME, CHARLES, THAT SOD'S ALREADY MADE UP HIS MIND. REGISTRATION OF MUTANTS TODAY, GAS CHAMBERS TOMORROW.

BE CHARITABLE, MOIRA. HE'S SCARED.

WE MUST TEACH HIM THAT HIS FEAR IS UNFOUNDED.

COMING THROUGH THE DOOR-- PETER, ORORO AND... KITTY! I'D BEST CONTACT THEM TELEPATHICALLY.

STORM, WHAT ARE YOU DOING HERE? IS SOMETHING WRONG?

YOU MIGHT SAY THAT, PROFESSOR.

OPEN YOUR MIND TO ME, CHILD. YOUR MEMORIES WILL EXPLAIN MATTERS FAR MORE EFFECTIVELY THAN YOUR WORDS.

OVER-COMING AN INSTINCTIVE FLASH OF RELUCTANCE AND DISTASTE, STORM DOES AS SHE'S TOLD.

OHO! THIS HEARING'S GETTING INTERESTING. THAT'S *WARREN WORTHINGTON.* HE'S A MUTIE. HIS HANDLE'S *THE ANGEL.* HE USED TO BANKROLL A WEST COAST SUPER-GROUP CALLED *THE CHAMPIONS.*

TELL LOIS TO TRY FOR AN INTERVIEW.

SENATOR, IN ALL HONESTY, I FAIL TO SEE THE NEED FOR THIS HEARING, OR YOUR CONCERN.

THE NEED IS SIMPLE, Dr. MacTAGGERT. I MERELY WONDER IF-- IN A WORLD OF BEINGS LIKE Dr. DOOM, MAGNETO, THE FANTASTIC FOUR, THE AVENGERS, AND LORD KNOWS HOW MANY OTHERS--

--THERE'S ANY PLACE FOR ORDINARY MEN AND WOMEN.

I WONDER, AS WELL, DOCTOR, IF THIS SAME QUESTION WASN'T ASKED BY THE LAST NEANDERTHAL ABOUT THE FIRST CRO-MAGNON?

≩?!?≨

HOLEE--!

GET OUTTA HERE, YOU PEOPLE! RUN FOR IT!!

THAT WALL'S COMIN' DOWN!!

YYIIII--!

HELP!

AND, WHEN THE AVALANCHE HAS RUN ITS COURSE...

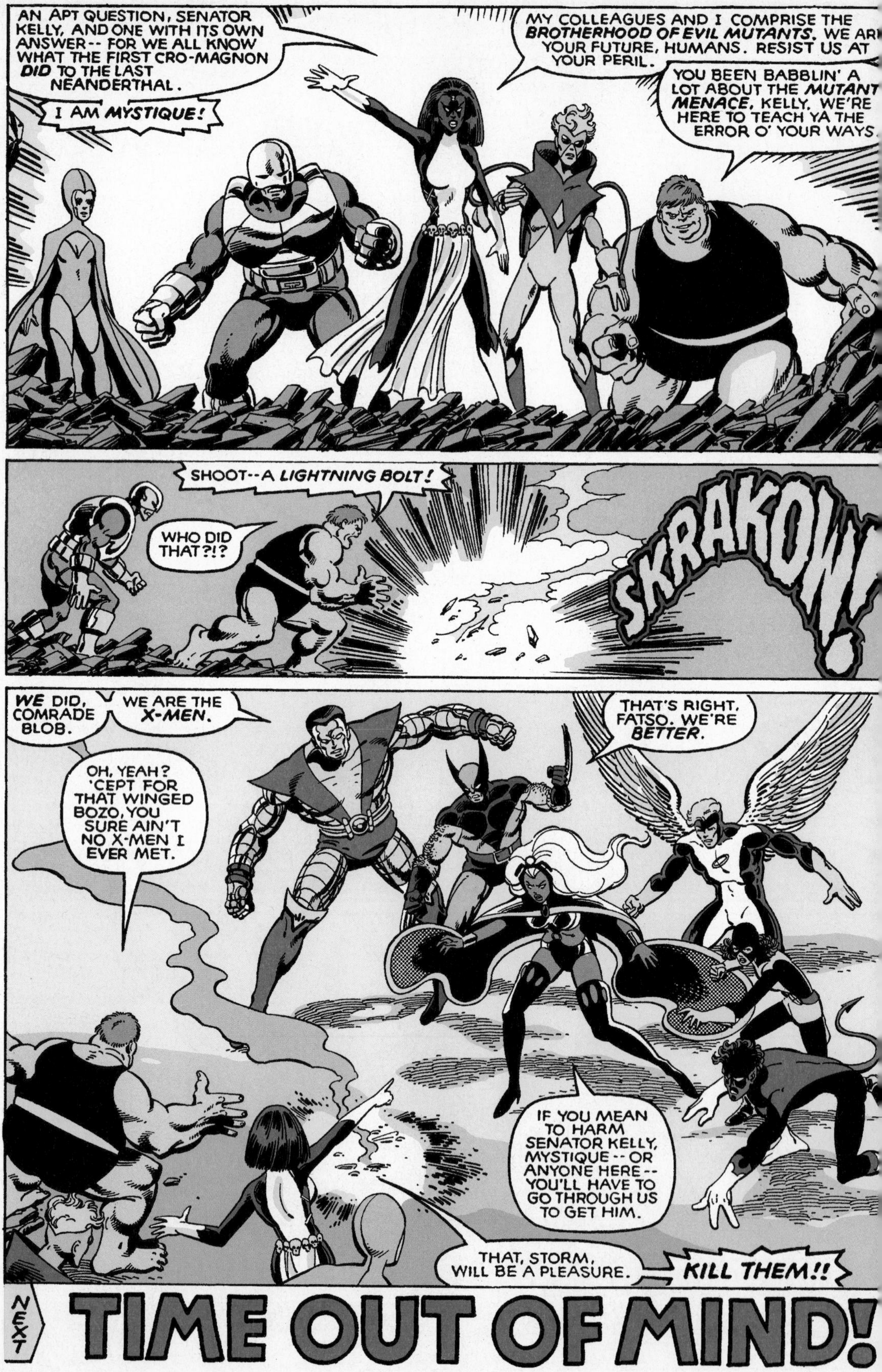

AN APT QUESTION, SENATOR KELLY, AND ONE WITH ITS OWN ANSWER-- FOR WE ALL KNOW WHAT THE FIRST CRO-MAGNON DID TO THE LAST NEANDERTHAL.
I AM MYSTIQUE!
MY COLLEAGUES AND I COMPRISE THE BROTHERHOOD OF EVIL MUTANTS. WE ARE YOUR FUTURE, HUMANS. RESIST US AT YOUR PERIL.
YOU BEEN BABBLIN' A LOT ABOUT THE MUTANT MENACE, KELLY. WE'RE HERE TO TEACH YA THE ERROR O' YOUR WAYS.
SHOOT--A LIGHTNING BOLT!
WHO DID THAT?!?
SKRAKOW!
WE DID, COMRADE BLOB.
WE ARE THE X-MEN.
THAT'S RIGHT, FATSO. WE'RE BETTER.
OH, YEAH? 'CEPT FOR THAT WINGED BOZO, YOU SURE AIN'T NO X-MEN I EVER MET.
IF YOU MEAN TO HARM SENATOR KELLY, MYSTIQUE -- OR ANYONE HERE -- YOU'LL HAVE TO GO THROUGH US TO GET HIM.
THAT, STORM, WILL BE A PLEASURE.
KILL THEM!!
NEXT
TIME OUT OF MIND!

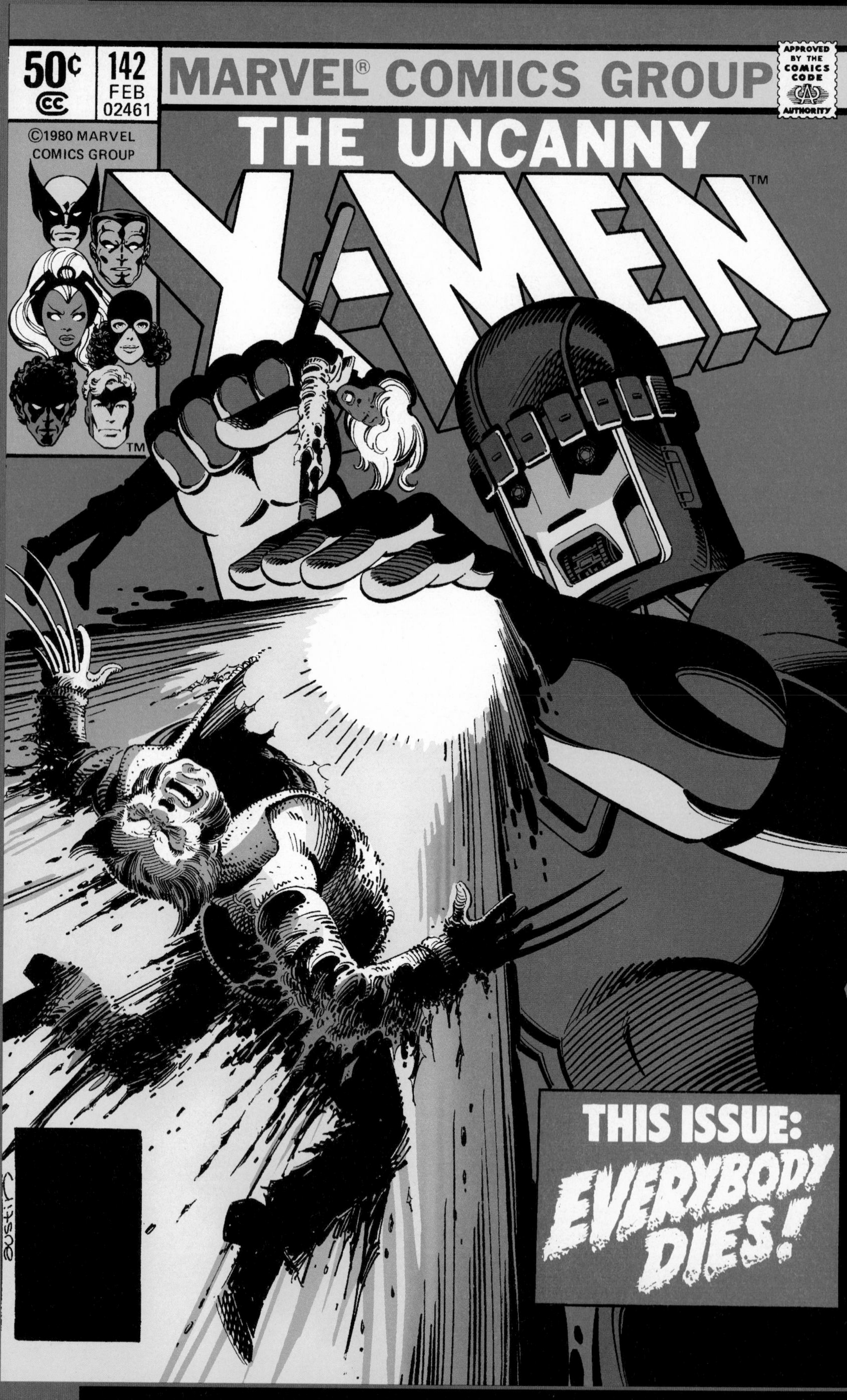
50¢
CC
142
FEB
02461
MARVEL® COMICS GROUP
APPROVED BY THE COMICS CODE AUTHORITY
©1980 MARVEL COMICS GROUP
THE UNCANNY
X-MEN™
TM
THIS ISSUE:
EVERYBODY DIES!
austin

STAN LEE presents: THE UNCANNY X-MEN!

CHRIS CLAREMONT • JOHN BYRNE | TERRY AUSTIN | GLYNIS WEIN, colorist | LOUISE JONES | JIM SHOOTER
WRITER / CO-PLOTTERS / PENCILER | INKER | TOM ORZECHOWSKI, letterer | EDITOR | Ed.-IN-CHIEF

THIS IS A TALE OF TWO WORLDS -- AND OF THE CHILD/WOMAN WHO SOUGHT TO SAVE THEM.

MIND OUT OF TIME!

1980-- THE UNCANNY X-MEN (WOLVERINE, COLOSSUS, STORM, ANGEL, SPRITE & NIGHTCRAWLER) FACE OFF AGAINST THE NEWLY-RECONSTITUTED BROTHERHOOD OF EVIL MUTANTS IN A HEARING ROOM OF THE UNITED STATES SENATE.

2013-- THE REMNANTS OF THAT SELF-SAME TEAM OF MUTANT SUPER-HEROES FIGHT FOR THEIR LIVES AGAINST THE NIGH-IRRESISTIBLE MIGHT OF THE SENTINELS...

...IN A LAST-DITCH ATTEMPT TO SAVE THEIR WORLD FROM IMMINENT NUCLEAR ARMAGEDDON.

AND LINKING THESE TWO WORLDS, THESE TWO DESPERATE BATTLES, IS KATHERINE PRYDE. IN HER HANDS LIES THE FATE OF MUTANTKIND, OF HUMANITY, OF THE EARTH ITSELF. FAILURE IS UNTHINKABLE, YET SUCCESS MAY WELL BE IMPOSSIBLE -- FOR SHE SEEKS TO CHANGE HISTORY.

OF THE ORIGINAL BROTHERHOOD, ONLY THE BLOB REMAINS, JOINED NOW BY THE BLIND PRECOG, *DESTINY,* WHO CAN SEE THE FUTURE.

PYRO-- MASTER OF THE LIVING FLAME.

AVALANCHE-- WHOSE TOUCH DISINTEGRATES INANIMATE OBJECTS.

AND THE GROUP'S LEADER, THE MYSTERIOUS SHAPE-CHANGER CALLED *MYSTIQUE.*

SENATOR KELLY IS FOND OF SPEAKING AGAINST THE MUTA MENACE. MY COLLEAGUES AN I ARE THAT MENACE INCARNA AS AN EXAMPLE OF OUR DRE POWER-- AS AN OBJECT LESSO TO THOSE WHO WOULD OPPOS US-- WE INTEND TO *KILL HIM*

THIS IS MONSTROUS! HOW *DARE* YOU FREAKS TURN THE UNITED STATES SENATE INTO A BATTLE- FIELD?!

HOW DARE YOU THREATEN ME! MARSHALS, *ARREST* THOSE... PEOPLE!

KELLY, YOU'RE EITHER THE BRAVEST MAN I EVER SEEN, OR THE DUMBEST. EITHER WAY, YOU'RE GONNA *DIE* TODAY!

THAT'S ENOUGH OUTTA YOU, FATSO. YOU AN' YOUR MUTIE PLAYMATES HAVE GONE TOO FAR THIS TIME, AN' YOU'RE GONNA PAY FOR IT!

COME ALONG QUIETLY-- ALL OF YOU-- OR ELSE!

WHOOO--EE! YOU GOT ME SHAKIN' IN MY BOOTS, COP! CHUMP, YOU'RE TALKIN' TA THE *BLOB!*

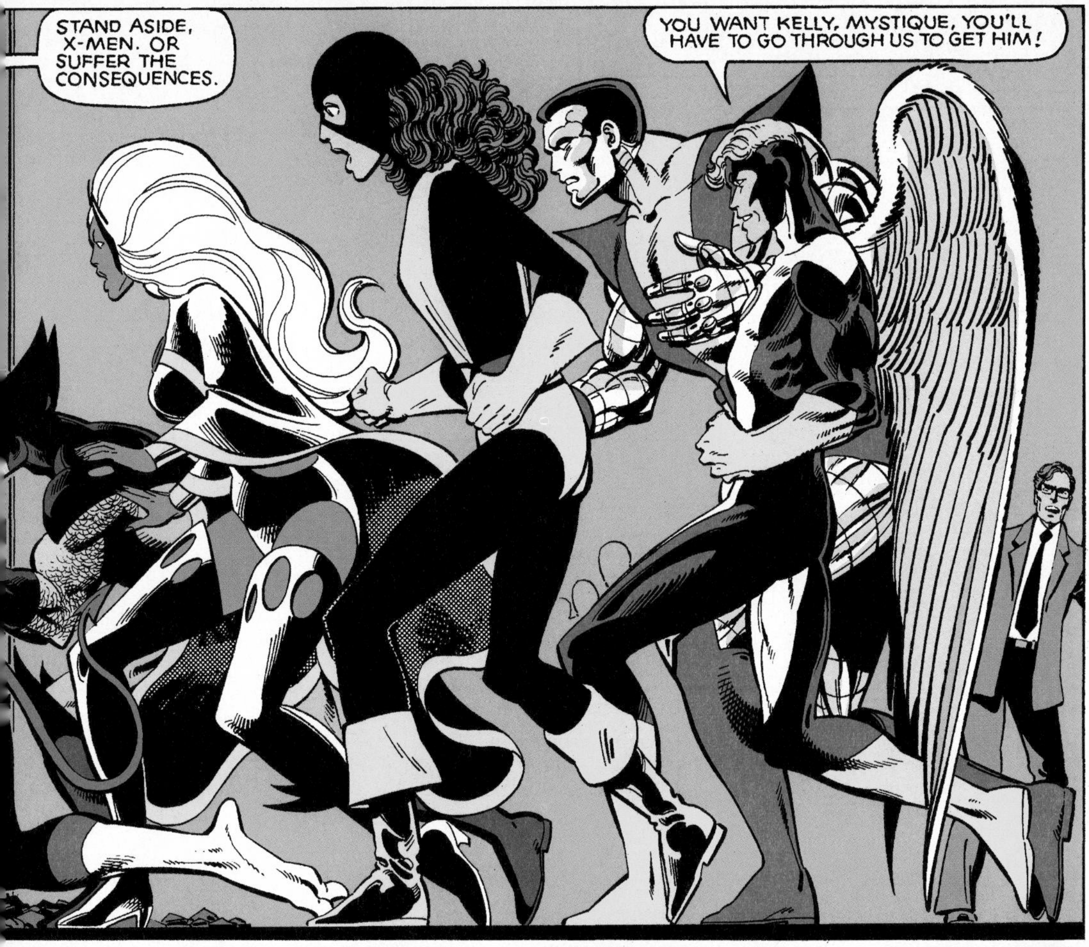
STAND ASIDE, X-MEN. OR SUFFER THE CONSEQUENCES.
YOU WANT KELLY, MYSTIQUE, YOU'LL HAVE TO GO THROUGH US TO GET HIM!

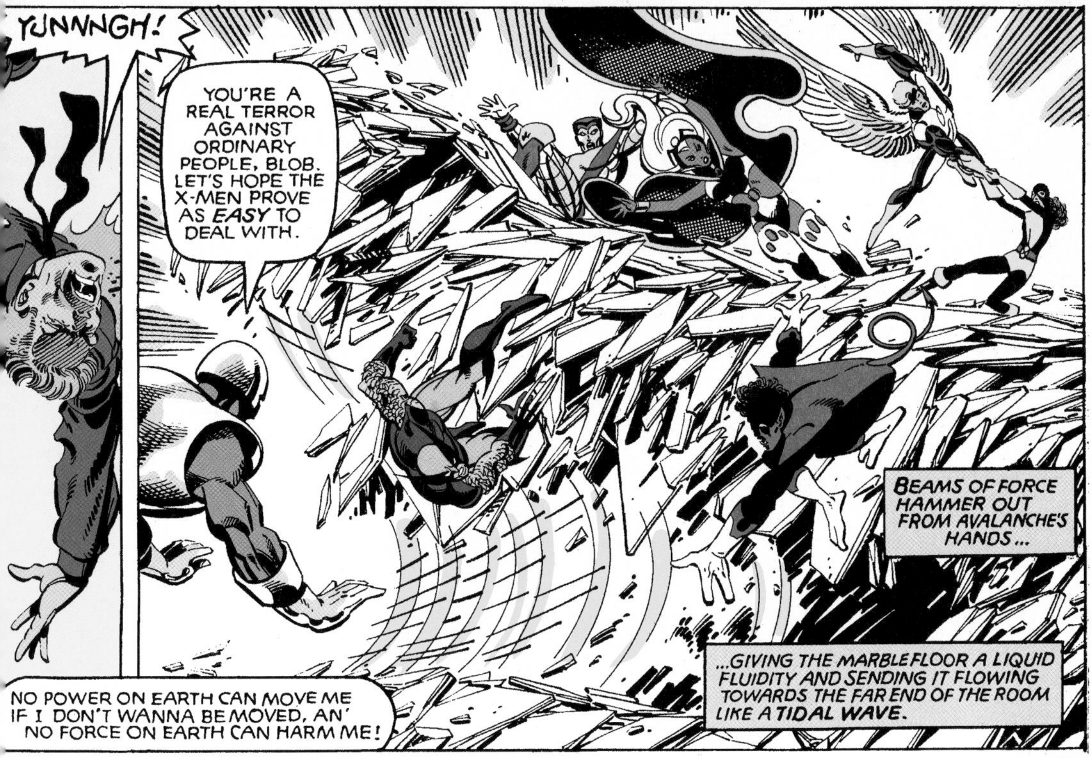
YUNNNGH!
YOU'RE A REAL TERROR AGAINST ORDINARY PEOPLE, BLOB. LET'S HOPE THE X-MEN PROVE AS EASY TO DEAL WITH.
NO POWER ON EARTH CAN MOVE ME IF I DON'T WANNA BE MOVED, AN' NO FORCE ON EARTH CAN HARM ME!
BEAMS OF FORCE HAMMER OUT FROM AVALANCHE'S HANDS...
...GIVING THE MARBLE FLOOR A LIQUID FLUIDITY AND SENDING IT FLOWING TOWARDS THE FAR END OF THE ROOM LIKE A TIDAL WAVE.

NIGHTCRAWLER REACTS FIRST, USING ACROBATIC SKILLS HONED BY A LIFETIME IN THE CIRCUS TO KEEP HIS BALANCE ON THE SWIFTLY TILTING FLOOR.

THEN, HE ATTACKS-- IN A STYLE UNIQUELY HIS OWN.

BAMF

HE TELEPORTS...

... MATERIALIZING AGAIN AND AGAIN RIGHT BEHIND AVALANCHE.

I CAN PUNCH AND DISAPPEAR FAR FASTER THAN YOU CAN REACT, HERR LAWINE. EVEN YOUR ARMOR WON'T PROTECT YOU FOR LONG AGAINST THIS FIERCE AN ASSAULT.

AVALANCHE, STRIKE TO YOUR LEFT!

THAT IS WHERE NIGHTCRAWLER WILL REAPPEAR!

WHOULFF!!

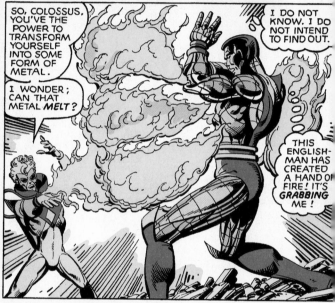

SO, COLOSSUS, YOU'VE THE POWER TO TRANSFORM YOURSELF INTO SOME FORM OF METAL.

I WONDER; CAN THAT METAL MELT?

I DO NOT KNOW. I DO NOT INTEND TO FIND OUT.

THIS ENGLISH-MAN HAS CREATED A HAND OF FIRE! IT'S GRABBING ME!

THAT'S A FANCY FLAME-THROWER YOU'RE PACKIN', BUB.

I WONDER WHAT'LL HAPPEN IF I PUNCH MY CLAWS THROUGH THE FUEL TANK AND INTO YOUR STINKIN' HIDE!

WOLVERINE'S RETRACTABLE CLAWS ARE FORGED OF ADAMANTIUM, THE STRONGEST METAL KNOWN. AND HE HAS NO COMPUNCTION ABOUT USING THEM.

WOLVERINE, DON'T!

STORM-- HAVE YOU FLIPPED?! WHADDAYA THINK YOU'RE DOIN'?!

THE X-MEN'S NEWLY-APPOINTED TEAM LEADER IGNORES WOLVERINE'S IMPASSIONED PROTESTS, AS SHE USES HER ELEMENTAL POWERS...

... TO SIMULTANEOUSLY CREATE A WHIRLWIND THAT YANKS WOLVERINE AWAY FROM PYRO, AND A TORRENTIAL BLAST OF RAIN TO DOUSE THE FLAME HAND AROUND COLOSSUS.

NICE MOVE, STORM. WITH THE COUNTRY'S GROWING ANTI-MUTANT SENTIMENT, THE LAST THING WE NEED IS WOLVIE CARVING SOMEONE UP-- EVEN IF IT IS A VILLAIN.

ANGEL, FIND SENATOR KELLY! HE MUST BE PROTECTED AT ANY COST!

*NEARBY, SCRAMBLING FOR THEIR LIVES, ARE THE X-MEN'S FOUNDER AND MENTOR, **PROFESSOR CHARLES XAVIER**, AND HIS COLLEAGUE IN MUTANT RESEARCH -- ALSO, HIS ONE-TIME LOVE -- MOIRA MacTAGGERT.*

CHARLES, WHAT THE DEVIL IS HAPPENING?!

IT'S ALMOST TOO FANTASTIC TO BELIEVE. SOMEHOW, THE MIND AND PERSONA OF THE **ADULT** KATE PRYDE -- FROM 30 YEARS IN THE FUTURE -- HAS PSYCHICALLY EXCHANGED PLACES WITH THAT OF HER TEEN-AGED SELF.

THE BODY OF **SPRITE** IS INHABITED BY THE CONSCIOUSNESS OF THE WOMAN SHE WILL ONE DAY BECOME.

THAT'S DAFT!

MOIRA, I TELEPATHICALLY SCANNED HER MIND. IT IS THE **TRUTH**.

PROFESSOR XAVIER, LET'S GET YOU AND Dr. MacTAGGERT OUT OF HERE!

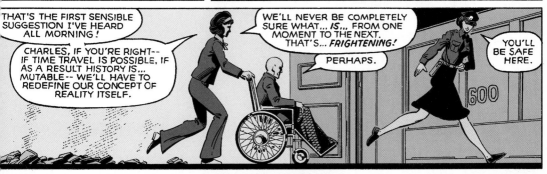

THAT'S THE FIRST SENSIBLE SUGGESTION I'VE HEARD ALL MORNING!

CHARLES, IF YOU'RE RIGHT-- IF TIME TRAVEL IS POSSIBLE, IF AS A RESULT HISTORY IS... MUTABLE-- WE'LL HAVE TO REDEFINE OUR CONCEPT OF REALITY ITSELF.

WE'LL NEVER BE COMPLETELY SURE WHAT... IS... FROM ONE MOMENT TO THE NEXT. THAT'S... **FRIGHTENING!**

PERHAPS.

YOU'LL BE SAFE HERE.

600

THANK GOODNESS.

WAIT! MOIRA, I SENSE SOME SORT OF ENERGY FIELD AROUND THIS WOMAN. SHE IS **NOT** WHAT SHE SEEMS--

AARGKGH!

YOU SPOTTED THE ELECTRONIC **DAMPER FIELD** WHICH KEPT YOU FROM READING MY MIND, XAVIER...

...UNTIL IT WAS **TOO LATE** TO DO YOU ANY GOOD.

THAT SHOT OF NERVE GAS INSTANTLY PARALYZED YOU. NOW, DEPRIVED OF YOUR TELEPATHIC GUIDANCE, WITH ONLY THE WOEFULLY INEXPERIENCED *STORM* TO LEAD THEM, THE X-MEN WILL BE FATALLY CRIPPLED.

YOU ARE MY MOST DANGEROUS FOE, XAVIER. I SHOULD KILL YOU WHILE I HAVE THE CHANCE, BUT FOR THE MOMENT, I THINK, YOU'RE OF MORE USE AS A POTENTIAL *HOSTAGE*.

HOW FARES OUR FUTURE, DESTINY?

I AM NOT SURE. BEYOND A CERTAIN POINT, THE IMAGES BECOME JUMBLED, DIFFICULT TO READ.

THERE IS A RANDOM FACTOR PRESENT, MYSTIQUE, AN *ANOMALY* THAT STRIKES TO THE VERY HEART OF THE TIME STREAM. SO LONG AS IT EXISTS, *NOTHING* IS CERTAIN. I'VE TRIED TO PINPOINT IT, WITHOUT SUCCESS.

NO MATTER. WITH OR WITHOUT YOUR FORSEEING HELP, MY FRIEND, THE BROTHERHOOD WILL PREVAIL.

AND, SPEAKING OF DESTINY'S TEMPORAL "ANOMALY"...

SOMETHING'S GONE TERRIBLY WRONG! MY PRESENCE HERE HASN'T CHANGED A BLESSED THING! HAVE I ENDURED-- AND GAMBLED--SO MUCH...

...ONLY TO *FAIL*?!?

KATE PRYDE'S THOUGHTS TWIST FORWARD ACROSS THE DECADES TO HER HOME -- A NORTH AMERICA RULED BY *SENTINELS* (GIANT, SUPER-SOPHISTICATED ROBOTS PROGRAMMED TO STAMP OUT MUTANT-KIND).

BY THE TURN OF THE CENTURY, VIRTUALLY EVERY MUTANT, SUPER HERO AND SUPER-VILLAIN IN THE UNITED STATES AND CANADA HAD BEEN EITHER SLAIN OR IMPRISONED. NOW, THE SENTINELS PREPARED TO EXPAND THEIR OPERATIONS TO THE REST OF THE WORLD.

OTHER NATIONS, HOWEVER, VIEWED THAT AS AN ACT OF WAR.

TO HEAD OFF THAT WORLD-DESTROYING CONFRONTATION, THE FEW SURVIVING X-MEN -- JOINED NOW BY MAGNETO -- HATCHED A DESPERATE PLAN. THE SEMINAL EVENT THAT LED TO THE SENTINELS' RE-CREATION...

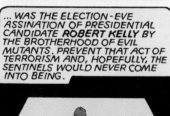

...WAS THE ELECTION-EVE ASSINATION OF PRESIDENTIAL CANDIDATE *ROBERT KELLY* BY THE BROTHERHOOD OF EVIL MUTANTS. PREVENT THAT ACT OF TERRORISM AND, HOPEFULLY, THE SENTINELS WOULD NEVER COME INTO BEING.

THE TIME-SWITCH HAD BEEN MADE...

... AND THE X-MEN PURSUADED TO RUSH TO WASHINGTON TO BLOCK THE BROTHERHOOD'S ATTACK. BUT AS THE BATTLE WEARS ON...

... KATE REALIZES BITTERLY THAT HISTORY IS PROVING FAR *HARDER* TO CHANGE THAN SHE ANTICIPATED. *

*FOR DETAILS, SEE LAST ISH -- LOUISE.

IN THAT FUTURE, THE FOUR PEOPLE WHOM KATE PRYDE LOVES MOST, SLOWLY, CAREFULLY PICK THEIR WAY THROUGH THE RUINS OF MIDTOWN MANHATTAN. WOLVERINE, STORM AND RACHEL ARE THE TRUEST FRIENDS SHE COULD EVER WISH FOR -- BUT *PETER RASPUTIN (COLOSSUS)* IS HER BELOVED *HUSBAND*.

FOR KATE, THE MOST TERRIBLE IRONY OF THEIR PLAN IS THAT, IF IT SUCEEDS, THE LOVE SHE AND PETER SHARED MIGHT VANISH ALONG WITH THE SENTINELS. BUT THE RISK -- THE POTENTIAL LOSS -- WAS ACCEPTED. THERE WAS SIMPLY NO ALTERNATIVE.

HOLD IT! ANOTHER PATROL!

THE SENTINELS ARE BUSY TONIGHT.

NOT SURPRISING, CONSIDERING I SUCCESSFULLY BUSTED YOU OUT OF YOUR SOUTH BRONX CONCENTRATION CAMP, TRASHING MORE'N OUR FAIR SHARE O' SENTINELS IN THE PROCESS.

THEY'LL BE EXPECTING US TO TRY TO MAKE CONTACT WITH MY OUTFIT, THE CANADIAN RESISTANCE ARMY.

THEY WON'T BE EXPECTING AN ATTACK ON THEIR MAIN HEADQUARTERS, THE *BAXTER BUILDING*.

IF WE KNOCK THAT OUT, WE'LL HAMSTRING THEIR OPERATIONS ACROSS THE ENTIRE CONTINENT. WE'LL HAVE TO HIT HARD AN' FAST...

I WILL TAKE THE LEAD, LOGAN.

OKAY, 'RORO. GOOD LUCK.

MY FRIEND, I STOPPED BELIEVING IN LUCK THE DAY I SAW MY PARENTS SLAIN BEFORE MY EYES, WHILE I SURVIVED. *

*X-MEN #102 -- LOUISE.

ALL MY LIFE, I'VE FLOWN WITH DEATH. I, WHO ONCE SWORE NEVER TO KILL, *HAVE* KILLED.

AND, IF I MUST, I WILL KILL AGAIN.

IN MY OWN WAY, I'VE BE- COME AS HARD, AS RUTHLESS, AS MERCILESS AS WOLVERINE.

I'VE BECOME SO NUMB I CAN'T EVEN HATE MYSELF ANYMORE. IF ANYTHING, MY SOUL FEELS... *TIRED*.

BUT SO LONG AS BREATH REMAINS WITHIN ME, I WILL DO WHAT MUST BE DONE.

RAW ENERGY FLOWS THROUGH STORM-- AUTOMATICALLY SHAPED AND FOCUSED BY HER MIND AND HER MUTANT METABOLISM--MANIFESTING ITSELF AT LAST AS AN AWESOME, IRRESISTIBLE BOLT OF LIGHTNING!

Squarrrrrrrk!

137

THE SENTINEL NEVER KNOWS WHAT HITS IT.

KONG!

RACHEL, YOU REMAIN HERE, TO PROTECT KITTY AS BEST YOU CAN. I WISH I KNEW HOW KATE IS FARING IN THE PAST. WHY IS IT TAKING SO LONG?

I DON'T KNOW, COLOSSUS. *OUR* WORLD MAY NOT CHANGE AT ALL. INSTEAD, KATE'S ACTIONS COULD CREATE AN ENTIRELY *DIFFERENT* TIMELINE... AN ALTERNATE, PARALLEL EARTH.

SO THE TIMESWITCH COULD BE A WASTED EFFORT. GREAT.

WOLVERINE, I'M SORRY. I JUST DON'T KNOW!

STORM, THESE DOORS ARE LOCKED. YOU'LL HAVE TO GIMMICK THE LOCKS AN' ALARMS.

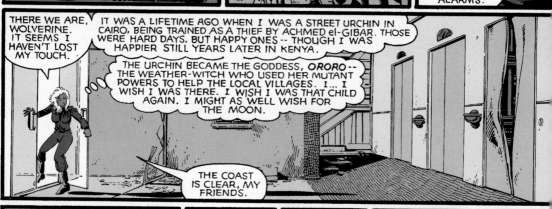
THERE WE ARE, WOLVERINE. IT SEEMS I HAVEN'T LOST MY TOUCH.

IT WAS A LIFETIME AGO WHEN I WAS A STREET URCHIN IN CAIRO, BEING TRAINED AS A THIEF BY ACHMED el-GIBAR. THOSE WERE HARD DAYS, BUT HAPPY ONES -- THOUGH I WAS HAPPIER STILL YEARS LATER IN KENYA.

THE URCHIN BECAME THE GODDESS, *ORORO* -- THE WEATHER-WITCH WHO USED HER MUTANT POWERS TO HELP THE LOCAL VILLAGES. I... I WISH I WAS THERE. I WISH I WAS THAT CHILD AGAIN. I MIGHT AS WELL WISH FOR THE MOON.

THE COAST IS CLEAR, MY FRIENDS.

THE BAXTER BUILDING -- THE OLD H.Q. OF THE *FANTASTIC FOUR* -- CONTAINS SOME OF THE MOST SOPHISTICATED ELECTRONICS LASH-UPS ON EARTH. THAT'S WHY THE SENTINELS CHOSE IT AS THEIR PRIMARY BASE.

BUT IT'S A BASE WITH AN *ACHILLES' HEEL*...

...IF OUR INTELLIGENCE REPORTS ARE ACCURATE, AND THE HOUSEKEEPING SYSTEM'S STILL OPERATIONAL.

THIS ELECTRIC EYE BEAM IN MY BELT BUCKLE SHOULD ACTIVATE THE F.F.'S PRIVATE ELEVATOR.

BINGO! ALL ABOARD! NEXT STOP, THE ROOF --

-- AND THE FIGHT OF OUR LIVES.

NERVOUS, ORORO?

A BIT. MY CLAUSTROPHOBIA. CONFINED SPACES STILL PUT ME ON EDGE. AND I CAN'T HELP THINKING ...

... THAT IT WOULDN'T TAKE MUCH TO TURN THIS TINY BOX... INTO A *DEATHTRAP*.

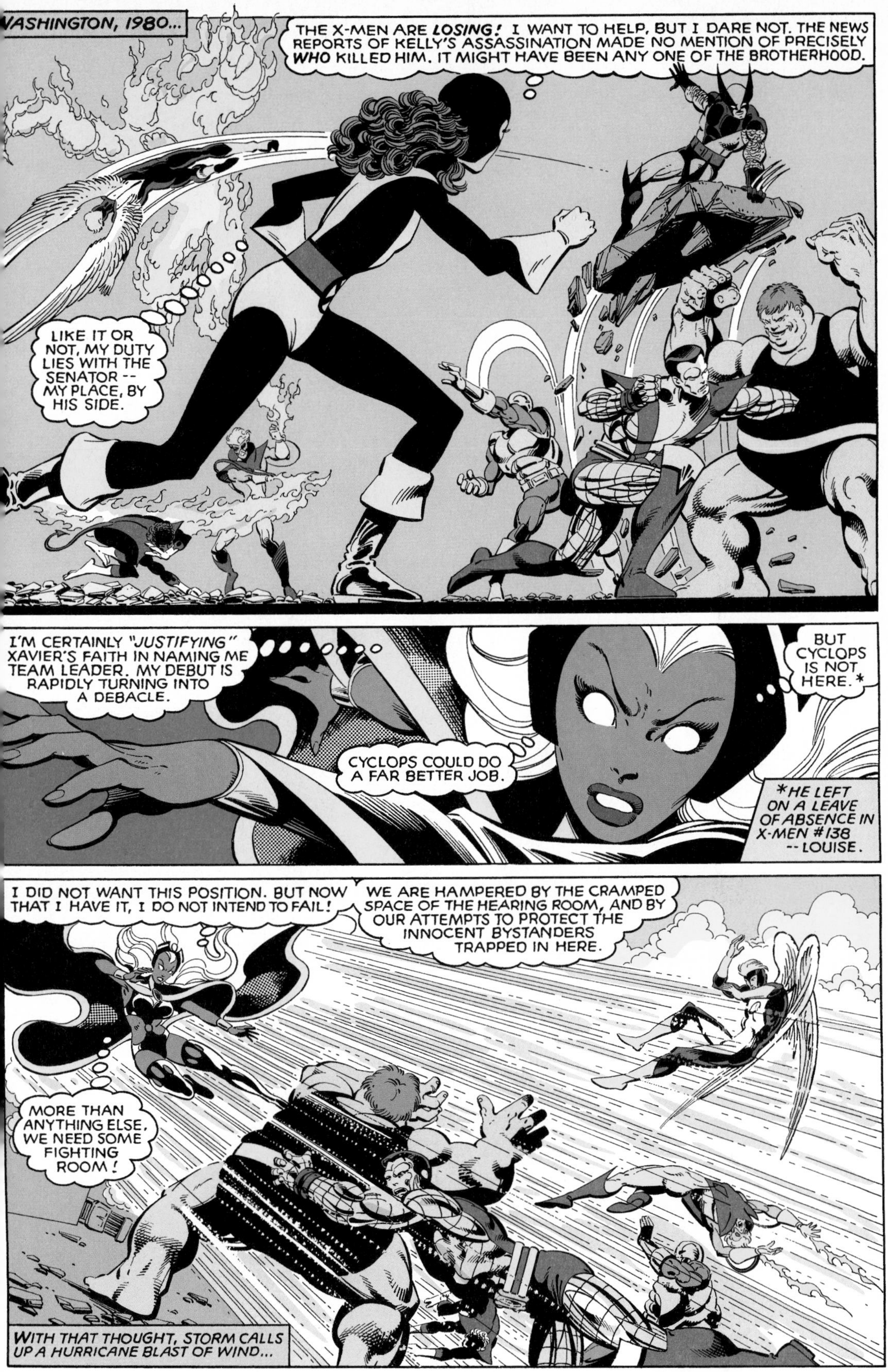
WASHINGTON, 1980...
THE X-MEN ARE LOSING! I WANT TO HELP, BUT I DARE NOT. THE NEWS REPORTS OF KELLY'S ASSASSINATION MADE NO MENTION OF PRECISELY WHO KILLED HIM. IT MIGHT HAVE BEEN ANY ONE OF THE BROTHERHOOD.
LIKE IT OR NOT, MY DUTY LIES WITH THE SENATOR -- MY PLACE, BY HIS SIDE.
I'M CERTAINLY "JUSTIFYING" XAVIER'S FAITH IN NAMING ME TEAM LEADER. MY DEBUT IS RAPIDLY TURNING INTO A DEBACLE.
BUT CYCLOPS IS NOT HERE.*
CYCLOPS COULD DO A FAR BETTER JOB.
*HE LEFT ON A LEAVE OF ABSENCE IN X-MEN #138 -- LOUISE.
I DID NOT WANT THIS POSITION. BUT NOW THAT I HAVE IT, I DO NOT INTEND TO FAIL!
WE ARE HAMPERED BY THE CRAMPED SPACE OF THE HEARING ROOM, AND BY OUR ATTEMPTS TO PROTECT THE INNOCENT BYSTANDERS TRAPPED IN HERE.
MORE THAN ANYTHING ELSE, WE NEED SOME FIGHTING ROOM!
WITH THAT THOUGHT, STORM CALLS UP A HURRICANE BLAST OF WIND...

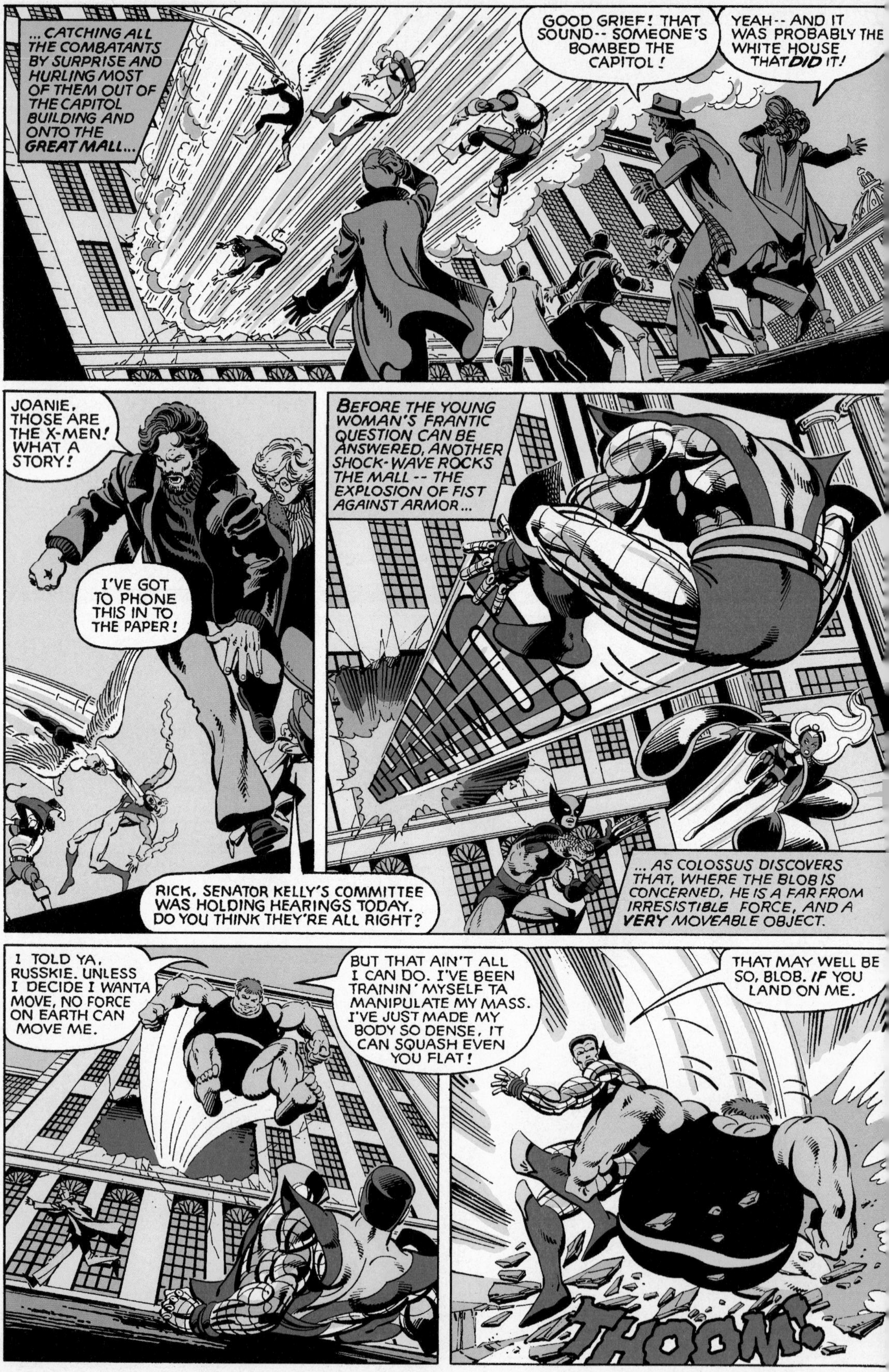
...CATCHING ALL THE COMBATANTS BY SURPRISE AND HURLING MOST OF THEM OUT OF THE CAPITOL BUILDING AND ONTO THE GREAT MALL...
GOOD GRIEF! THAT SOUND-- SOMEONE'S BOMBED THE CAPITOL!
YEAH-- AND IT WAS PROBABLY THE WHITE HOUSE THAT DID IT!
JOANIE, THOSE ARE THE X-MEN! WHAT A STORY!
I'VE GOT TO PHONE THIS IN TO THE PAPER!
RICK, SENATOR KELLY'S COMMITTEE WAS HOLDING HEARINGS TODAY. DO YOU THINK THEY'RE ALL RIGHT?
BEFORE THE YOUNG WOMAN'S FRANTIC QUESTION CAN BE ANSWERED, ANOTHER SHOCK-WAVE ROCKS THE MALL -- THE EXPLOSION OF FIST AGAINST ARMOR...
...AS COLOSSUS DISCOVERS THAT, WHERE THE BLOB IS CONCERNED, HE IS A FAR FROM IRRESISTIBLE FORCE, AND A VERY MOVEABLE OBJECT.
I TOLD YA, RUSSKIE. UNLESS I DECIDE I WANTA MOVE, NO FORCE ON EARTH CAN MOVE ME.
BUT THAT AIN'T ALL I CAN DO. I'VE BEEN TRAININ' MYSELF TA MANIPULATE MY MASS. I'VE JUST MADE MY BODY SO DENSE, IT CAN SQUASH EVEN YOU FLAT!
THAT MAY WELL BE SO, BLOB. IF YOU LAND ON ME.
THOOM!

I'VE BEEN HITTING HIM AS HARD AS I CAN--TO NO EFFECT. IT IS LIKE PUNCHING A BODY MADE OF PORRIDGE.

PERHAPS THE IMPACT HAS STUNNED--

BY THE WHITE WOLF!

SURPRISE, SONNY!

REMEMBER, I NOT ONLY CAN'T BE MOVED, I CAN'T BE HURT, EITHER. *SHEEE-OOT,* I COULD PROBABLY TRASH ALL'A YOU "*NEW*" X-MEN ALL BY MY LONESOME!

UNNOTICED BY EITHER THE X-MEN OR THE BROTHERHOOD, AN ARMY FAST-REACTION, SPECIAL WEAPONS TEAM HAS ARRIVED FROM FORT MYERS.

MAJOR, WHO ARE THE GOOD GUYS AN' WHO ARE THE BAD? WHO DO WE SHOOT AT?!

IT DOESN'T MATTER, SERGEANT. TRASH 'EM ALL! WE'LL SORT OUT THE DETAILS LATER.

CONCUSSION CANNON--*FIRE!*

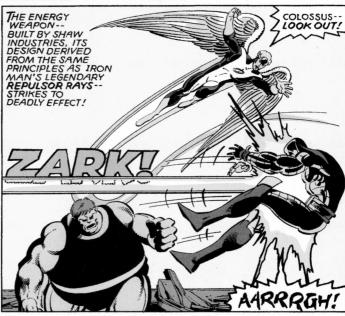

THE ENERGY WEAPON-- BUILT BY SHAW INDUSTRIES, ITS DESIGN DERIVED FROM THE SAME PRINCIPLES AS IRON MAN'S LEGENDARY *REPULSOR RAYS*-- STRIKES TO DEADLY EFFECT!

COLOSSUS-- *LOOK OUT!*

ZARK!

AARRRGH!

THAT'S ONE DOWN. LET'S SEE IF WE CAN'T PERSUADE THE OTHERS...

...THAT THEIR FIGHTING DAYS ARE OVER.

TSK. TSK. A BAD MOVE, GENTLE-MEN--USING FIRE AGAINST ONE WHO CAN SHAPE THOSE FLAMES INTO ANYTHING HE CHOOSES... AND THEN TURN THEM AGAINST YOU.

I TRUST YOU ALL HAVE ADEQUATE PENSIONS. YOUR FAMILIES WILL SOON NEED THEM.

S-SARGE--!!

141

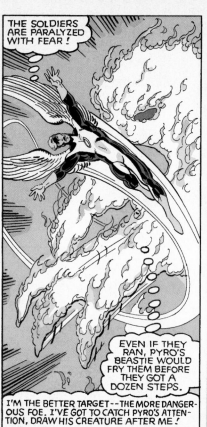

THE SOLDIERS ARE PARALYZED WITH FEAR!

EVEN IF THEY RAN, PYRO'S BEASTIE WOULD FRY THEM BEFORE THEY GOT A DOZEN STEPS.

I'M THE BETTER TARGET--THE MORE DANGEROUS FOE. I'VE GOT TO CATCH PYRO'S ATTENTION, DRAW HIS CREATURE AFTER ME!

ANGEL'S PLOY WORKS-- IN A WAY. WHILE THE FIRE DEMON REACHES FOR THE RETREATING ANGEL, PYRO SEES THAT HIS COMRADE IS IN TROUBLE... AND *ONE* FIRE MONSTER SPLITS INTO *TWO*.

WHAT'S'A MATTER, BUB?! IF YOU'RE SO INVULNERABLE, HOW COME YOU'RE SO SCARED O' MY CLAWS?

WITH THE SPEED OF THOUGHT, THE DEMON LASHES OUT...

ONLY SECONDS TO ACT. EVEN WOLVERINE'S MUTANT *FAST-HEALING* ABILITY CAN'T COPE WITH THE DAMAGE THAT FLAME HAND WILL DO.

PYRO'S FIRE MONSTER IS HUGE. I'LL NEED A CONSIDERABLE AMOUNT OF POWER TO COUNTER IT.

AND I'LL HAVE TO DO IT ON THE FIRST PASS. WOLVERINE WON'T SURVIVE LONG ENOUGH FOR ME TO TRY A SECOND.

IN THE BLINK OF AN EYE, STORM CLIMBS HIGH ABOVE THE MALL, GATHERING SPEED AND STRENGTH AS SHE GOES. IN ANOTHER BLINK, SHE SLAMS DOWN THROUGH THE HEART OF PYRO'S CREATION.

...BLASTING IT APART WITH A MASSIVE WEDGE OF AIR THAT HITS WITH THE FORCE OF A BATTERING RAM.

WOLVERINE-- MEIN VERRUCKT FREUND -- ARE YOU ALL RIGHT?!

I'LL... LIVE, ELF. THE FIREPROOF UNSTABLE MOLECULES OF MY COSTUME SHIELDED ME FROM MOST O' THE FLAMES. AN' MY FAST-HEALING ABILITY'S ALREADY DEALIN' WITH MY BURNS.

I OWE STORM, PAL. A FEW MORE SECONDS AND... I'D HAVE BEEN A GONER.

OH, MAN-- 'CRAWLER, THIS... HURTS!

FOR YOU TO ADMIT THAT, WOLVERINE, YOU MUST BE IN AGONY. LET ME HELP--

WHAT THE DEVIL?!

WOLVERINE, BEWARE! THAT'S NOT ME-- I'M ME! ONE OF THE BROTHERHOOD MUST BE A SHAPE-CHANGER!

WHOEVER YOU ARE, VILLAIN, YOU'VE JUST BITTEN OFF MORE THAN YOU CAN CHEW. I LIKE BEING UNIQUE. I DON'T TAKE KINDLY TO DOPPELGANGERS.

NEITHER DO I!

THIS IS CRAZY! WHICH IS WHICH?!

I'M STILL TOO WOOZY FROM MY BURNS-- MY SENSES CAN'T TELL 'EM APART.

BUT I FIGURE THE REAL NIGHTCRAWLER OUGHT'A BE ABLE TA TELEPORT OUTTA THE RANGE OF MY CLAWS.

WOLVERINE, SHEATHE YOUR CLAWS!

SNIKT!

NOT A CHANCE. WE'RE IN THE MIDDLE OF A FIGHT, STORM. I'M IN NO MOOD FER A DEBATE!

SHEATHE THEM-- OR USE THEM ON ME.

THAT CAN BE ARRANGED, BABE!

GODDESS, HE MEANS IT!

I AM LEADER OF THE X-MEN. WHILE THAT IS SO, YOU WILL USE YOUR CLAWS WHEN I COMMAND. NO OTHER TIME.

I WOULDN'T TAKE THAT FROM CYCLOPS!

YOU WILL TAKE IT FROM ME. YOU POSSESS SPEED, STRENGTH-- YOUR UNBREAKABLE ADAMANTIUM SKELETON MAKES YOU NEARLY INVULNERABLE. YOU SHOULD NOT NEED YOUR CLAWS--

--EXCEPT IN THE MOST EXTREME OF SITUATIONS, AGAINST THE DEADLIEST AND MOST POWERFUL OF FOES.

ALL RIGHT, STORM. I'LL DO IT YER WAY-- FER NOW.

BUT THIS CONVERSATION AIN'T FINISHED. NOT BY A LONG SHOT.

SNAKT!

LADY, SINCE YOU AND YOUR PINT-SIZED PAL WOULD OBVIOUSLY MUCH RATHER FEUD THAN FIGHT--

--IT SEEMS ONLY FAIR THAT I SEND YOU FAR AWAY FROM HERE, WHERE YOU CAN DO IT IN PEACE.

AVALANCHE! GRAB MY HAND, WOLVERINE! I'LL FLY YOU TO SAFETY!

IF YOU HADN'T CHOSEN SUCH A STUPID MOMENT TA GET SQUEAMISH, LADY, WE WOULDN'T BE IN THIS MESS IN THE FIRST PLACE!

WHAT ABOUT NIGHT-CRAWLER?! WHO'S GONNA HELP *HIM*?!

I WANT NO HELP, WOLVERINE! I INTEND TO FINISH THIS FIGHT ON MY OWN!

PYRO'S FLAME DEMON HAS GIVEN UP ON ME! HE'S ENDANGERING MORE SOLDIERS!

I'VE GOT TO AIRLIFT THEM OUT OF THE WAY.

WOLVERINE, COME WITH ME! I NEED YOUR ASSISTANCE TO DEFEAT THE BLOB!

FINE BY ME, BUB. I'M IN A MOOD TA DEFEAT SOME-ONE.

THE BIGGER, THE BETTER!

THE BLOB BOASTS THAT NO POWER ON EARTH CAN MOVE HIM--BUT SUPPOSE WE MOVE THE EARTH HE STANDS ON?

LIKE ARCHIMEDES SAID, PAL: GIMME A BIG ENOUGH LEVER AN' I CAN MOVE THE WORLD!

IT'S SMART O' PETEY TA USE ME AS THE FULCRUM OF HIS LEVER. THAT I-BEAM WILL CRACK BEFORE MY ADAMAN-TIUM STEEL BONES WILL.

YEEEOWW!

YA GOT HIM IN THE AIR, COLOSSUS. WHAT ARE YA GONNA DO WHEN HE COMES DOWN?!

YOU GONNA *DIE*, RUSSKIE! THAT'S A *PROMISE*!

I INTEND TO PROVE THAT NO MATTER HOW AWESOME THE BLOB THINKS HIS POWER HAS BECOME--

-- COLOSSUS WILL NOT BE CRUSHED. BY HIM. BY *ANYONE!*

BLOB-- OH, *NO!*

KROM!

EXCELLENT, PETER! THAT'S TWO OF THE OPPOSITION BEATEN.

-- WATER *DOUSES* FIRE!

IT TAKES VIRTUALLY ALL HER STRENGTH OF BODY AND WILL-- NOT MERELY TO CREATE THIS STORM, BUT, MORE IMPORTANTLY, TO CONTROL IT-- AND TO DO SO, SHE WARPS WEATHER PATTERNS FOR MILES AROUND THE DISTRICT OF COLUMBIA.

SHE CREATES A *MONSOON,* CONFINING IT TO A TINY SECTION OF THE MALL. HIT BY THIS RAW, PRIMAL, ELEMENTAL FORCE...

ANGEL RESCUED THOSE SOLDIERS. NOW TO DEAL WITH PYRO. HE THINKS HIMSELF PROTECTED BY HIS FLAME CREATURE. HE FORGETS THAT-- WHILE FIRE BURNS ANYTHING--

...NEITHER THE FIRE-DEMON-- NOR THE MAN WHO BROUGHT IT INTO BEING-- CAN STAND AGAINST IT FOR VERY LONG.

THREE OF THE BROTHERHOOD ARE DOWN.

NOW, A FOURTH JOINS THEM.

PERHAPS.

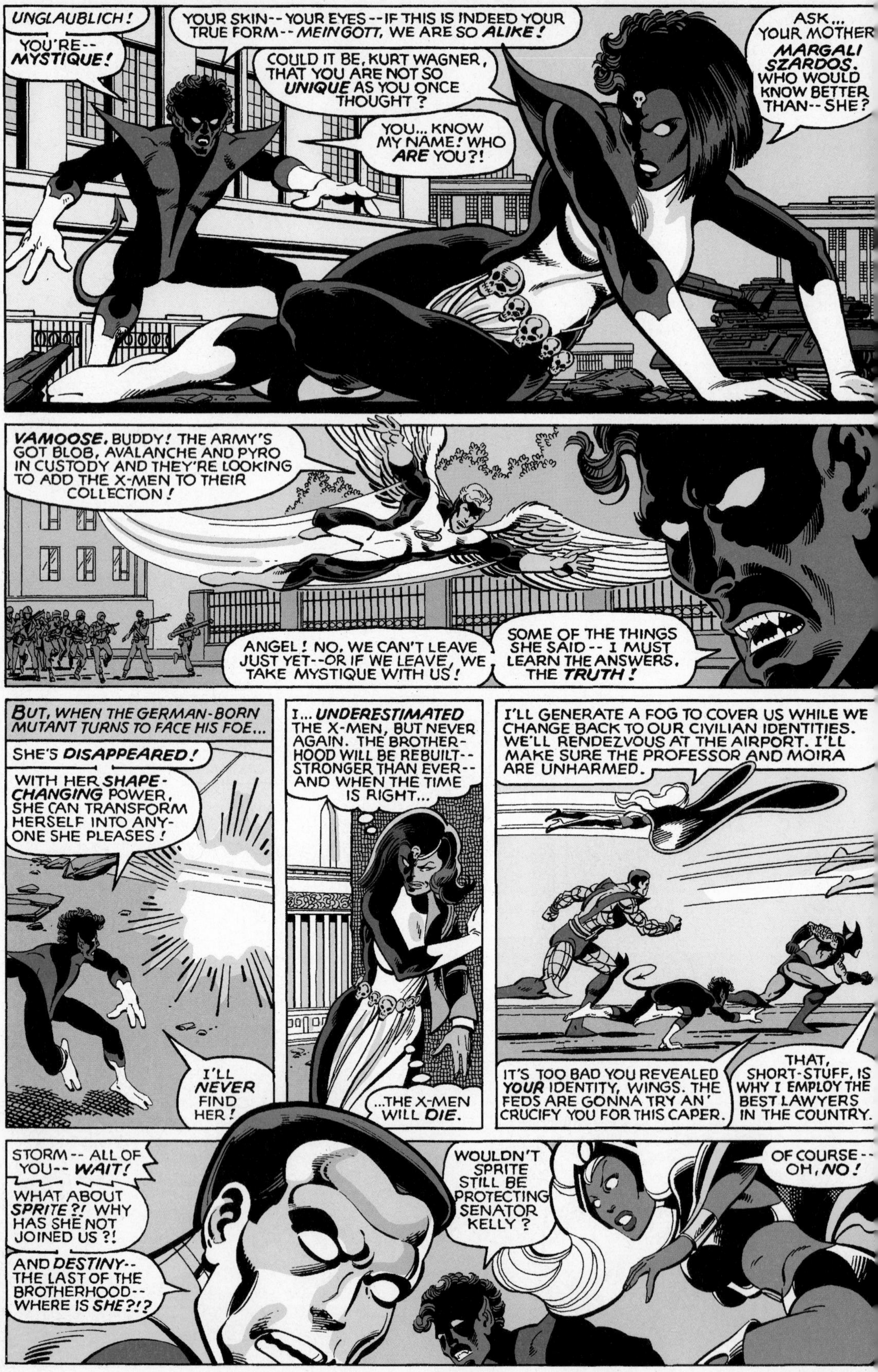
UNGLAUBLICH!
YOU'RE-- MYSTIQUE!
YOUR SKIN-- YOUR EYES --IF THIS IS INDEED YOUR TRUE FORM-- MEINGOTT, WE ARE SO ALIKE!
COULD IT BE, KURT WAGNER, THAT YOU ARE NOT SO UNIQUE AS YOU ONCE THOUGHT?
YOU... KNOW MY NAME! WHO ARE YOU?!
ASK... YOUR MOTHER MARGALI SZARDOS. WHO WOULD KNOW BETTER THAN-- SHE?
VAMOOSE, BUDDY! THE ARMY'S GOT BLOB, AVALANCHE AND PYRO IN CUSTODY AND THEY'RE LOOKING TO ADD THE X-MEN TO THEIR COLLECTION!
ANGEL! NO, WE CAN'T LEAVE JUST YET--OR IF WE LEAVE, WE TAKE MYSTIQUE WITH US!
SOME OF THE THINGS SHE SAID -- I MUST LEARN THE ANSWERS. THE TRUTH!
BUT, WHEN THE GERMAN-BORN MUTANT TURNS TO FACE HIS FOE...
SHE'S DISAPPEARED!
WITH HER SHAPE-CHANGING POWER, SHE CAN TRANSFORM HERSELF INTO ANYONE SHE PLEASES!
I'LL NEVER FIND HER!
I... UNDERESTIMATED THE X-MEN, BUT NEVER AGAIN. THE BROTHERHOOD WILL BE REBUILT-- STRONGER THAN EVER-- AND WHEN THE TIME IS RIGHT...
...THE X-MEN WILL DIE.
I'LL GENERATE A FOG TO COVER US WHILE WE CHANGE BACK TO OUR CIVILIAN IDENTITIES. WE'LL RENDEZVOUS AT THE AIRPORT. I'LL MAKE SURE THE PROFESSOR AND MOIRA ARE UNHARMED.
IT'S TOO BAD YOU REVEALED YOUR IDENTITY, WINGS. THE FEDS ARE GONNA TRY AN' CRUCIFY YOU FOR THIS CAPER.
THAT, SHORT-STUFF, IS WHY I EMPLOY THE BEST LAWYERS IN THE COUNTRY.
STORM -- ALL OF YOU-- WAIT!
WHAT ABOUT SPRITE?! WHY HAS SHE NOT JOINED US?!
AND DESTINY-- THE LAST OF THE BROTHERHOOD-- WHERE IS SHE?!?
WOULDN'T SPRITE STILL BE PROTECTING SENATOR KELLY?
OF COURSE-- OH, NO!

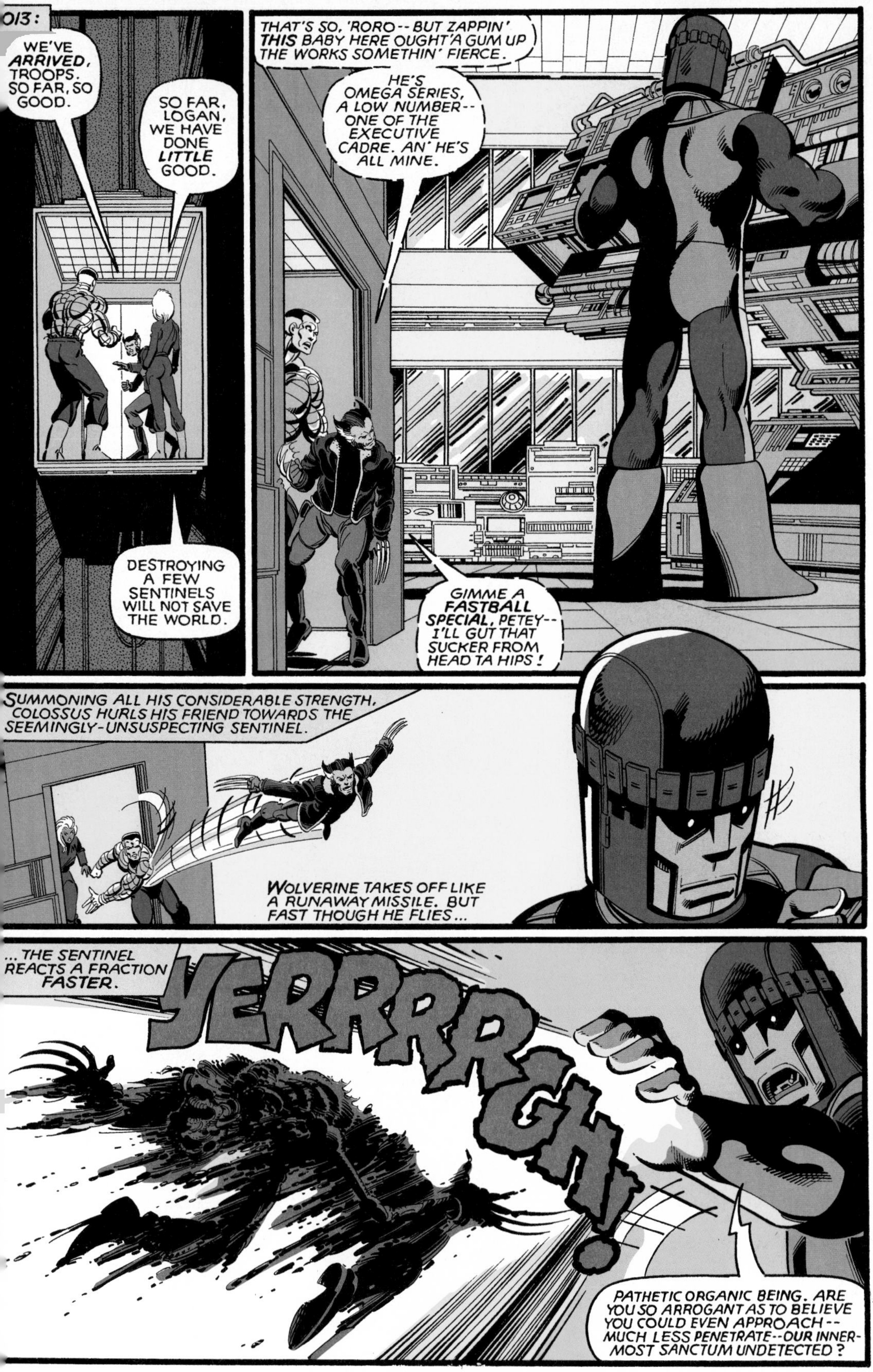
013:
WE'VE ARRIVED, TROOPS. SO FAR, SO GOOD.
SO FAR, LOGAN, WE HAVE DONE LITTLE GOOD.
DESTROYING A FEW SENTINELS WILL NOT SAVE THE WORLD.
THAT'S SO, 'RORO-- BUT ZAPPIN' THIS BABY HERE OUGHT'A GUM UP THE WORKS SOMETHIN' FIERCE.
HE'S OMEGA SERIES, A LOW NUMBER-- ONE OF THE EXECUTIVE CADRE. AN' HE'S ALL MINE.
GIMME A FASTBALL SPECIAL, PETEY-- I'LL GUT THAT SUCKER FROM HEAD TA HIPS!
SUMMONING ALL HIS CONSIDERABLE STRENGTH, COLOSSUS HURLS HIS FRIEND TOWARDS THE SEEMINGLY-UNSUSPECTING SENTINEL.
WOLVERINE TAKES OFF LIKE A RUNAWAY MISSILE. BUT FAST THOUGH HE FLIES...
...THE SENTINEL REACTS A FRACTION FASTER.
YERRRRGH!
PATHETIC ORGANIC BEING. ARE YOU SO ARROGANT AS TO BELIEVE YOU COULD EVEN APPROACH -- MUCH LESS PENETRATE--OUR INNER-MOST SANCTUM UNDETECTED?

NOT SO. YOU ARE HERE BECAUSE WE *ALLOWED* YOU TO BE HERE, THE BETTER TO TERMINATE YOU.

YIELD, X-MEN. OR SUFFER A SIMILAR FATE.

NEVER!

SQUARRRZZZZK!!

SENTINEL OMEGA FIVE HAS BEEN TERMINATED. ADDITIONAL ALPHA COMBAT UNITS RESPOND TO THIS LOCATION -- IMMEDIATELY!

WE MAY BE HURT, SENTINEL. BUT WE ARE NOT BEATEN!

WE HAVE FACED *GREATER* ODDS -- AND *TRIUMPHED!*

TERMINATE ONE SENTINEL-- TERMINATE ONE THOUSAND-- IT MAKES NO DIFFERENCE. OUR NUMBERS ARE TOO GREAT.

EVENTUALLY, MUTANTS, WE WILL OVER-WHELM YOU.

STORM, I'VE TOPPLED HIM! *FREEZE HIM!*

WITH A TREMENDOUS EFFORT, STORM SURROUNDS THE SENTINEL WITH A FEARSOME BLIZZARD -- DROPPING ITS SURFACE TEMPERATURE FAR BELOW ZERO IN A MATTER OF SECONDS, MAKING ITS METAL SKIN DANGEROUSLY BRITTLE. ONE PUNCH FROM COLOSSUS WILL SHATTER IT.

WHILE SHE CONCENTRATES ON THIS ROBOT, SHE COUNTS ON HER AIRBORN MANEUVERABILITY TO PROTECT HER FROM ITS COMPANION.

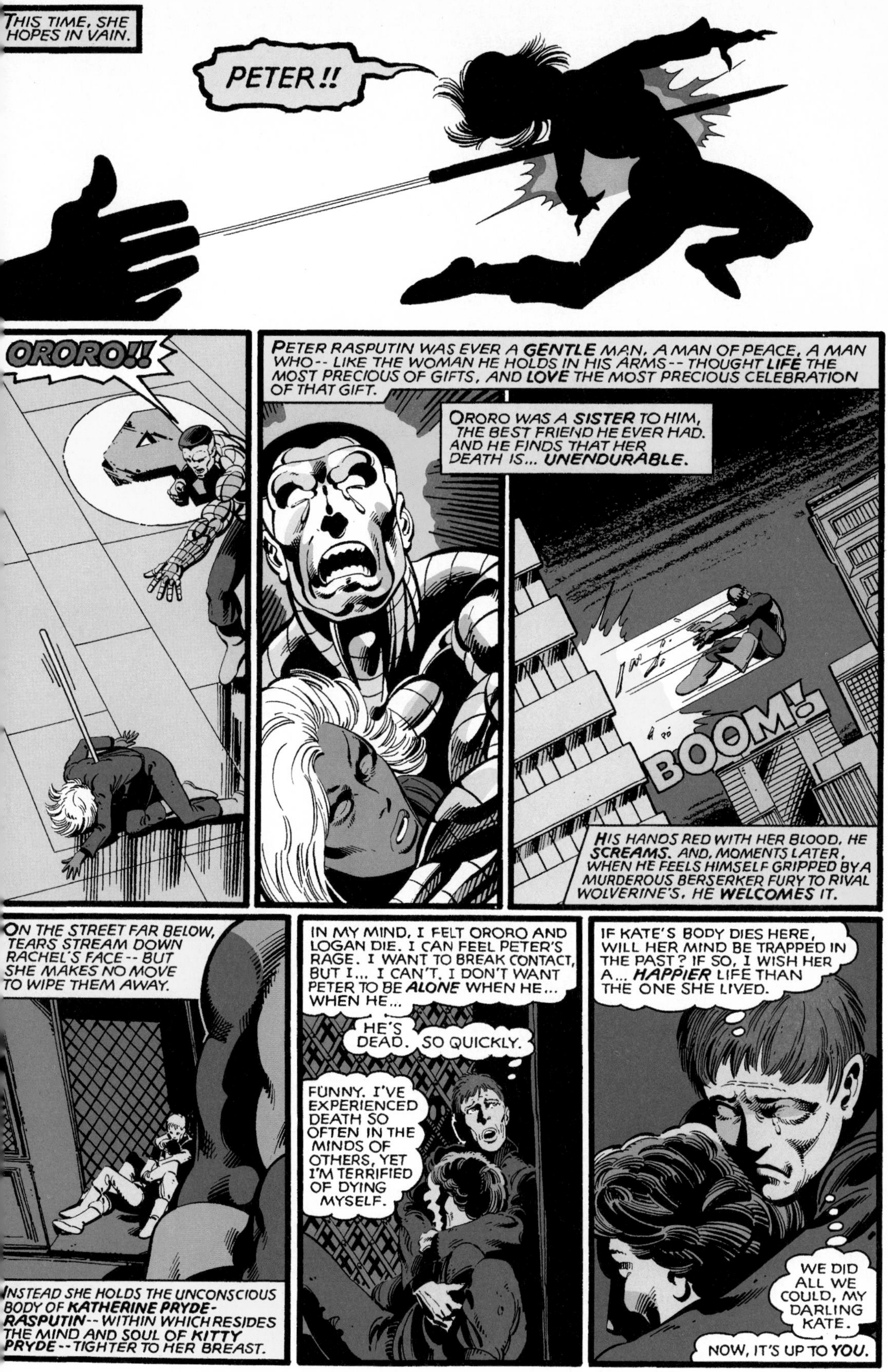
THIS TIME, SHE HOPES IN VAIN.
PETER!!
ORORO!!
PETER RASPUTIN WAS EVER A GENTLE MAN, A MAN OF PEACE, A MAN WHO-- LIKE THE WOMAN HE HOLDS IN HIS ARMS-- THOUGHT LIFE THE MOST PRECIOUS OF GIFTS, AND LOVE THE MOST PRECIOUS CELEBRATION OF THAT GIFT.
ORORO WAS A SISTER TO HIM, THE BEST FRIEND HE EVER HAD. AND HE FINDS THAT HER DEATH IS... UNENDURABLE.
BOOM!
HIS HANDS RED WITH HER BLOOD, HE SCREAMS. AND, MOMENTS LATER, WHEN HE FEELS HIMSELF GRIPPED BY A MURDEROUS BERSERKER FURY TO RIVAL WOLVERINE'S, HE WELCOMES IT.
ON THE STREET FAR BELOW, TEARS STREAM DOWN RACHEL'S FACE -- BUT SHE MAKES NO MOVE TO WIPE THEM AWAY.
INSTEAD SHE HOLDS THE UNCONSCIOUS BODY OF KATHERINE PRYDE-RASPUTIN -- WITHIN WHICH RESIDES THE MIND AND SOUL OF KITTY PRYDE -- TIGHTER TO HER BREAST.
IN MY MIND, I FELT ORORO AND LOGAN DIE. I CAN FEEL PETER'S RAGE. I WANT TO BREAK CONTACT, BUT I... I CAN'T. I DON'T WANT PETER TO BE ALONE WHEN HE... WHEN HE...
HE'S DEAD.
SO QUICKLY.
FUNNY. I'VE EXPERIENCED DEATH SO OFTEN IN THE MINDS OF OTHERS, YET I'M TERRIFIED OF DYING MYSELF.
IF KATE'S BODY DIES HERE, WILL HER MIND BE TRAPPED IN THE PAST? IF SO, I WISH HER A... HAPPIER LIFE THAN THE ONE SHE LIVED.
WE DID ALL WE COULD, MY DARLING KATE.
NOW, IT'S UP TO YOU.

1980:

THE BLIND PRECOG, *DESTINY*, HAS SENATOR KELLY CORNERED. BUT... IF SHE CAN PSYCHICALLY SCAN THE FUTURE, WHY HASN'T SHE SPOTTED ME?! UNLESS...

...THE TIMESWITCH HAS MADE ME SOMEHOW *INVISIBLE* TO HER PRESCIENT ABILITIES!

MY COLLEAGUES HAVE BEEN DEFEATED, YET VICTORY WILL STILL BE OURS-- WITH YOUR DEATH.

MURDERING ME WILL ACCOMPLISH *NOTHING*. TRUE, PEOPLE WILL FEAR MUTANTS, AS THEY FEAR *ALL* TERRORISTS --

--BUT THEY WON'T BE *COWED* BY THAT FEAR. THEY'LL FIGHT BACK. THEY'LL *DESTROY* YOU, DESTINY !

POSSIBLY. BUT YOU ARE A GREATER THREAT ALIVE.

DO NOT TRY TO EVADE MY CROSSBOW BOLT, SENATOR. I WILL SENSE YOUR PLANS A HEARTBEAT BEFORE YOU EVEN FORMULATE THEM, AND FIRE WHERE YOU ARE *GOING* TO BE.

I WOULDN'T GIVE YOU THAT SATISFACTION. IF I GOT MY HANDS ON YOU, MUTANT, I'D PROBABLY BREAK YOUR NECK...

...BUT I WON'T RUN.

DESTINY LAUGHS SOFTLY, AND TIGHTENS HER FINGER ON THE TRIGGER.

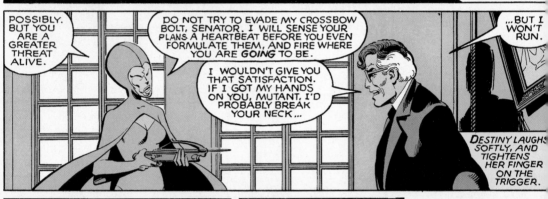

BUT, AS DESTINY FIRES, KATE "PHASES" WRAITH-LIKE THROUGH HER, CALLING UPON HER DECADES OF TRAINING AND EXPERIENCE TO ACT AS HER CHILD SELF COULD NOT...

MY--MY-- *MIND!*

THE TEMPORAL ANOMALY-- A PART OF ME-- CONSUMING ME!

SENATOR-- *DUCK!*

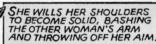

SHE WILLS HER SHOULDERS TO BECOME SOLID, BASHING THE OTHER WOMAN'S ARM AND THROWING OFF HER AIM.

IN THAT SPLIT-SECOND, A ABYSS OPENS WITHIN KATE PRYDE. REALITY TWISTS INSIDE-OUT AND, SUDDENLY SHE COMES FACE-TO-FACE WITH HERSELF AS A CHILD: SO INNOCENT, SO VULNERABLE, SO YOUNG.

IMPULSIVE SHE GIVES HERSELF KISS...

...AND LETS THE WINDS OF ETERNITY SWEEP HER HOME

KI-- I MEAN, SPRITE, ARE YOU *ALL RIGHT*?!

SENATOR KELLY, HAVE YOU BEEN HARMED?

S-STORM? WH-WHERE... AM I? THIS ISN'T THE DANGER ROOM.

I... FEEL... AWFULLL...

I AM STORM, LEADER OF THE X-MEN. AND I SUSPECT THIS... CHILD IS THE PERSON WHO JUST SAVED YOUR LIFE.

MUTANTS, LIKE PEOPLE, ARE BOTH GOOD AND BAD. YOU WOULD DO WELL TO REMEMBER THAT, SENATOR, BEFORE YOU SEEK TO CONDEMN US *ALL*.

WHO ARE YOU, YOUNG WOMAN? WHO IS THIS CHILD?!

S-STORM...?

PROFESSOR, THE AUTHORITIES ARE COMING. I MUST LEAVE.

WE WILL RENDEZVOUS AT ANGEL'S PRIVATE AIRCRAFT.

XAVIER, DR. MAC-TAGGERT-- THANK HEAVEN YOU'RE ALL RIGHT!

DESTINY-- CAPTURED AS WELL!

HAVE NO FEAR, MY DEAR FRIEND. NEITHER YOU NOR THE BROTHER-HOOD WILL BE IN PRISON FOR LONG. THIS, MYSTIQUE SWEARS!

LATER, EN ROUTE TO THE WESTCHESTER, NEW YORK MANSION THAT SERVES BOTH AS PROFESSOR XAVIER'S SCHOOL FOR GIFTED YOUNGSTERS AND THE SECRET HEADQUARTERS OF THE X-MEN, PROFESSOR X EXPLAINS ALL THAT HAS TRANSPIRED TO A DUMBFOUNDED SPRITE...

YOU REMEMBER *NOTHING* AFTER BLACKING OUT IN THE DANGER ROOM?

NOPE. EXCEPT, WELL, I THINK I FELT SOME-ONE KISS ME JUST BE-FORE I WOKE UP.

PERHAPS IT IS FOR THE BEST. I THINK IF I KNEW *MY* FUTURE, I WOULD SPEND MY LIFE TRYING TO *CHANGE* IT.

YOU SAID YOU MINDSCANNED ME, PROFESSOR. WHAT DID YOU FIND OUT-- ABOUT ME, I MEAN?

THAT *KATE* PRYDE IS AS DELIGHTFUL AND ADMIRABLE A PERSON AS *KITTY* PRYDE. THE REST YOU WILL DISCOVER IN DUE COURSE.

PROFESSOR, WE SAVED SENATOR KELLY. KITTY'S MIND HAS BEEN RETURNED TO HER BODY.

DOES THAT MEAN WE CHANGED THE FUTURE?

I DO NOT KNOW, WARREN. CLICHE *THOUGH* IT *SOUNDS*, ONLY *TIME* WILL TELL.

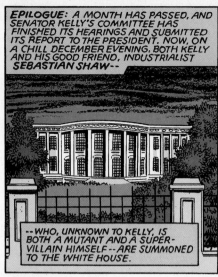

EPILOGUE: A MONTH HAS PASSED, AND SENATOR KELLY'S COMMITTEE HAS FINISHED ITS HEARINGS AND SUBMITTED ITS REPORT TO THE PRESIDENT. NOW, ON A CHILL DECEMBER EVENING, BOTH KELLY AND HIS GOOD FRIEND, INDUSTRIALIST SEBASTIAN SHAW--

--WHO, UNKNOWN TO KELLY, IS BOTH A MUTANT AND A SUPER-VILLAIN HIMSELF--ARE SUMMONED TO THE WHITE HOUSE.

COME IN, ROBERT, SEBASTIAN.

I WON'T BANDY WORDS, GENTLEMEN. I'VE READ YOUR REPORT, ROBERT. ITS RECOMMENDATIONS ARE DANGEROUS. THEY MAY BE UNCONSTITUTIONAL, EVEN CRIMINAL -- A DRACONIAN ATTITUDE FOR SOMEONE WHO OWES HIS LIFE TO THE MUTANT X-MEN.

A LIFE THAT WAS THREATENED INITIALLY, MISTER PRESIDENT, BY THE BROTHERHOOD OF EVIL MUTANTS.

IF THERE WERE NO MUTANTS, PERIOD, MY LIFE WOULDN'T HAVE BEEN THREATENED AT ALL.

THERE IS ALSO THE NATIONAL SECURITY ASPECT, SIR.

AN ANTI-GOVERNMENT GROUP OF SUPER-POWERED BEINGS-- MUTANT OR OTHERWISE-- OR SUCH A GROUP IN THE SERVICE OF A FOREIGN ENEMY, WOULD BE A SERIOUS THREAT TO OUR NATION.

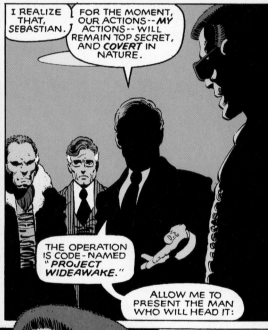

I REALIZE THAT, SEBASTIAN.

FOR THE MOMENT, OUR ACTIONS-- MY ACTIONS-- WILL REMAIN TOP SECRET, AND COVERT IN NATURE.

THE OPERATION IS CODE-NAMED "PROJECT WIDEAWAKE."

ALLOW ME TO PRESENT THE MAN WHO WILL HEAD IT:

HENRY PETER GYRICH.

HE WILL BE RESPONSIBLE TO ME ALONE, AND HIS AUTHORITY IN THIS MATTER WILL BE ABSOLUTE.

YOUR FIRST PRIORITY, HENRY, WILL BE TO WORK WITH SHAW INDUSTRIES TO DESIGN AND CONSTRUCT A NEW SERIES OF ROBOT SENTINELS.

YOU'LL HAVE THEM, SIR. AND YOU HAVE MY WORD...

...THIS MUTANT CONTROVERSY WILL BE RESOLVED. IF WE FIND THEM TO BE A THREAT TO THIS REPUBLIC-- A THREAT TO THE WORLD, A THREAT TO THE HUMAN RACE-- THEY WILL BE DEALT WITH.

PERMANENTLY.

NEXT: **DEMON**

WHEN YOU'RE ALONE, KITTY PRYDE, NO ONE CAN HEAR YOU SCREAM

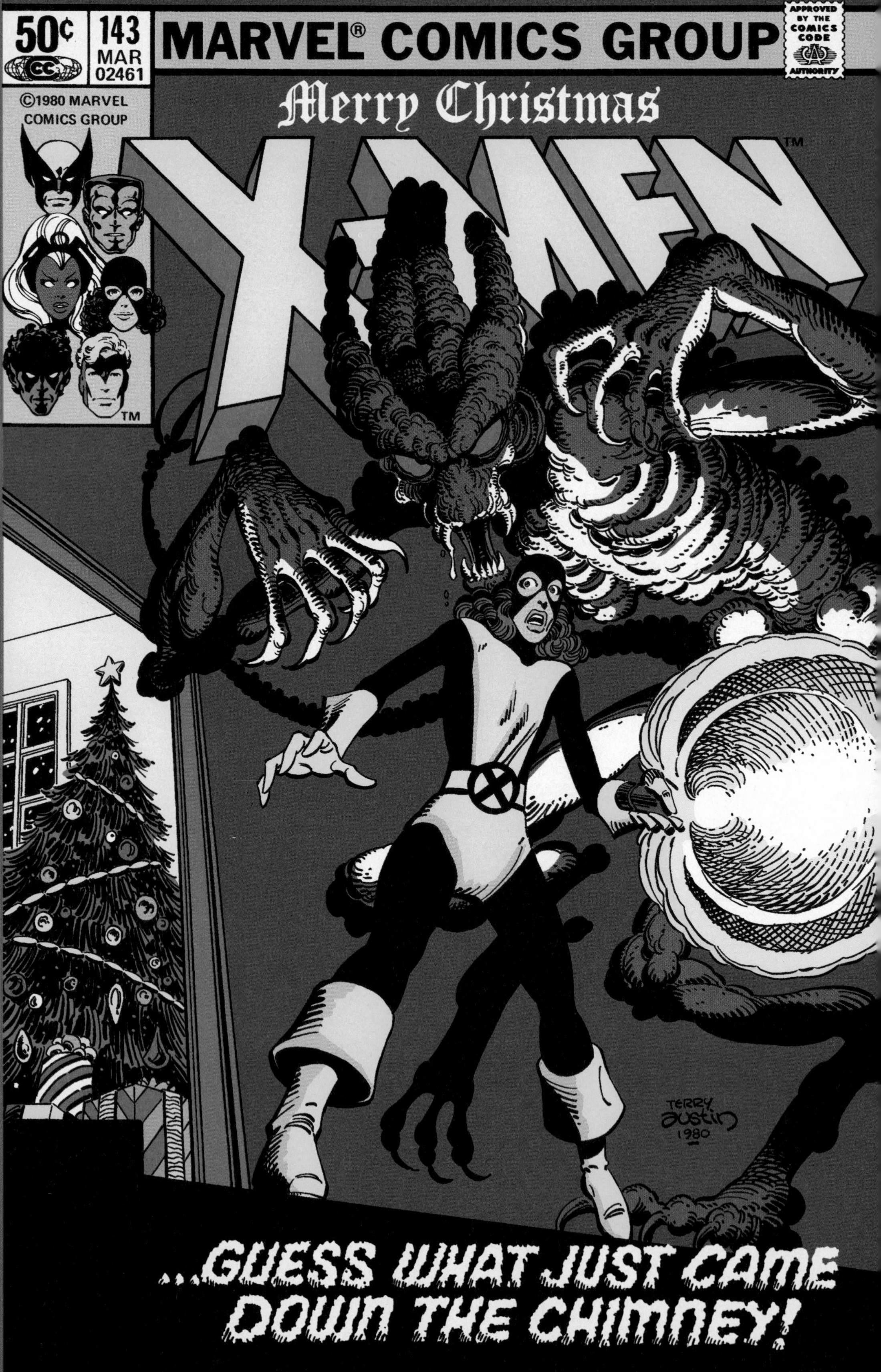

50¢
143
MAR
02461
MARVEL® COMICS GROUP
APPROVED BY THE COMICS CODE AUTHORITY
©1980 MARVEL COMICS GROUP
Merry Christmas
X-MEN™
TERRY AUSTIN 1980
...GUESS WHAT JUST CAME DOWN THE CHIMNEY!

STAN LEE PRESENTS: THE UNCANNY X-MEN! ™

HER NAME IS STORM, AND ALTHOUGH IN HER YOUNG LIFE SHE HAS BEEN HAILED AS A GODDESS, SHE IS IN TRUTH A MUTANT-- MISTRESS OF THE WIND AND WEATHER AND NOW A MEMBER OF THE UNCANNY X-MEN, A TEAM OF MUTANT SUPER-HEROES.

ARRGHH!

THIS AUTUMN NIGHT, IN THE SKY ABOVE NEW YORK'S WESTCHESTER COUNTY, SHE HAS COME FACE TO FACE WITH BEINGS AS FOUL AS THE PIT THAT SPAWNED THEM --

-- MEMBERS OF AN ANCIENT RACE THAT ONCE RULED THE EARTH AND WHO MEAN TO RULE IT AGAIN.

THEY ARE THE N'GARAI--THE ELDER GODS OF LEGEND, THE ULTIMATE EVIL. ONE OF THEIR NUMBER HAS ATTACKED THE X-MEN IN THE MANSION THAT SERVES AS THE MUTANTS' SECRET HEADQUARTERS.

I... CAN'T LET THESE MONSTERS HIT ME AGAIN. NEVER FELT... SUCH AGONY.

BELOW STORM IS AN AGES-OLD CAIRN, WHOSE MALEFIC POWER SUSTAINS THE CREATURE THAT THREATENS HER FRIENDS.

UNLESS SHE DESTROYS IT UTTERLY, THE X-MEN ARE DOOMED.

BUT WHAT ARE THESE CREATURES?! THEY AREN'T REAL!

THEY'RE JUST THINGS OF SMOKE AND LIGHT, CREATED BY THE CAIRN. HOW CAN I FIGHT THEM?!

THAT BOLT OF ENERGY-- NO TIME TO AVOID IT--!

UNNNGNH!!

SHAKEN TO HER SOUL BY HER NARROW ESCAPE, STORM SOARS WEARILY HOME*...

*FOR DETAILS, SEE X-MEN #96 -- LOUISE.

... AS PROFESSOR XAVIER -- THE X-MEN'S FOUNDER AND MENTOR-- TELEPATHICALLY ASSURES HER THAT THE BATTLE IS OVER, THE VICTORY WON.

MONTHS PASS, AND NATURE BEGINS TO HEAL THE TERRIBLE WOUNDS INFLICTED BY THAT BRIEF, FIERCE COMBAT.

THE X-MEN MOVE ON NEW CHALLENGES, NE FOES. THEY KNOW TRIUMPH, AND TRAGEDY

156

MY MIND...FUZZY...NOTHING FITS TOGETHER...I CAN'T ...CONCENTRATE...

GODDESS-- *NO!* I'M BEING PULLED INTO THE CAIRN-- INTO THE *DARK!* AND NO MATTER HOW HARD I TRY, I CAN'T BREAK LOOSE! BUT I *MUST!*

I MUST BE *FREE!*

AND I *SHALL* BE FREE!

IT'S AS IF THE SUN HAD MOMENTARILY TOUCHED THE EARTH. RAW ENERGY-- FUELED IN PART BY STORM'S CLAUSTROPHOBIC FEAR OF BEING BURIED ALIVE, IN PART BY AN ATAVISTIC TERROR BORN OF SUB- CONSCIOUS RACIAL MEMORIES OF THE N'GARAI-- EXPLODES AROUND HER...

...SHATTERING THE CAIRN. AT THE SAME INSTANT, THE THING SPAWNED BY THAT CAIRN SIMPLY...CEASES TO EXIST.

AND, IN TIME, THEIR BATTLE WITH N'GARAI-- ONE OF THE FIRST THE "NEW" X-MEN FOUGHT-- IS FORGOTTEN

FORGOTTEN IT MAY BE-- BY THE X-MEN BUT IT IS *FAR* FROM OVER.

PROFESSOR XAVIER BELIEVED THAT DESTROYING THE CAIRN WOULD FOREVER SEAL THIS GATEWAY BETWEEN THE N'GARAI DIMENSION AND EARTH.

HE WAS WRONG.

DOUGLAS, YOU ARE A HOPELESS ROMANTIC!

SO SUE ME!

ELLIE, IT'S OUR FIRST CHRISTMAS. WE'LL HAVE YEARS AND YEARS TO GET PRE-CHOPPED TREES OR PLASTIC ONES.

I WANT THIS ONE TO BE *SPECIAL*.

I WASN'T ARGUING, DOUG, JUST STATING A FACT. HOW'S THIS?

WELLLL...

WE LIVE IN AN APARTMENT, REMEMBER?

SAVE THE BIG ONE FOR OUR FIRST HOUSE.

I THINK IT'S SWEET.

I THINK *YOU'RE* SWEET.

I THINK VERY NAUGHTY THOUGHTS.

OH, YEAH? LIKE...

...*WHAT'S THAT?!*

SOMETHING IN THE TREES.

I'LL TAKE A LOOK.

DOUG, BE CAREFUL!

RELAX, ELLIE. IT'S A FALSE ALARM, I THINK.

I'M GLAD THE MOON IS FULL. THINGS ARE LIT UP SO BRIGHT I DON'T NEED MY FLASH --

!URRRGH!

FOR DOUGLAS MOORE, DEATH IS VIRTUALLY INSTANTANEOUS.

HIS WIFE HAS TIME FOR A CHOKED CRY...

...THAT IS ENDED AS QUICKLY, AS ABRUPTLY, AS HER LIFE.

AND WHEN THE KILLING IS DONE, THE N'GARAI FEEDS...

...ON BOTH BODY AND SOUL.

THESE VICTIMS ARE BUT THE FIRST... OF MANY.

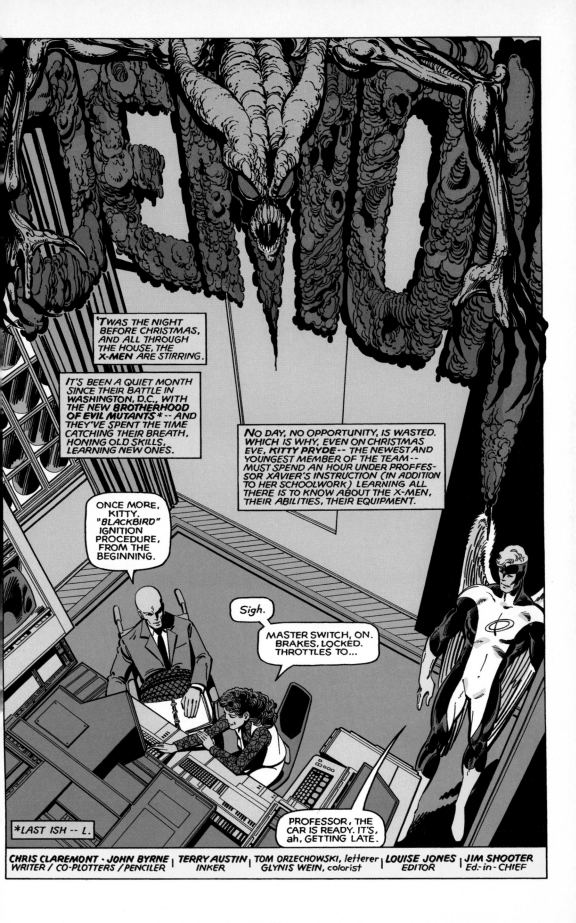

'TWAS THE NIGHT BEFORE CHRISTMAS, AND ALL THROUGH THE HOUSE, THE X-MEN ARE STIRRING.

IT'S BEEN A QUIET MONTH SINCE THEIR BATTLE IN WASHINGTON, D.C., WITH THE NEW *BROTHERHOOD OF EVIL MUTANTS* * -- AND THEY'VE SPENT THE TIME CATCHING THEIR BREATH, HONING OLD SKILLS, LEARNING NEW ONES.

NO DAY, NO OPPORTUNITY, IS WASTED. WHICH IS WHY, EVEN ON CHRISTMAS EVE, *KITTY PRYDE* -- THE NEWEST AND YOUNGEST MEMBER OF THE TEAM -- MUST SPEND AN HOUR UNDER PROFFES-SOR XAVIER'S INSTRUCTION (IN ADDITION TO HER SCHOOLWORK) LEARNING ALL THERE IS TO KNOW ABOUT THE X-MEN, THEIR ABILITIES, THEIR EQUIPMENT.

ONCE MORE, KITTY. "BLACKBIRD" IGNITION PROCEDURE, FROM THE BEGINNING.

Sigh.

MASTER SWITCH, ON. BRAKES, LOCKED. THROTTLES TO...

*LAST ISH -- L.

PROFESSOR, THE CAR IS READY. IT'S, ah, GETTING LATE.

CHRIS CLAREMONT · JOHN BYRNE | TERRY AUSTIN | TOM ORZECHOWSKI, letterer | LOUISE JONES | JIM SHOOTER
WRITER / CO-PLOTTERS / PENCILER | INKER | GLYNIS WEIN, colorist | EDITOR | Ed.- in - CHIEF

159

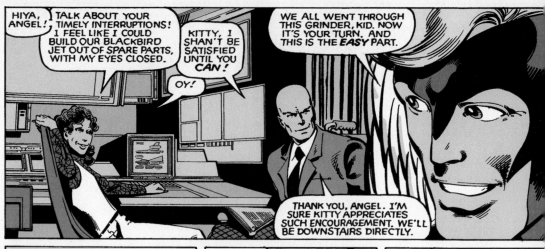

HIYA, ANGEL! TALK ABOUT YOUR TIMELY INTERRUPTIONS! I FEEL LIKE I COULD BUILD OUR *BLACKBIRD* JET OUT OF SPARE PARTS, WITH MY EYES CLOSED.

KITTY, I SHAN'T BE SATISFIED UNTIL YOU *CAN*!

OY!

WE ALL WENT THROUGH THIS GRINDER, KID. NOW IT'S YOUR TURN. AND THIS IS THE *EASY* PART.

THANK YOU, ANGEL. I'M SURE KITTY APPRECIATES SUCH ENCOURAGEMENT. WE'LL BE DOWNSTAIRS DIRECTLY.

SOON, IN THE MANSION'S FOYER...

PROF, I'D LIKE TO INTRODUCE MY, um, LADY. CHARLES XAVIER-- *MARIKO YASHIDA*.

KOM-BAN-WA, KYOJU. HAJIMEMASHITE.

GOOD EVENING, PROFESSOR. I AM PLEASED TO MEET YOU.

AS AM I, MISS YASHIDA.

MARIKO! LONG TIME, NO SEE! AND YOU LOOK AS BEAUTIFUL AS EVER!

Eh--?! *NIGHTCRAWLER-SAN!*

BACK OFF, ELF!

WHADDYA THINK YER DOIN'?! MARIKO'S MY LADY!

BAMF

RETRACTABLE ADAMANTIUM CLAWS FLASH FROM THE BACKS OF WOLVERINE'S HANDS, AND ONLY NIGHTCRAWLER'S ABILITY TO TELEPORT SAVES HIM FROM SOME NASTY WOUNDS.

INSTANTLY REACTING WITH A SPEED THAT BELIES HIS MASSIVE FORM, PETER RASPUTIN SHIFTS TO THE ARMORED FORM OF COLOSSUS, AND...

LEGGO'A'ME, YA TIN-PLATED-LUMMOX!

WOLVERINE, WHAT DO YOU THINK *YOU* ARE DOING?! KURT IS OUR *FRIEND!*

WOLVERINE, SHEATHE YOUR CLAWS!

KURT MEANT NO HARM YOU KNOW THAT. HIS WAS AN INNOCENT CHRISTMAS GREETING...

...NOT SOME ENEMY'S *ATTACK!*

AS ABRUPTLY AS WOLVERINE'S SUDDEN BERSERKER RAGE BEGINS, IT ENDS...

I'M OBLIGED, CHARLEY. YOUR TELEPATHIC MINDTOUCH DID THE TRICK. I'M...CALM NOW. EVERYTHING'S COOL. MISFIT--KURT, I... I'M SORRY. I LOST MY HEAD.

I GUESS THE OLD WAYS, THE OLD HABITS, DIE A LOT HARDER'N WE FIGURED.

MINE ARE A KILLER'S INSTINCTS. ALWAYS HAVE BEEN. ALWAYS WILL BE. I THOUGHT-- I HOPED-- THAT COULD BE CHANGED.

I WAS WRONG.

THE MOOD HERE HAS GOTTEN A WEE BIT HEAVY. I DON'T KNOW IF I SHOULD, BUT I'M GONNA TRY TO LIGHTEN IT UP A LITTLE.

MERRY CHRISTMAS, SEXY.

KITTY!

PETER, YOU'RE BLUSHING!

GOOD THING YOU ONLY KISSED HIM ON THE CHEEK, KITTEN. ANYWHERE ELSE AND HE'D HAVE PROBABLY DROPPED DEAD FROM SHOCK.

YOU KNOW, KURT, I AM BEGINNING TO REGRET RESCUING YOU JUST NOW.

ARE YOU INDEED?

I'VE BROUGHT THE AUTOMOBILE AROUND, PROFESSOR.

THANK YOU, ORORO.

IT'S A LOVELY NIGHT, ORORO. YOUR DOING?

WHAT GOOD IS BEING A MUTANT "WEATHER WITCH" IF ONE CAN'T CONJURE UP A CRYSTAL CLEAR CHRISTMAS EVE?

WAY TO GO, ORORO!

HAVE A NICE TIME, YOU GUYS!

SEE YOU LATER, KID!

MY LADY, CANDY SOUTHERN, AND I HAVE A LONG OVERDUE DATE. YOU MAY NOT SEE ME AGAIN 'TIL EASTER.

ENJOY YOURSELF, ANGEL.

FINALLY, THEY'RE ALL GONE.

OMIGOSH! WHAT AM I SAYING?! THEY ARE ALL GONE!

I'M ALL ALONE!

GREAT. THE KID HERE MAY HAVE A GENIUS I.Q. BUT SHE'S ABOUT AS QUICK ON THE UPTAKE AS A CLAM.

I'VE NEVER SPENT CHANUKAH AWAY FROM HOME BEFORE. I WONDER HOW MOM AND DAD ARE DOING?

I KNOW! I'LL CALL THEM!

IT'S FUNNY. SOMETIMES, I DON'T MISS 'EM AT ALL.

SOMETIMES I DO.

NO ANSWER.

THE PHONE--!

MOM?! DAD?!?

Oh, IT'S YOU. SORRY. HI, SCOTT.

THIS IS KITTY PRYDE. DO YOU REMEMBER--?

ON THE OTHER END OF THE LINE, IN THE FLORIDA SEACOAST TOWN OF SHARK BAY, IS SCOTT SUMMERS. AS CYCLOPS, HE ONCE LED THE X-MEN--UNTIL THE DEATH OF THE WOMAN HE LOVED, JEAN GREY. AFTER THAT-- DRIVEN BY NEEDS HE BARELY UNDERSTOOD AND A GRIEF ALMOST TOO TERRIBLE TO ENDURE -- HE TOOK A LEAVE OF ABSENCE FROM THE TEAM. * HE'S BEEN ON THE ROAD EVER SINCE.

OF COURSE I REMEMBER YOU, KITTY. HOW'RE THINGS?

NO ONE'S HOME BUT YOU? I... SEE.

WELL, GIVE EVERYONE MY LOVE, WISH THEM A MERRY CHRISTMAS AND TELL THEM I'LL TRY TO PHONE AGAIN TOMORROW.

'BYE, KITTY. TAKE CARE.

*IN X-MEN #138 -- L.

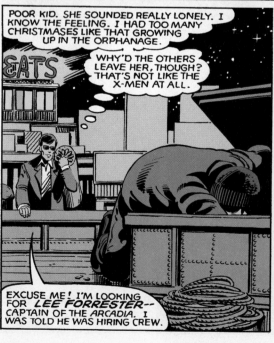

POOR KID. SHE SOUNDED REALLY LONELY. I KNOW THE FEELING. I HAD TOO MANY CHRISTMASES LIKE THAT GROWING UP IN THE ORPHANAGE.

WHY'D THE OTHERS LEAVE HER, THOUGH? THAT'S NOT LIKE THE X-MEN AT ALL.

EXCUSE ME! I'M LOOKING FOR LEE FORRESTER-- CAPTAIN OF THE ARCADIA. I WAS TOLD HE WAS HIRING CREW.

I'M LEE FORRESTER-- "ALEYTYS" TO MY RELATIVES-- AND YOU HEARD RIGHT.

YOU'RE A GIRL--!

CARE TO TRY AGAIN, SPORT?

I... I'M SORRY. I MEAN, I...

APOLOGY ACCEPTED...

...SCOTT. SCOTT SUMMERS.

C'MON ABOARD, SCOTT. WE'LL SPLIT A POT OF COFFEE AND TALK.

MEANWHILE, BACK IN NEW YORK...

ENOUGH WITH THE MOPES, A'READY!

I'M A BIG GIRL NOW, AND WHEN BIG GIRLS-- WHO ALSO HAPPEN TO BE *X-MEN*-- FEEL AS MISERABLE AS I DO, THEY DON'T ACT SORRY FOR THEM- SELVES AND GET ALL WEEPY- WAILY.

THEY *HIT* SOME- THING.

PRIMITIVE-- BUT OH SO CATHARTIC.

SINCE NO ONE'S AROUND TO MONITOR ME IN THE *DANGER ROOM*, I CAN'T RUN A COMBAT WORKOUT.

0776
DANGER ROOM
PRIMARY CYCLE
GYMNASIUM
TIME CYCLE: 60 min

BUT I DON'T REALLY MIND.

SHE CONCENTRATES, TRYING TO BE SERIOUS BUT UNABLE TO REPRESS A GIGGLE OF EXCITEMENT AS SHE PHASES THROUGH THE FLOOR OF THE CONTROL BOOTH --

-- LITERALLY FALLING THROUGH THE VAST, EMPTY SPACES BE- TWEEN ATOMS, THOSE OF HER BODY SLIDING BETWEEN THOSE OF THE METAL--

-- AND FLOATS DOWN TO THE FLOOR OF THE DANGER ROOM. SHE HASN'T BEEN AN X-MAN VERY LONG. SHE'S NOT USED TO HER NASCENT SUPER- POWERS, AND USING THEM STILL GIVES HER A THRILL.

AWAITING HER IS ENOUGH EQUIPMENT TO STOCK A TOP- RATED SPA. AFTER A SERIES OF WARM- UP EXERCISES, KITTY GOES TO WORK.

ONCE UPON A TIME -- TWO, THREE, FOUR-- I THOUGHT THE LIFE OF A SUPER-HERO WAS ALL FUN AND GAMES.

HAH!

NO ONE TOLD ME I'D BE SPENDING AN HOUR A DAY -- PLUS SCHOOLWORK --STUDYING.

OR ANOTHER HOUR, EVERY DAY, EXERCISING. AND THIS ISN'T JUST FOR ME, EITHER. ALL THE X-MEN WORK OUT. I DON'T SEE THE POINT. IT'S OUR SUPER-POWERS THAT NEED TRAININ', NOT OUR BODIES. I'M IN *GREAT* SHAPE.

THE WAY THINGS ARE GOING, I'LL PROBABLY TURN INTO A TEEN- AGE, FEMALE *ARNOLD SCHWARZE- NEGGER.*

ALLEZ- *OOP!*

OW!

BETTER EASE OFF A LITTLE. SOMETHING WENT TWINGE IN MY THIGH.

I SHOULDN'T JOKE SO MUCH ABOUT THE X-MEN. THIS ISN'T A GAME TO THEM. THEY HIDE THEIR FEELINGS AROUND ME, BUT WHENEVER THEY MENTION JEAN GREY, THEY SOUND SO... *SAD.*

SHE DIED. AS AN X-MAN.

I COULD DIE.

I WISH I'D KNOWN HER BETTER -- HUNH?!

BRRRANG!

THAT'S THE *BURGLAR ALARM!* THE HOUSE COMPUTER SHOULD BE PRINTING OUT THE DETAILS ON THE WALL SCANSCREEN -- AH, THERE IT IS!

POSSIBLE INTRUDER ZONE 4

ZONE 4 IS UPSTAIRS-- ORORO'S ATTIC!

IF THERE'S AN INTRUDER WHEN I'M BY MYSELF, I'M SUPPOSED TO CALL THE POLICE, BUT I THINK I'D BETTER CHECK THINGS OUT FIRST.

I CALLED 'EM LAST SEPTEMBER DURING A BIG WINDSTORM...

...AND IT TURNED OUT TO BE A FALSE ALARM. A TREE BRANCH HAD BLOWN THROUGH THE SKYLIGHT. THE COPS TOOK IT IN STRIDE BUT I FELT LIKE A JERK.

THIS TIME I'M GOING TO MAKE SURE!

RUNNING UP AIR MOLECULES IS A LOT MORE FUN THAN WALK-ING UP STAIRS!

EVEN IF I *DO* FIND A BURGLAR, THERE'S NOTHING TO WORRY ABOUT. WITH MY PHASING POWER, THERE'S *NO WAY* I CAN BE HARMED.

GEE -- IT'S GOTTEN AWFUL *COLD* ALL OF A SUDDEN.

AND *NO WONDER!* MY COSTUME'S INSULATED, AND I CAN *STILL* FEEL THE COLD. ICICLE CITY.

OH, NO! ORORO'S FLOWERS!

THEY'RE ALL DEAD, POOR THINGS. BUT-- THIS ISN'T RIGHT. GRANTED, THIS ATTIC WAS LIKE A HOTHOUSE AND THE WINTER AIR OUTSIDE WILL KILL THE PLANTS BUT... NOT SO QUICKLY, SO COMPLETELY!

YUCK!

WHAT THE HECK IS *THIS?!*

THE FLOOR'S COVERED WITH THIS GOOP!

THAT SOUND--! SOMEONE'S IN HERE! BUT WHO--?!

164

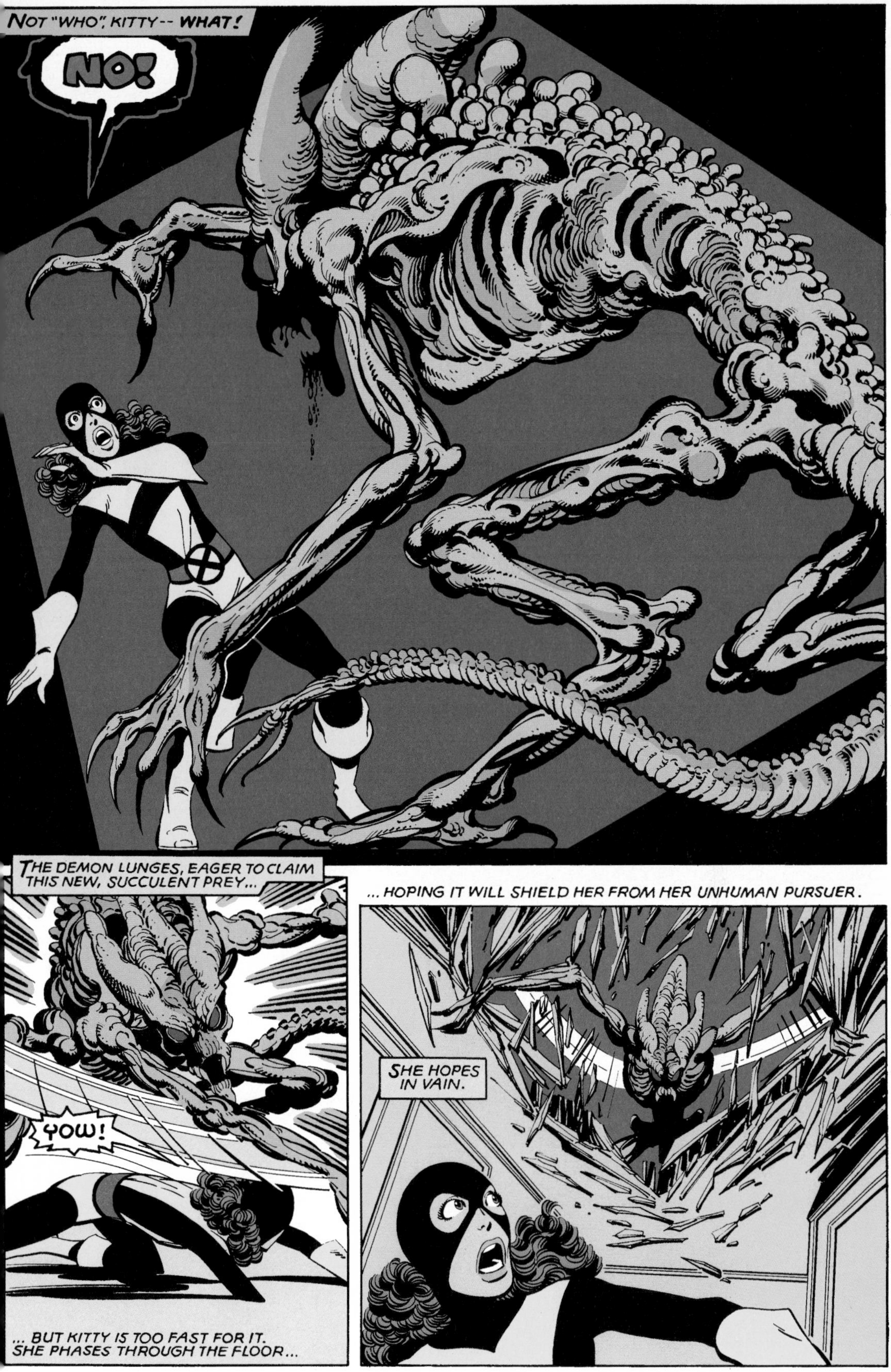
NOT "WHO", KITTY -- WHAT!
NO!
THE DEMON LUNGES, EAGER TO CLAIM THIS NEW, SUCCULENT PREY...
YOW!
... BUT KITTY IS TOO FAST FOR IT. SHE PHASES THROUGH THE FLOOR...
... HOPING IT WILL SHIELD HER FROM HER UNHUMAN PURSUER.
SHE HOPES IN VAIN.

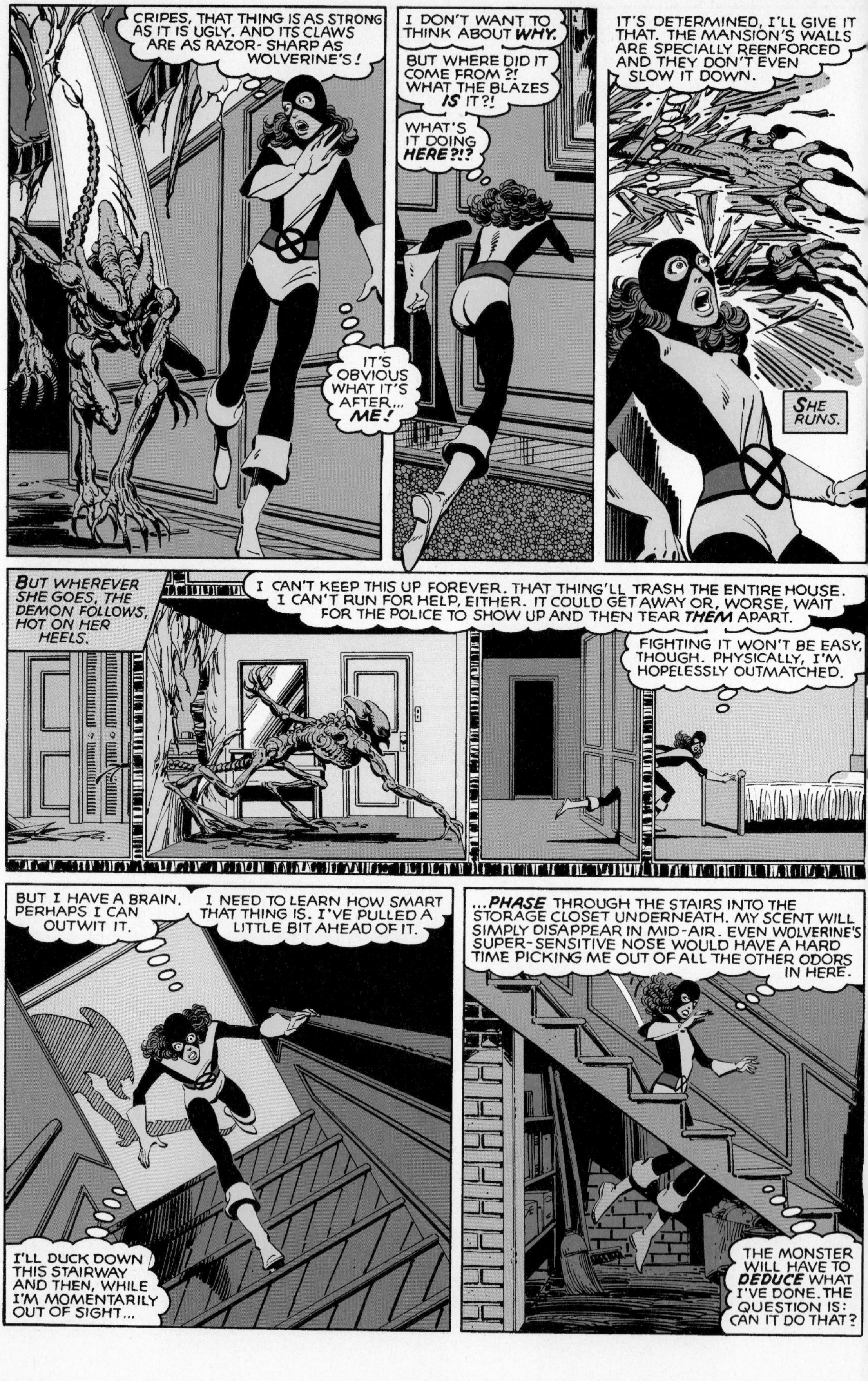
CRIPES, THAT THING IS AS STRONG AS IT IS UGLY. AND ITS CLAWS ARE AS RAZOR-SHARP AS WOLVERINE'S!
IT'S OBVIOUS WHAT IT'S AFTER... ME!
I DON'T WANT TO THINK ABOUT WHY.
BUT WHERE DID IT COME FROM?! WHAT THE BLAZES IS IT?!
WHAT'S IT DOING HERE?!?
IT'S DETERMINED, I'LL GIVE IT THAT. THE MANSION'S WALLS ARE SPECIALLY REENFORCED AND THEY DON'T EVEN SLOW IT DOWN.
SHE RUNS.
BUT WHEREVER SHE GOES, THE DEMON FOLLOWS, HOT ON HER HEELS.
I CAN'T KEEP THIS UP FOREVER. THAT THING'LL TRASH THE ENTIRE HOUSE. I CAN'T RUN FOR HELP, EITHER. IT COULD GET AWAY OR, WORSE, WAIT FOR THE POLICE TO SHOW UP AND THEN TEAR THEM APART.
FIGHTING IT WON'T BE EASY, THOUGH. PHYSICALLY, I'M HOPELESSLY OUTMATCHED.
BUT I HAVE A BRAIN. PERHAPS I CAN OUTWIT IT.
I NEED TO LEARN HOW SMART THAT THING IS. I'VE PULLED A LITTLE BIT AHEAD OF IT.
I'LL DUCK DOWN THIS STAIRWAY AND THEN, WHILE I'M MOMENTARILY OUT OF SIGHT...
...PHASE THROUGH THE STAIRS INTO THE STORAGE CLOSET UNDERNEATH. MY SCENT WILL SIMPLY DISAPPEAR IN MID-AIR. EVEN WOLVERINE'S SUPER-SENSITIVE NOSE WOULD HAVE A HARD TIME PICKING ME OUT OF ALL THE OTHER ODORS IN HERE.
THE MONSTER WILL HAVE TO DEDUCE WHAT I'VE DONE. THE QUESTION IS: CAN IT DO THAT?

I CAN'T HEAR ANYTHING. MY PLOY WORKED. NEXT I'LL PHASE THROUGH THE FLOOR INTO THE CLOSET BELOW--THE ONE THAT'S NEXT TO THE PHONE!

IF THIS WAS A MOVIE, THE MONSTER WOULD BE WAITING RIGHT OUTSIDE THE DOOR, READY TO BITE MY HEAD OFF THE MOMENT I SHOW MYSELF.

ISN'T THAT A CHEERY THOUGHT? WELL, HERE GOES NOTHIN'!

I DON'T BELIEVE I'M TAKING THIS SO MUCH IN STRIDE. I'M SCARED, YET... I'M COPING.

I'M OUT, AND SO FAR, I'M SAFE. ALL I NEED ARE A FEW SECONDS' GRACE, TO CALL THE PROFESSOR ON THE ROLLS' CAR-PHONE AND I FIGURE I'M HOME FREE.

X-MEN TO THE RESCUE. BYE-BYE BEASTIE.

OH-- NO!

THE DEMON TIMES ITS ATTACK PERFECTLY, SMASHING THROUGH THE DOOR BEHIND HER. BEFORE SPRITE CAN MOVE, MUCH LESS ESCAPE...

...ITS CLAWS RIP THROUGH HER. SHE SCREAMS--

--BUT DOES NOT DIE.

I-- FELT THAT! I... MANAGED TO PHASE THE INSTANT BEFORE IT HIT ME, BUT ITS ATTACK STILL HURT. HURT--HAH! I'VE... NEVER FELT SUCH AGONY.

MY RIGHT ARM'S NUMB, FROZEN-- USELESS!

167

SOMEHOW, THAT CREATURE CAN REACH ME-- HURT ME-- EVEN IN MY EPHEMERAL STATE. THIS CHANGES EVERYTHING.

MY GUTS FEEL LIKE THEY'VE BEEN TWISTED INSIDE-OUT. I FEEL SICK-- PHYSICALLY AND PSYCHICALLY. IT'S AN EFFORT JUST TO STAY ON MY FEET.

DANGER ROOM INACTIVE

I CAN'T LET IT TOUCH ME AGAIN.

IT'S *SMART*, TOO. IT ANTICIPATED MY MOVE AND TURNED THE TABLES ON ME. I DAREN'T UNDER-ESTIMATE IT A SECOND TIME.

I CAN'T CALL FOR HELP. I CAN'T RUN. I'VE NO ALTERNATIVE.

I HAVE TO FIGHT IT-- AND BEAT IT-- ON MY OWN.

I'LL MAKE MY STAND HERE IN THE *DANGER ROOM.* MY TRAIL WILL LEAD IT INSIDE.

ONCE MORE USING HER PHASING ABILITY TO LITERALLY WALK ON INDIVIDUAL MOLECULES OF AIR, KITTY ASCENDS FROM THE FLOOR TO THE CONTROL BOOTH.

I'LL PROGRAM THE MOST DANGEROUS SEQUENCES POSSIBLE-- BLAST! I'M NOT USED TO DOING THIS ONE-HANDED. THIS IS HARDER THAN I THOUGHT. IT'S TAKING SO LONG-- TOO LONG.

THE SYSTEM HAS BUILT-IN SAFETY INTERLOCKS, TO PREVENT ANYONE FROM BEING SERIOUSLY INJURED. BUT IF I HIT THE MONSTER OFTEN ENOUGH, WITH EVERYTHING THE ROOM HAS, I THINK I CAN KNOCK IT SILLY!

AT THE VERY LEAST, THIS SHOULD KEEP IT OCCUPIED LONG ENOUGH FOR ME TO CONTACT THE PROFESSOR.

THERE. IT'S ALL SET. THE ONLY THING MISSING IS MY MONSTER. THAT SUCKER'S SURE TAKING ITS TIME.

Oh. SUPPOSE IT SUSPECTS A TRAP? THAT'S RIDICULOUS. THERE'S NO REASON WHY IT SHOULD. WHEN LAST IT SAW ME, I WAS CRIPPLED AND ON THE RUN.

UNLESS... IT ISN'T MERELY SMART, IT'S *REAL* SMART.

CRASH!

I THINK I JUST GOT MY ANSWER.

KITTY DIVES BACKWARDS, PHASING THROUGH THE FACE OF THE BOOTH.

THE DEMON CHARGES AFTER HER...

...SHATTERING THE ARMORED, SUPPOSEDLY UNBREAKABLE GLASS WITH TERRIFYING EASE, LEAVING SHATTERED, SAVAGED COMPUTERS SHORT-CIRCUITING IN ITS WAKE.

AS KITTY LANDS, SHE FEELS THE ROOM COME TO LIFE AROUND HER.

THE DEMON CLOSES IN FOR THE KILL, BELIEVING IT HAS HER CORNERED...

... AND THEN IT IS THE N'GARAI'S TURN TO YOWL IN SURPRISE AND PAIN AS THE TRAP SO CAREFULLY LAID BY KITTY...

...IS SPRUNG!

NAILED THE CREEP!

BUT, ALTHOUGH STAGGERED BY THE MULTIPLE ASSAULTS, THE DEMON IS FAR FROM BEATEN.

IT'S RIPPING UP THE FLOOR!

BAD MOVE, UGLY. REACTING THAT WAY IS SURE TO THROW THE DANGER ROOM SYSTEMS OUT OF CONTROL AND CANCEL THE SAFETY INTERLOCKS.

UNFORTUNATELY, WHEN THE DEVICES IN HERE RUN WILD, THEY CAN NOT ONLY KILL *YOU*...

...THEY CAN KILL *ME*, AS WELL.

MY PHASING ABILITY WILL PROTECT ME FROM THE MECHANICAL THREATS. I'LL SIMPLY SLIP RIGHT THROUGH 'EM. I'LL BE LESS ABLE TO HANDLE GAS OR SONIC ATTACKS, OR THE HALLUCINOGENIC LIGHTSHOWS.

AND, AT THE SAME TIME, I'VE GOT TO STAY AWAY FROM THE CREATURE. I DIDN'T EXPECT TO BE HERE WITH IT WHEN THE ROOM ACTIVATED. I THOUGHT I'D BE WATCHING FROM THE SAFETY OF THE BOOTH.

BUT PERHAPS I CAN TURN THAT TO MY ADVANTAGE. THE MONSTER SEEMS PREPARED TO ENDURE ANYTHING TO GET ME. I CAN LEAD IT INTO THE WORST OF THE ASSAULT SYSTEMS.

THEY SHOULDN'T AFFECT ME, BUT THEY OUGHT TO CAUSE MY MONSTER A WHOLE LOT OF PROBLEMS. *FATAL* ONES, I HOPE.

≶WHUNFFF!≶

I WAS SAYING--!

A FORCE FIELD WALL! IT'S A RANDOM ENERGY PATTERN. IT'LL TAKE CONCENTRATION TO PHASE THROUGH IT...

...AND THAT KIND OF TIME...

I ...SIMPLY DO NOT HAVE.

DOESN'T THIS WALKING HORROR EVER SLOW UP?! I'M PUSHING MYSELF AS HARD AS I CAN, AND I'M BARELY STAYING AHEAD OF IT.

THE MONSTER'S GETTING MAD-- AND I'M GETTING *TIRED*.

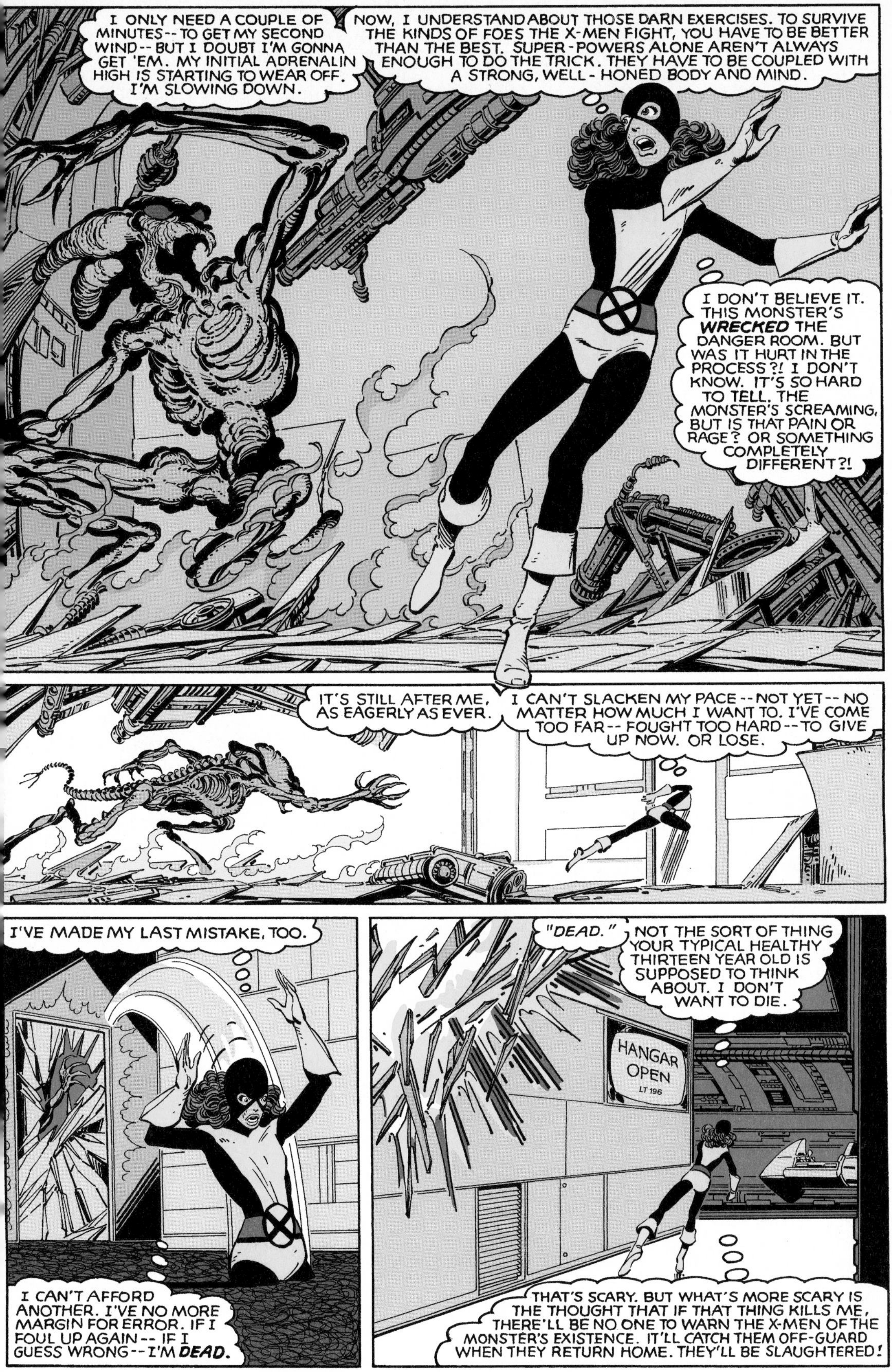
I ONLY NEED A COUPLE OF MINUTES--TO GET MY SECOND WIND--BUT I DOUBT I'M GONNA GET 'EM. MY INITIAL ADRENALIN HIGH IS STARTING TO WEAR OFF. I'M SLOWING DOWN.
NOW, I UNDERSTAND ABOUT THOSE DARN EXERCISES. TO SURVIVE THE KINDS OF FOES THE X-MEN FIGHT, YOU HAVE TO BE BETTER THAN THE BEST. SUPER-POWERS ALONE AREN'T ALWAYS ENOUGH TO DO THE TRICK. THEY HAVE TO BE COUPLED WITH A STRONG, WELL-HONED BODY AND MIND.
I DON'T BELIEVE IT. THIS MONSTER'S ***WRECKED*** THE DANGER ROOM. BUT WAS IT HURT IN THE PROCESS?! I DON'T KNOW. IT'S SO HARD TO TELL. THE MONSTER'S SCREAMING, BUT IS THAT PAIN OR RAGE? OR SOMETHING COMPLETELY DIFFERENT?!
IT'S STILL AFTER ME, AS EAGERLY AS EVER.
I CAN'T SLACKEN MY PACE--NOT YET--NO MATTER HOW MUCH I WANT TO. I'VE COME TOO FAR--FOUGHT TOO HARD--TO GIVE UP NOW. OR LOSE.
I'VE MADE MY LAST MISTAKE, TOO.
I CAN'T AFFORD ANOTHER. I'VE NO MORE MARGIN FOR ERROR. IF I FOUL UP AGAIN--IF I GUESS WRONG--I'M ***DEAD.***
"DEAD."
NOT THE SORT OF THING YOUR TYPICAL HEALTHY THIRTEEN YEAR OLD IS SUPPOSED TO THINK ABOUT. I DON'T WANT TO DIE.
HANGAR OPEN
LT 196
THAT'S SCARY. BUT WHAT'S MORE SCARY IS THE THOUGHT THAT IF THAT THING KILLS ME, THERE'LL BE NO ONE TO WARN THE X-MEN OF THE MONSTER'S EXISTENCE. IT'LL CATCH THEM OFF-GUARD WHEN THEY RETURN HOME. THEY'LL BE SLAUGHTERED!

IN THE DANGER ROOM, IT ALMOST CAUGHT ME, BUT *FIRE* FORCED IT AWAY. IS IT VULNERABLE TO INTENSE HEAT? TOO BAD I DON'T HAVE SOME KING-SIZED *FLAME-THROWERS* HANDY!

THEY USED *THEM* TO FIGHT THE MONSTER IN THAT *MOVIE!* IT DIDN'T WORK, THOUGH--

--BUT I REMEMBER WHAT *DID!* OH *BOY!* I JUST HOPE IT WORKS AS WELL FOR *ME!*

THE UNDERGROUND HANGAR COMPLEX IS A MILE FROM THE MANSION, CONNECTED BY A HIGH-SPEED SUBWAY. THIS MONOCAR CAN MAKE IT IN LESS THAN A MINUTE.

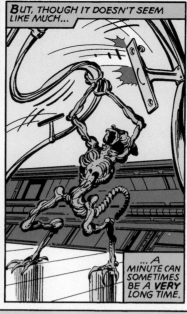

BUT, THOUGH IT DOESN'T SEEM LIKE MUCH...

...A MINUTE CAN SOMETIMES BE A *VERY* LONG TIME.

KITTY HASN'T EVEN GONE HALFWAY...

...BEFORE THE DEMON DERAILS HER MONOCAR.

SHE FINISHES THE JOURNEY ON FOOT-- NINE HUNDRED METERS IN THREE MINUTES* IGNORING THE WHITE HOT POKERS STABBING THROUGH HER CHEST WITH EVERY GASPING BREATH, AND THE BLINDING SHARDS OF PAIN FROM HER LEFT KNEE THAT REDUCE HER TO A HOBBLE BY THE TIME SHE REACHES THE HANGAR.

*1 METER = 3.3 FEET -- L.

THERE, IN THE LAUNCH BAY-- ON THE ELEVATOR THAT LIFTS IT TO THE SURFACE FOR TAKE-OFF-- SITS THE X-MEN'S MODIFIED SR-71 BLACKBIRD. PROBABLY THE MOST POWERFUL AIRCRAFT ON EARTH, IT IS CAPABLE OF CIRCLING THE GLOBE WITHOUT REFUELING, OR SOARING TO THE EDGE OF SPACE, OF FLYING AT HYPERSONIC SPEEDS, OVER FIVE TIMES THE SPEED OF SOUND.

IF THE MONSTER WANTS ME, IT'LL HAVE TO COME DOWN THE TRANSIT TUNNEL. THERE'S NO OTHER ENTRANCE TO THE HANGAR COMPLEX FROM THE MANSION.

THE HANGAR IS CONSTRUCTED OF STEEL AND CONCRETE-- A COUPLE OF METERS THICK. EVEN THAT CREATURE WOULD HAVE A HARD TIME DIGGING ITS WAY IN HERE.

I'M COUNTING ON IT BEING TOO ANGRY TO TRY...

...OR WANTING ME SO BADLY THAT IT'LL FOLLOW THE PATH OF LEAST RESISTANCE, CERTAIN THAT I CAN DO NOTHING TO DESTROY IT.

SUPPOSE IT'S RIGHT?

I DON'T SEE IT YET, IN THE TAIL CAMERA. NOW TO RUN THROUGH THE IGNITION CHECK LIST. PLEASE, LORD, DON'T LET ME FORGET ANYTHING.

172

MASTER SWITCH, ON. INTERNAL POWER, ON. BRAKES, LOCKED. FUEL PUMPS, ON. WHAT'S NEXT? I... I -- *DON'T KNOW!*

THINK! THINK!

"IT'S COMING!"

"WHAT'LL I DO?!"

STOP IT!

RELAX! RELAX. DEEP BREATH. CALM, STAY CALM.

DON'T RUSH. TAKE YOUR TIME.

"EVERY-THING'LL BE ALL RIGHT.

WAIT!

THE BLACKBIRD'S ON A TURNTABLE. I CAN FOLLOW THE MONSTER ANYWHERE INSIDE THE LAUNCH BAY.

BUT I HAVE TO WAIT 'TIL THE LAST POSSIBLE INSTANT-- 'TIL IT'S RIGHT ON TOP OF ME. THAT'S THE SPIRIT, YOU SLIMY HORROR, YOU.

COME TO KITTY. JUST A LITTLE CLOSER, SUCKER, A COUPLE OF MORE LOUSY STEPS...

GOT YOU!

TWO ENGINES, EACH RATED AT TWENTY THOUSAND KILOGRAMS OF THRUST, FLARE TO LIFE AT THE TOUCH OF A BUTTON. THEY'RE AT FULL EMERGENCY POWER, AFTERBURNERS PUNCHING TWIN PILLARS OF FLAME FROM THE HUGE EXHAUSTS.

FROM BEHIND THE BLACK-BIRD, IT'S LIKE SUDDENLY FINDING ONESELF TRANS-PORTED TO THE GATES OF HELL, OR PLUNGED INTO THE HEART OF A STAR.

173

A HOWLING BASSO ROAR FILLS THE HANGAR, AS AWESOME IN ITS OWN WAY AS THE ENGINES' FIRE. THE ENGINES WERE NEVER MEANT TO BE FIRED UNDERGROUND -- AND ESPECIALLY NOT AT MAXIMUM THRUST.

THEY CREATE BLAST WAVES THAT SHAKE THE COMPLEX LIKE A SMALL EARTHQUAKE.

METAL -- STRESSED BEYOND ENDURANCE -- BENDS, SHRIEKS. TELLTALES IN THE COCKPIT FLASH URGENT WARNINGS. KITTY IGNORES THEM UNTIL FINALLY, WITH AN ALMOST HUMAN SCREAM, THE LANDING GEAR BUCKLES AND THE BLACKBIRD HURLS ITSELF FORWARD ACROSS THE LAUNCH BAY, INTO THE FAR WALL.

THEN, AND ONLY THEN -- AS SHE FEELS THE UNDERCARRIAGE COLLAPSE -- DOES KITTY SHUT DOWN THE ENGINES, FLOODING THEM WITH FOAM TO PREVENT A FIRE. THE SILENCE IS DEAFENING.

I'M... SORRY, BLACK-BIRD. I WISH I COULD'VE THOUGHT OF ANOTHER WAY.

KOFF! KOFF!

I MUST'VE KAYOED THE AIR CYCLERS. THE HANGAR IS SO THICK WITH SMOKE I CAN HARDLY SEE.

THE AUTOMATIC SPRINKLERS HAVE MALFUNCTIONED, TOO. I'LL HAVE TO ACTIVATE THEM MANUALLY.

I'D BETTER WALK ON AIR. THINGS ARE STILL BURNING. AND THE FLOOR'S SO HOT I CAN FEEL IT THROUGH THE SOLES OF MY INSULATED BOOTS.

WHERE'S THE MONSTER?! DID I KILL IT?!?

I HAD TO. NOTHING COULD HAVE SURVIVED THIS HOLOCAUST. NOTHING!

SHE HAS TIME TO SCREAM.

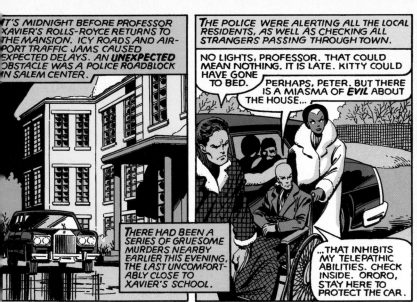

IT'S MIDNIGHT BEFORE PROFESSOR XAVIER'S ROLLS-ROYCE RETURNS TO THE MANSION. ICY ROADS AND AIRPORT TRAFFIC JAMS CAUSED EXPECTED DELAYS. AN *UNEXPECTED* OBSTACLE WAS A POLICE ROADBLOCK IN SALEM CENTER.

THERE HAD BEEN A SERIES OF GRUESOME MURDERS NEARBY EARLIER THIS EVENING, THE LAST UNCOMFORTABLY CLOSE TO XAVIER'S SCHOOL.

THE POLICE WERE ALERTING ALL THE LOCAL RESIDENTS, AS WELL AS CHECKING ALL STRANGERS PASSING THROUGH TOWN.

NO LIGHTS, PROFESSOR. THAT COULD MEAN NOTHING. IT IS LATE. KITTY COULD HAVE GONE TO BED.

PERHAPS, PETER. BUT THERE IS A MIASMA OF *EVIL* ABOUT THE HOUSE...

...THAT INHIBITS MY TELEPATHIC ABILITIES. CHECK INSIDE. ORORO, STAY HERE TO PROTECT THE CAR.

THIS IS STRANGE.

IT IS SIGNIFICANTLY COLDER *INSIDE* THE HOUSE THAN OUTSIDE.

I SWEAR I'VE SENSED THIS PARTICULAR EVIL BEFORE, BUT FOR THE LIFE OF ME, I CAN'T REMEMBER WHEN. IT'S INFURIATING.

ALL SEEMS PEACEFUL, PROFESSOR.

WAIT! I HEAR THE TELEVISION. SOMEONE MUST BE IN THE LIVING ROOM.

KITTY!

Yawn!

Hmh... ??? OH -- HI, PETER.

PETER!!

OH, *WOW!* OH, THANK HEAVENS! IT'S *YOU!*

WAIT'LL YOU HEAR WHAT HAPPENED TONIGHT! YOU HAVE NO IDEA HOW HAPPY I AM TO SEE YOU!

KITTY... PLEASE...

MOM!! DAD!!

YOU GREW A *BEARD!*

IF YOU'RE HAPPY TO SEE PETER, KITTEN, HOW D'YOU FEEL ABOUT US?

SHORTLY...

I'M SO GLAD YOU BOTH COULD MAKE THE TRIP, CARMEN. YOUR PRESENCE HAS DONE WONDERS FOR KITTY'S MORALE.

CHARLES, TO BE HONEST, YOU COULDN'T HAVE KEPT US AWAY. I DIDN'T REALIZE I'D--WE'D--MISS OUR KITTEN SO MUCH. OUR VISIT-- YOUR SPECIAL CHANUKAH SURPRISE--IS AS MUCH A GIFT TO US AS TO HER.

KITTY, I'VE JUST BEEN UP-STAIRS TO MY ATTIC.

Uh-oh.

WHAT PRECISELY HAPPENED WHILE WE WERE GONE?

I WAS ATTACKED BY A BIG, UGLY MONSTER.

A--MONSTER?!

ORORO, YOU HAD TO SEE IT TO BELIEVE IT. WE FOUGHT. I GOT LUCKY. I WON.

BUT, IN THE PROCESS, WE KIND'A WRECKED THE DANGER ROOM.

"WRECKED...THE DANGER ROOM?!"

AND THE BLACKBIRD. AND THE HANGAR. AND A LOT OF THE HOUSE.

OH. MY.

ARE YOU ANGRY?

I'M NOT QUITE SURE. BUT FROM THE SOUND OF THINGS, I'M FAIRLY CERTAIN I SHOULD FEEL TERRIBLY PROUD OF YOU.

GEE.

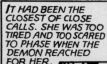

IT HAD BEEN THE CLOSEST OF CLOSE CALLS. SHE WAS TOO TIRED AND TOO SCARED TO PHASE WHEN THE DEMON REACHED FOR HER.

IT COULD HAVE KILLED HER, HAD IT GOT ITS HANDS ON HER.

BUT IT WAS DYING ON ITS FEET, ITS UNEARTH-LY FORM CRUMBLING INTO DUST WITH EVERY STEP.

IT TRIED. IT MADE A SUPREME EFFORT. IT FAILED.

ALONE, ON CHRISTMAS EVE, KITTY PRYDE UNDERWENT A RITE OF PASSAGE--

--A SUPREME TEST OF HER ABILITIES, HER INTELLECT, HER COURAGE, HER... SELF.

SHE PASSED.

NEXT THE RETURN OF CYCLOPS!

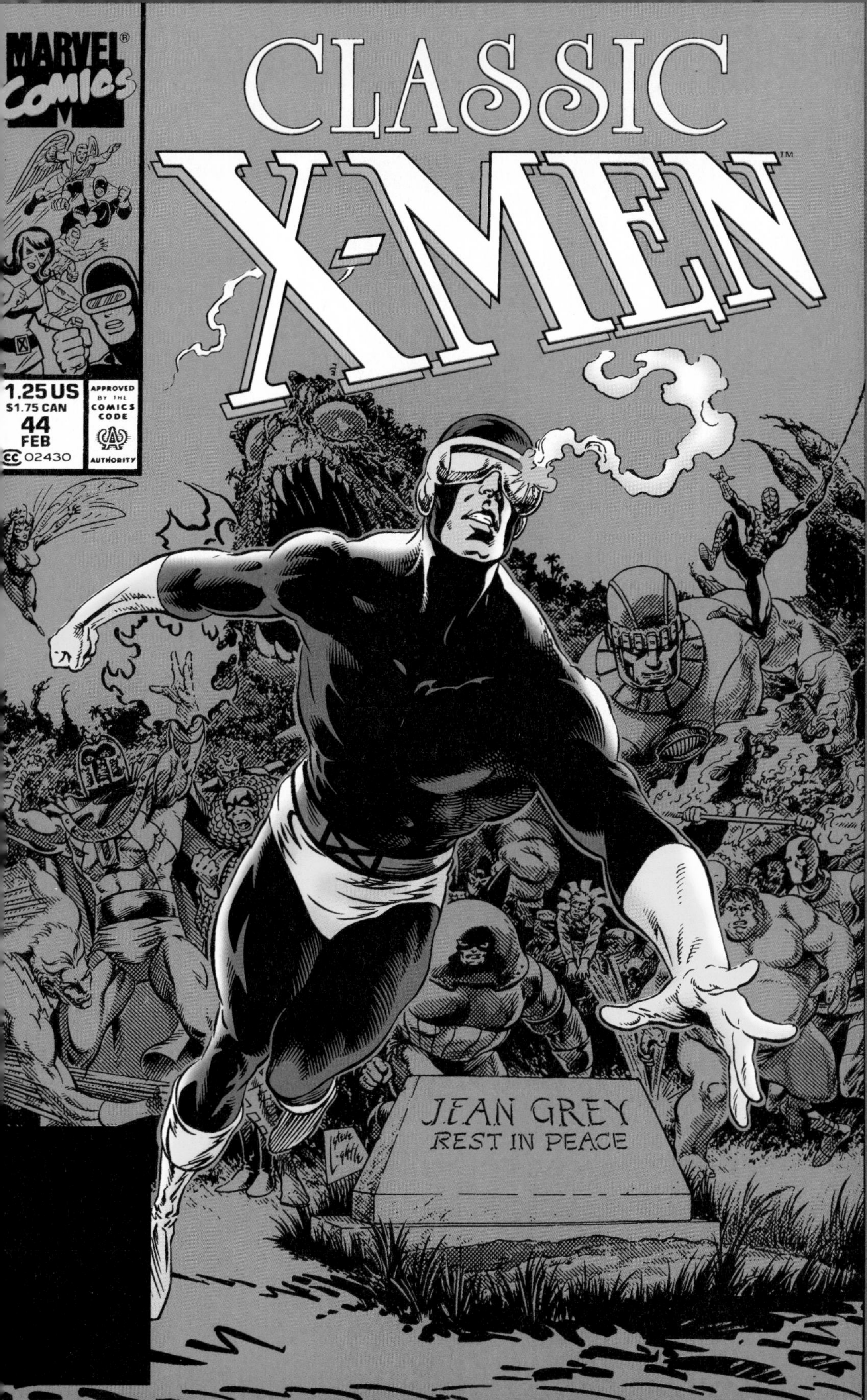
MARVEL COMICS
CLASSIC X-MEN
1.25 US
$1.75 CAN
44
FEB
02430
APPROVED BY THE COMICS CODE AUTHORITY
JEAN GREY
REST IN PEACE

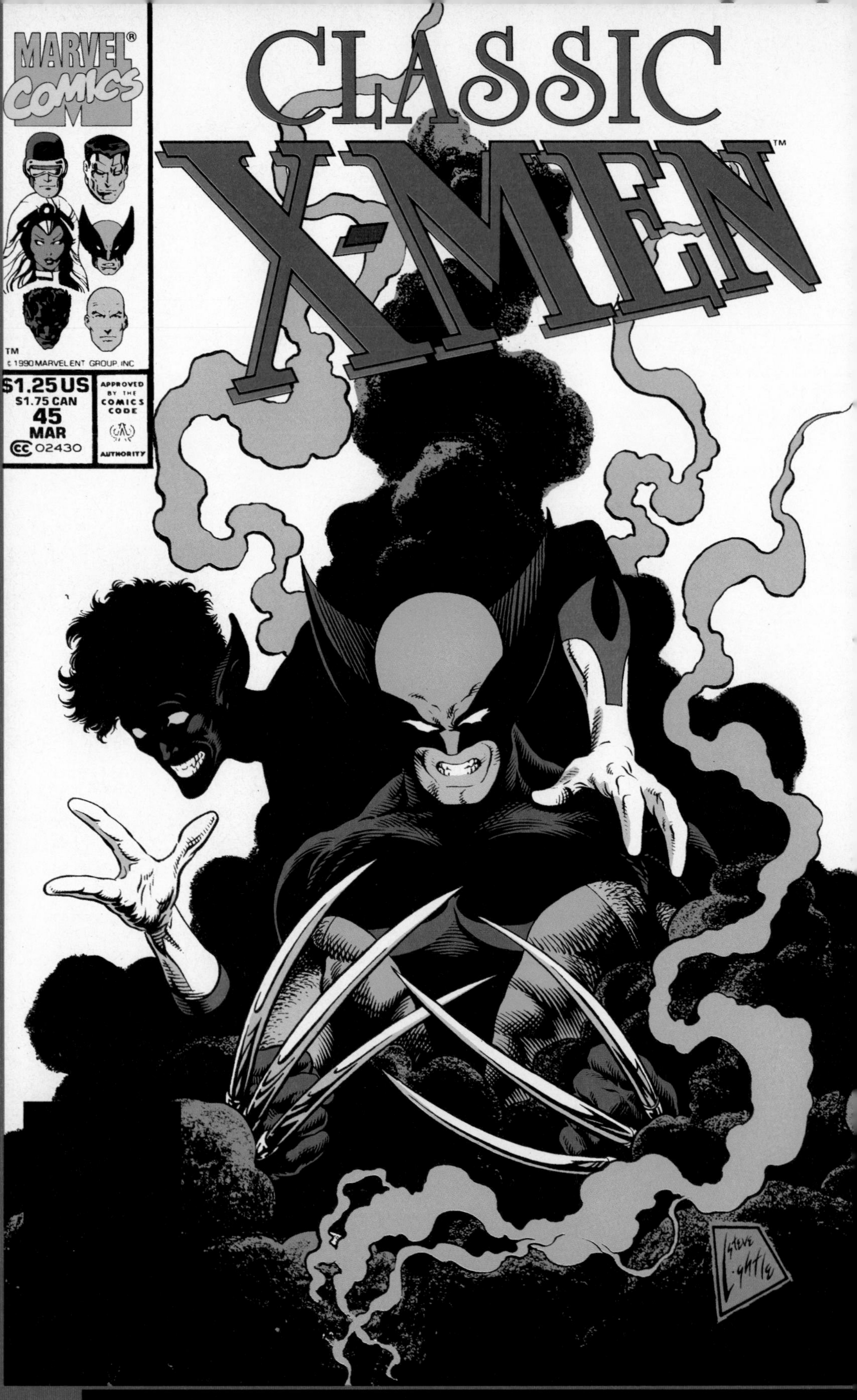
MARVEL® COMICS
CLASSIC
X-MEN™
TM
© 1990 MARVEL ENT. GROUP, INC.
$1.25 US
$1.75 CAN
45
MAR
02430
APPROVED BY THE COMICS CODE AUTHORITY
STEVE LIGHTLE

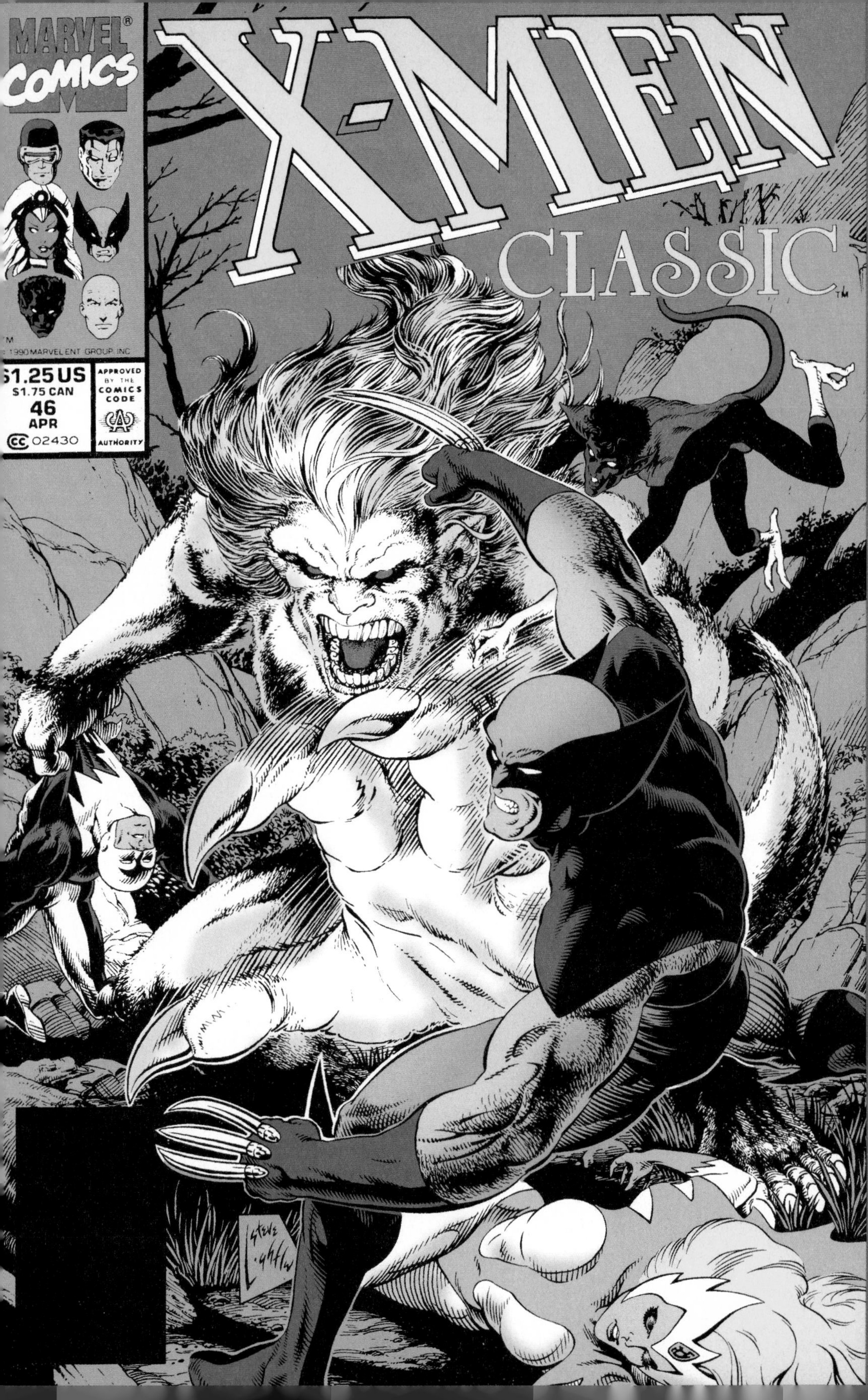
MARVEL COMICS
X-MEN
CLASSIC
© 1990 MARVEL ENT. GROUP, INC.
$1.25 US
$1.75 CAN
46
APR
CC 02430
APPROVED BY THE COMICS CODE AUTHORITY

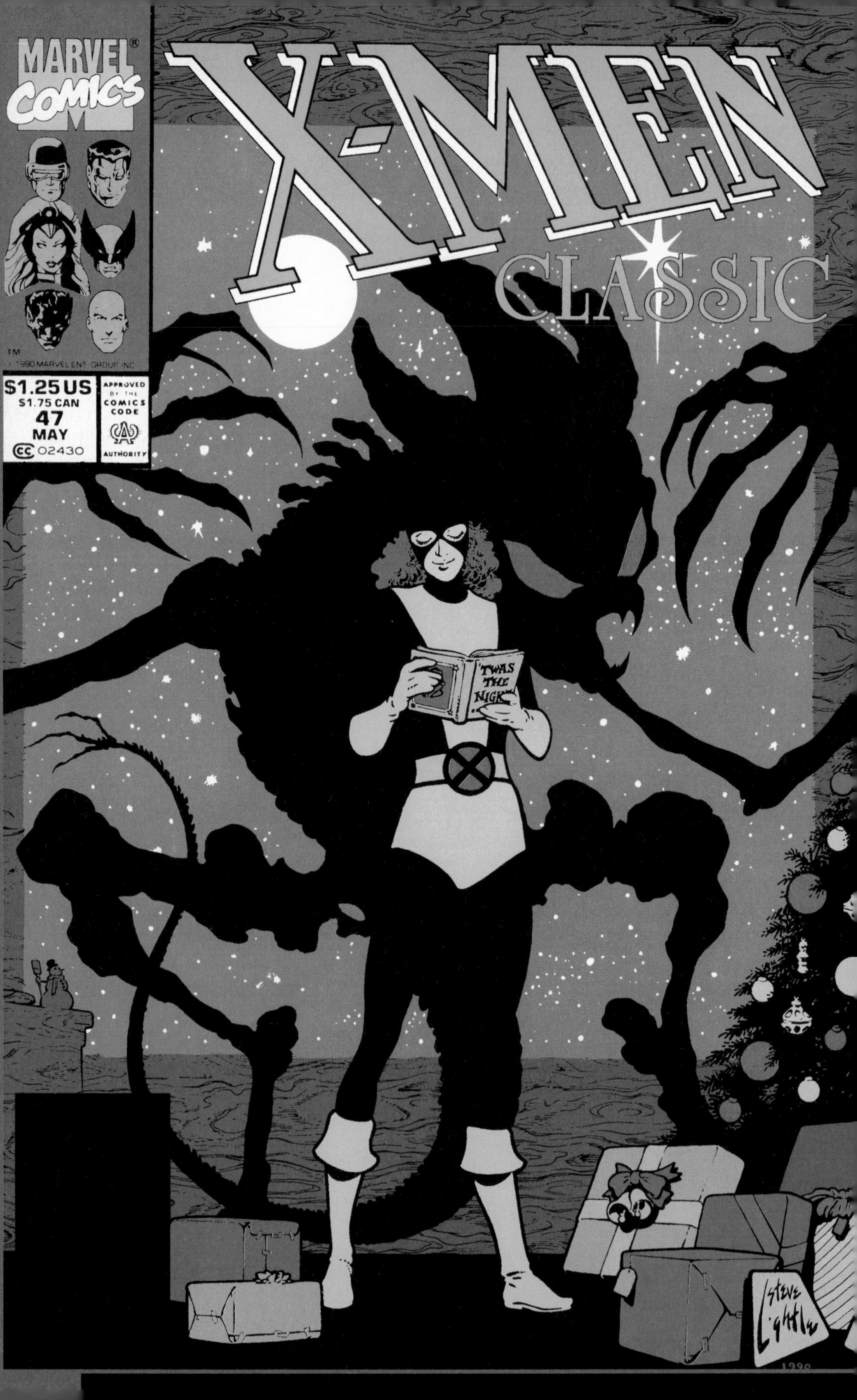

MARVEL COMICS
X-MEN
CLASSIC
TM
© 1990 MARVEL ENT. GROUP INC
$1.25 US
$1.75 CAN
47
MAY
CC 02430
APPROVED BY THE COMICS CODE AUTHORITY
TWAS THE NIGH
STEVE Lightle

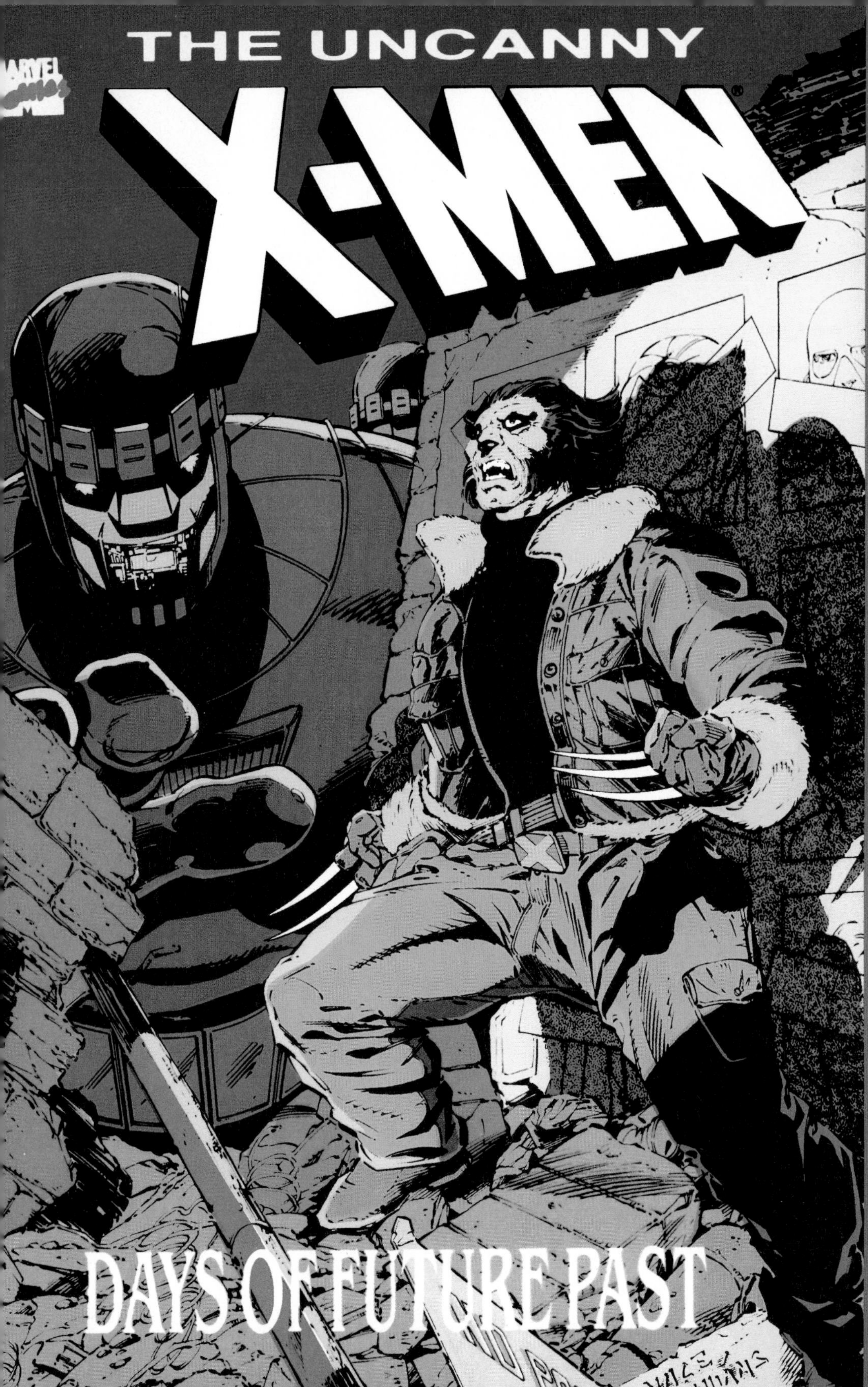
THE UNCANNY
X-MEN
DAYS OF FUTURE PAST

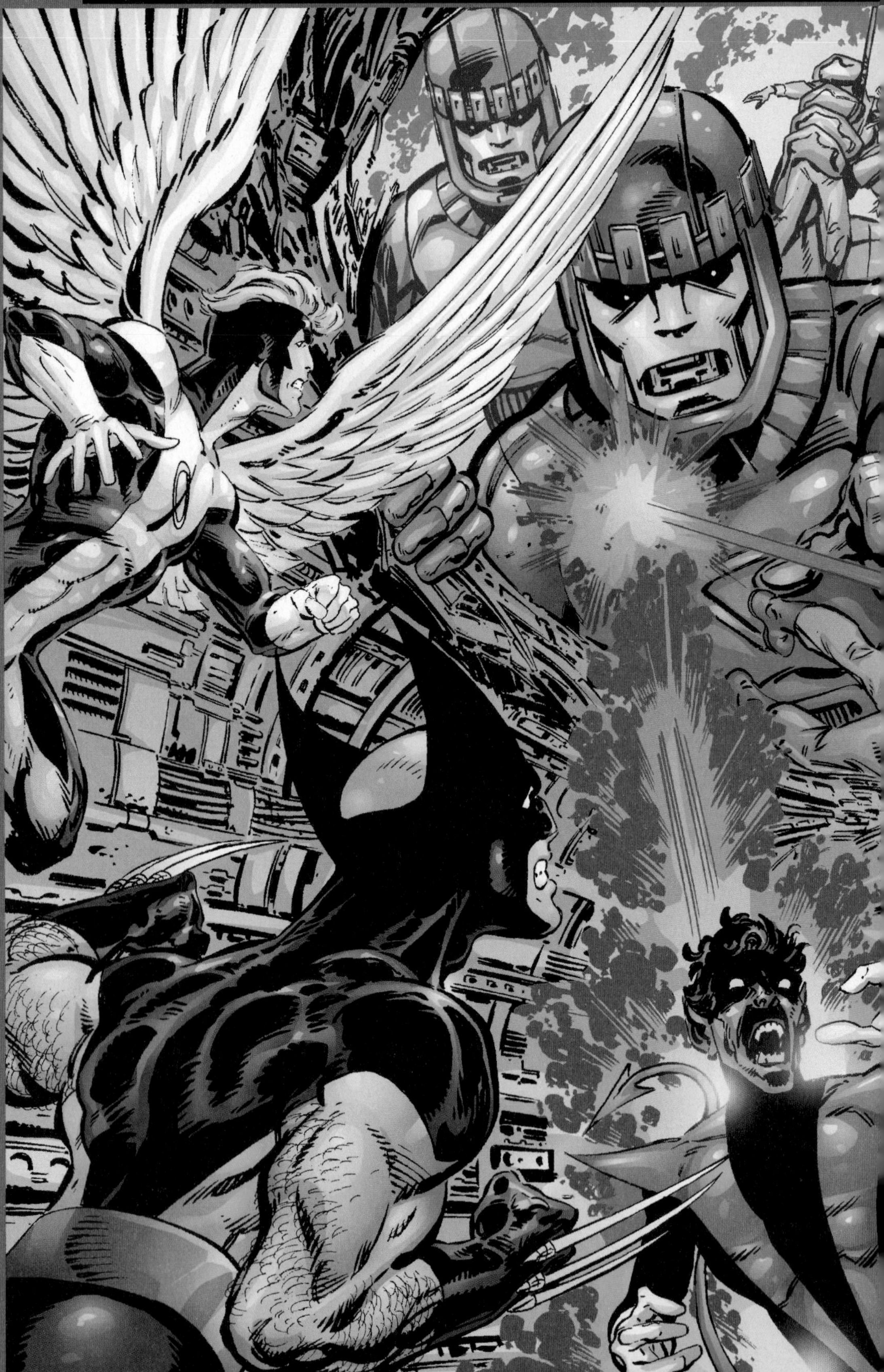